D0221570

Transnational Perspectives on Transformations in State and Society

edited by

Prof. Dr. Robert Kaiser, University of Siegen
Prof. Dr. Christian Lahusen, University of Siegen
Prof. Dr. Andrea Schneiker, University of Siegen

Volume 5

Robert Kaiser | Heiko Prange-Gstöhl

# The European Union Budget in Times of Crises

**The Deutsche Nationalbibliothek** lists this publication in the Deutsche Nationalbibliografie; detailed bibliographic data are available on the Internet at http://dnb.d-nb.de

ISBN 978-3-8487-5666-7 (Print)
978-3-8452-9811-5 (ePDF)

**British Library Cataloguing-in-Publication Data**
A catalogue record for this book is available from the British Library.

ISBN 978-3-8487-5666-7 (Print)
978-3-8452-9811-5 (ePDF)

**Library of Congress Cataloging-in-Publication Data**
Kaiser, Robert / Prange-Gstöhl, Heiko
The European Union Budget in Times of Crises
Robert Kaiser / Heiko Prange-Gstöhl
205 p.
Includes bibliographic references.

ISBN 978-3-8487-5666-7 (Print)
978-3-8452-9811-5 (ePDF)

1st Edition 2019

# Preface of the book series editors

The European Union (EU) remains a unique institutional system for transnational politics. No other international organization has obtained comparable regulative competences, and only in the process of European integration a specific structure for the joint exercise of national sovereignty has emerged. Its uniqueness is essentially reflected in the interdependence of supranational legislation and intergovernmental interest mediation. This interaction is particularly evident in the negotiation of the multiannual financial framework. Here, the EU and its member states not only define their political priority setting for the coming years, but also the degree of mutual solidarity among them for the strengthening of economic and social coherence. Because of the importance of the long-term financial planning, ambitious reform proposals have always been addressed for future multiannual financial frameworks. The present volume turns against those expectations from a theoretical and empirical perspective. It shows that the financial perspective over the past decades has developed a strongly path-dependent structure whose value lies precisely in realizing necessary changes in the context of institutional stability.

Siegen, June 2019

Robert Kaiser
Christian Lahusen
Andrea Schneiker

Contents

# Authors

Robert Kaiser holds a chair for comparative politics and political theory at the University of Siegen. His main research interests are the process of European integration, comparative public policies, and empirical political theory.

Heiko Prange-Gstöhl is a Senior Associate Researcher at the Institute for European Studies, Vrije Universiteit Brussel (VUB). His main research interests are processes of European integration, European public policies, and external governance of the European Union.

# 1. Building the long-term EU budget in times of crises: "much ado about nothing" or defending core national interests?

## *1.1 The ritual*

It has become a beloved ritual. Usually every seven years the European Union's (EU) member states and its institutions go on stage for the drama called "negotiation of the EU long-term budget", known as the multiannual financial framework (MFF). The plot (some call it "theatre season" or "battle"[1]) is always opened by the European Commission presenting its proposals, i.e. the overall MFF (which includes the expenditure and the revenue sides) and the sectoral proposals (or programmes), to the European Parliament and the member states in the Council (in that order). When doing so, the European Commission is keen to underline that the proposals focus on areas of European added-value, reflect the need to fund new priorities, while not hitting so-called old policies (meaning the Common Agricultural Policy and Regional and Cohesion policies) inadequately hard, and that spending will be done in the most effective and efficient way through more simplification and conditionality (see European Commission 2011a, 2018a).

The financing side of the MFF grabs normally less attention. Three-quarter of the MFF stem from national contributions based on the Gross National Income (GNI). Critics of the current system point out that it has led to an unhealthy emphasis on net balances between the member states (i.e. the so-called "juste retour"-principle) and to the introduction of national rebates and other correction mechanisms (for example, European Parliament 2014a: 5). Although with every new MFF the Commission is trying to reform the financing side towards a system of more genuine own resources[2], member states do not show any political willingness for a change. In a nutshell, the proposals are presented by the Commission as focused, modern, efficient, and effective reflecting Europe's realities.

---

1 See, for example, Pisani-Ferry (2018) and Wolff (2018).

2 The Commission tabled proposals for reform in the context of the 2014-2020 MFF as well as the post-2020 MFF; see European Commission (2011b, 2018b).

Swift reactions of member states and the European Parliament (and also of the myriad of interest organisations) are part of the ritual – and they are rarely positive. For some the proposed overall budget is too high (either in total or as a share of GNI), the financial burden sharing is "unfair", it is not focused enough on European added-value, it is not "modern" enough, for others the cuts in certain policy areas are too high, the budget is not "ambitious" enough, regional specificities have not been taken into account – and so on. The game is on – on the overall expenditure ceiling, the distribution of the money between the different clusters of policies ("headings"), the allocation of funds within each policy cluster –; and it unfolds at several levels: first within the institutions (in the Council between the member states, in EP Committees between political groups and nationalities, in the European Commission between departments[3]), second between the institutions. But why is there always so much of a drama? What conditions the outcome of the negotiations? Why has the EU always failed to re-orient its budget towards investing in public goods[4]? And what chances exist for an MFF that deserves to be called "modern"[5]?

While there is no lack of studies on how the EU budget architecture should look like (or, according to some authors, must look like) to be effective and efficient[6], there is still a knowledge gap in terms of analysing the conditions and likelihood for a MFF reform that could be called "modernization".[7] Still the puzzle of why "the EU budget is suffering from a

---

3 One should not forget that negotiations take place within the Commission, first before the official proposal is adopted, and second during the legislative process, which is a window of opportunity for Commission departments to still increase the budgets for programmes they are responsible for.

4 Based on Samuelson (1954), Tarschys (2011a: 27) defines public goods as follows: "A good is considered to be public if its consumption by one individual does not reduce its availability and usefulness to others". Collignon (2011: 45) elaborates on the differences between national and European public goods, such as the four freedoms or the use of the Euro, the latter being available for all European residents, but excluding non-Europeans.

5 Notably, the only legal requirement an MFF has to follow is that "the categories of expenditure, limited in number, shall correspond to the Union's major sectors of activity" (Article 312(3) TFEU).

6 On this normative approach of analysing the EU's budget, see for example Becker (2014), Blankart/Köster (2009), Danell/Östholl (2008), Heinemann et al. (2010), Kölling (2014), Tarschys (2011b), Thillaye (2016).

7 A few studies have focused on the explanation of annual budget dynamics (Citi 2013, 2015), the bargaining behaviour of member states during budget negotiations (Aksoy 2010; Schneider 2013) or the patterns of coalition building in the negotiations for the MFF (Blavoukos/Pagoulatos 2011). Analysing the pace of

significant mismatch between its means and the objectives the EU is tasked to pursue, both in terms of absolute and relative amounts of resources allocated to each chapter of expenditure" (Molino/Zuleeg 2011: 2) is not solved. Sapir (2014: 65) claims that the EU was, so far, unwilling and unable to adapt its policy agenda to the realities of the twenty-first century; and Begg and Heinemann (2006: 1) found that "the EU regularly ends up with budgets that are inefficient, badly targeted, ludicrously complicated and hardly worth the countless hours of political fighting that precede them".

With this book we want to fill this gap in the literature on the EU's long-term budget. To this end, we will provide a timely in-depth review of the potentials and impediments for change of the EU's future budget. We argue that institutionalizing the EU budget in form of a multiannual financial framework allows for stability and change in financing the EU at the same time. It represents a stable – path-dependent – structure providing security for the actors (in particular the member states) in terms of costs and benefits. It has proven stability also in times of major changes (for example, a series of enlargements) and crises (for example, the financial and economic crisis). Nevertheless, it is a flexible instrument as change within the overall framework, for example to react to crises, to support new policy areas, or to reflect new priorities, is a recurring feature in MFF negotiations. Stability and change being two sides of the same coin minimizes the conflict potential amongst actors. In order to explain the simultaneousness of stability and change and to grasp the options that are available for the post-2020 MFF, we will apply institutionalist theories (see Chapter 2) and offer reasoned scenarios on the MFFs potential look (see Chapter 9).

The EU applies the method of multi-annual financial planning since 1988 (see Laffan/Lindner 2014).[8] The main purpose was to overcome the EU budget crisis of the late 1970s and 1980s, which was characterised by the non-adoption of the EU annual budgets for 1980, 1985, 1986 and 1988 until the financial year was well under way (see Lindner 2006). While budgetary conflicts between the EP and the Council as a results over dif-

---

change in budget negotiations between 1988 and 2005, Schild (2008: 545) concluded that "changes in overall levels of the budget and in spending priorities were possible when budgetary decision-making was linked to major integration projects, and when net contributors to the budget were willing to accept side payments in order to advance their interests in non-budgetary policy fields (single market in 1988, monetary union in 1992)".

8 See De Feo (2017) for a comprehensive and long-term analysis of 40 years of EU budgetary decisions.

ferent Treaty interpretations already appeared during the period 1974-1978 (Lindner 2006: 46-58), De Feo argues that the escalation of this crisis could mainly be found in the first direct election of the European Parliament in 1979 (although with still very limited legal competences), "the ambiguity of the text of the Treaty[9], [...], the will to develop new policies under pressure from the new member states, which had the direct consequence of a lack of resources, and last but not least the problem of budgetary imbalances and requests for correction mechanisms" (De Feo 2017: 46).

According to Laffan (2000: 733) "the highly conflictual bargaining of the 1970s and 1980s was replaced by a more predictable, consensual and rule-bound system". In 1988, the so-called Delors-I-package introduced a multiannual financial perspective, a law on budgetary discipline to control the expenditures of the Common Agricultural Policy (CAP) in favour of structural and cohesion policy (following the introduction of "economic and social cohesion" as a new priority into the Treaty), and an inter-institutional agreement between the European Commission, the Council and the European Parliament to agree on budgetary procedures (Laffan 2000: 733f). The 1988 budget reform laid down the foundations for any future financial negotiations (Laffan 2000: 742).

With entry into force of the Lisbon Treaty the MFF has become legally binding through a Council Regulation (Article 312 TFEU). The Treaty (Art. 312(2) TFEU) stipulates that the regulation must be based on a Commission proposal and adopted by the Council by unanimity after obtaining the consent of the European Parliament. The Council may act by qualified majority when the European Council decides so (the so-called "passerelle" clause).[10] When presenting the MFF proposal the Commission has to respect that "the financial framework shall determine the amounts of the annual ceilings on commitment appropriations by category of expenditure and of the annual ceiling on payment appropriations" (Article 312(3) TFEU). Since 2016, these ceilings are set at 1.2% of the sum of the member states' GNIs for payments and 1.26% for commitments (European Commission 2016a). Moreover, so far, each long-term budget has been established in the shadow of the Fontainebleau European Council conclusions, which stipulated that "any member state sustaining a budget-

9 This remark refers to the vague definition of the so-called "compulsory expenditures" in the Treaty, on which the EP had no say (mainly agriculture).

10 For an overview of the changes introduced to the EU budgetary system by the Lisbon Treaty, see Benedetto (2012).

ary burden which is excessive in relation to its relative prosperity may benefit from a correction at the appropriate time" (European Council 1984)[11]. The famous rebates had been born.

With the financial perspective 2007-2013 the EU introduced a new instrument, the so-called budget review[12], to provide an additional option for strategic reorientation of the EU budget at mid-term (European Commission 2010a).[13] The European Commission was – for the first time ever – invited by the Council "to undertake a full, wide ranging review covering all aspects of EU spending" (Council of the European Union 2005, point 80) at the midst of the MFF 2007-2013. Rubio (2008: 14) argued that the review offered "member states the possibility of making unpopular decisions on the next financial perspective well before the start of negotiations, thus free from the political pressures that characterise the period of negotiation". This assumption turned out to be over-optimistic as the review fell victim to the economic and financial crisis during which member states significantly shifted their preferences (Kaiser/Prange-Gstöhl 2012). The finalisation of the budget review had to be postponed from the expected date in the first half of 2009 to October 2010, when preparations for the MFF 2014-2020 had already begun. Consequently, the budget review finally had little impact on the negotiations for the MFF 2014-2020 (Kaiser/Prange-Gstöhl 2010).

On 14 September 2016, the Commission has presented its mid-term review on the functioning of the MFF 2014-2020, including five legislative proposals to revise the framework (European Commission 2016b). The proposal sought to allocate an extra €6.33 billion to migration policies (40.3%), competitiveness and growth (22.1%, including research and higher education), security (21.9%), and youth unemployment (15.8%). The proposal for a mid-term review did not touch the reform of the revenue side of the MFF, but simply referred to the report of the High-Level Group on Own Resources (HLGOR 2016).

---

11 A reference to these Council conclusions has been made in the Council Decision on the EU's system of own resources of May 2014 (see Council of the European Union 2014)

12 With regard to the revenue side, all long-term EU budgets since 1988 foresaw some sort of assessment at mid-term on the functioning of the system (Cipriani 2007: 130).

13 Begg (2007: 24) argued that the budget review provided an opportunity to break the change-resistant decision-making system of previous rounds of budget negotiations and could therefore be the key to reform.

The main political elements of the Commission's proposal were the extension of the European Fund for Strategic Investments (EFSI) until 2020 and the doubling of its financing capacity, fresh money for programmes that experienced EFSI-related cuts in 2015 (like Horizon 2020 and the Connecting Europe Facility), extending the Youth Employment Facility, setting up a Partnership Framework with third countries under the European Agenda on Migration, and establishing a new European Fund and Guarantee for Sustainable Development to address migration and security challenges. The European Parliament criticised the Commission for not proposing to revise the MFF ceilings, but instead intending to use the budgetary margins available under the MFF to finance its revisions (European Parliament 2016a: points 7 and 8).

The mid-term review finally led to an upgrade of the MFF 2014-2020 of €6.01 billion (see Council of the European Union 2017a). While the members states left the Commission proposal on migration and security policies untouched, they increased the money for youth unemployment, and cut down significantly the area of competitiveness and growth (i.e. from €1.4 billion to €875 million). In sum, the Commission had been cautious with its proposals in terms of content and timing due to the referendum of the United Kingdom (UK) on Brexit and general negative sentiments about Brussels (cf. Thillaye 2016: 61). But even without these factors, a mid-term review cannot be expected to trigger major changes as "national" envelopes (for example, all structural funds and direct payments) are ring-fenced and revisions require unanimity in the Council. It is, therefore, also not surprising that the mid-term review remained vague on possible future directions. Nevertheless, the Commission at least pointed out the need to assess the effectiveness of existing policies (i.e. cohesion policy, the Common Agricultural Policy, external action instruments) and the importance of exploring potential new areas for contributions, such as the completion of the Economic and Monetary Union as well as defence and security (European Commission 2016b: 14).

On 2 May 2018 the European Commission opened the new negotiation season by presenting its proposals for the post-2020 MFF (European Commission 2018b, 2018c, 2018d, 2018e, 2018f). Until mid-June 2018 all legislative proposals for the sectoral programmes followed. Overall, for the period 2021-2027 the Commission proposed a budget of €1.135 billion in commitments (1.11% of the EU27 GNI) and €1.105 billion (1.08% of the EU27 GNI) in payments (both in 2018 prices)[14]. Compared to the Commission's proposal for the period 2014-2020 this is an increase of 10.7% in commitments (i.e. up from €1.025 billion in 2011 prices or 1.05% of the EU28 GNI) and 13.7% in payments (i.e. up from €972.2 billion in 2011 prices or 1% of EU28 GNI). The agreed MFF 2014-2020 finally represented a cut of 3.5% in commitments (€960 billion in 2011 prices) and 3.7% in payments (€908 billion in 2011 prices) compared to the 2007-2013 financial perspective.

The post-2020 MFF proposal has been split into seven headings (compared to five under the previous MFF).[15] A first heading, called "Single Market, Innovation and Digital", will include research and innovation funding (i.e. the new Framework Programme "Horizon Europe", Euratom, and the International Thermonuclear Experimental Reactor of €91 billion), European Strategic Investments (such as the InvestEU Fund – merging EFSI and other financial instruments into one single instrument[16] – and the Connecting Europe Facility of €44.4 billion), activities linked to the Single Market (€5.7 billion), and space policy (€14.4 billion). The total proposed budget for this heading is €166.3 billion or 14.7% of the overall MFF.

The second heading "Cohesion and Values" comprises regional development and cohesion funding (€242.2 billion), investing in people, social policy, and values (€123.5 billion), as well as new instruments to support the Economic and Monetary Union (€22.3 billion). The total proposed budget for this heading is €392 billion or 34.5% of the overall MFF.

The third heading "Natural Resources and Environment" includes agricultural (€324.3 billion) and maritime policies (€5.5 billion) as well as environmental and climate policies (€5.1 billion). The total proposed budget for this heading is €336.6 billion or 29.6% of the overall MFF.

---

14 Haas et al. (2018: 2) note that when deducting the UK from the MFF 2014-2020, the proposed post-2020 MFF is in fact smaller in relative terms than the MFF 2014-2020, which in that case would stand at 1.13% of the EU-27 GNI (or 1.16% if the European Development Fund is included).

15 In the following, all figures are commitments in 2018 prices. We will provide more in-depth analyses of the main sectoral programmes in Chapters 6-8.

16 As a novelty the Commission proposed is that the Fund will be able to provide an EU guarantee not only to the European Investment Bank (EIB), but also to other financial institutions, such as National Promotional Banks or the European Bank for Reconstruction and Development (European Commission 2018c: 9).

"Migration and Border Management" is the fourth heading. It has an overall proposed ceiling of €30.8 billion (2.7% of the overall MFF), including an Asylum and Migration Fund, an Integrated Border Management Fund, and provisions for strengthening the European Border and Coast Guard Agency (Frontex).

Heading five "Security and Defence" comes up with the three subheadings "Security" (Internal Security Fund; nuclear safety and decommissioning in Lithuania, Bulgaria, and Slovakia; the budget for decentralized agencies), "Defence" (European Defence Fund; Military Mobility), and "Crisis Response" (Union Civil Protection Mechanism). This heading has a proposed budget ceiling of €24.4 billion or 2.1% of the overall MFF.

In the future, the EU's external action (€93.2 billion) and its pre-accession assistance (€12.9 billion) should be funded through heading six – "Neighbourhood and the World". It is proposed to "budgetise" the European Development Fund (which has been outside the MFF so far) and merge it into a general instrument called "Neighbourhood, Development and International Cooperation Instrument". The overall budget for this heading would end up at €108.9 billion or 9.6% of the MFF.

Expenditures for the European public administration has been allocated to heading seven with a total amount of €75.6 billion, which is 6.7% of the MFF.

Last, but not least, the Commission proposed a new mechanism linking compliance with the rule of law to the disbursement of EU funds (European Commission 2018g). However, the Commission does not intend to directly sanction a breach of the rule of law (as this is the purpose of Article 7 TEU[17]), but "targets generalised deficiencies in the rule of law that threaten the EU's financial interests" (Haas et al. 2018: 5). The Commission's logic behind this approach is that any breach of the rule of law[18] would automatically result in inefficient or deceptive spending: "Whenev-

17 Article 7 TEU is a legal instrument seeking to remedy a situation of continuously and seriously breaches of democratic values (as defined in Article 2 TEU) in a member state. Applying this article could lead to a suspension of certain rights for the member state in question.

18 Article 3 (1) of the proposed regulation defines cases how generalized deficiencies as regards the rule of law could risk the principles of sound financial management or the protection of the financial interests of the Union, including the "proper functioning of investigation and public prosecution services" and the "effective judicial review by independent courts of actions or omissions by the authorities". Article 3 (2) defines generalised deficiencies as regards the rule of law, including "endangering the independence of judiciary".

er the member states implement the Union's budget, and whatever method of implementation they use, respect for the rule of law is an essential pre-condition to comply with the principles of sound financial management" (European Commission 2018g: 6).

The mechanism would be triggered by the Commission only. The Commission would need to decide whether the conditions for launching a procedure are fulfilled and what kind of sanctions would be proposed. A decision by the Commission would only be rejected if the Council votes against it by qualified majority ("reverse qualified majority" voting).

In sum, while the Commission proposed a few new instruments (for example, in the areas of the Economic and Monetary Union and defence) and re-named or merged others (mainly in the area of external action), the so-called traditional priorities of the EU budget – agriculture, regional development and cohesion – still account for half of the MFF during the period 2021-2027. In contrast to its narrative, the European Commission has refrained from suggesting a substantial reform of the overall post-2020 MFF architecture.

## 1.2 *The cleavages*

A number of crises of different kinds have challenged the EU since 2008 ranging from, inter alia, the economic and financial crisis, the conflict over immigration policies, to Brexit, and a crisis of democracy, becoming particularly visible by the support left- and right-wing populist parties gain across Europe for their anti-EU agendas.

Crises[19] accompany the European integration project since its birth. From the collapse of the European Defence Community in 1952, de Gaulle's "empty chair"-policy in 1965/1966, the economic and financial crisis in the 1970s, and Margaret Thatcher's fight for a new deal concerning the UK's contribution to the Community budget between 1981 and 1984, to the Treaty ratification crises of the 1990s and 2000s, culminating

19 There is an academic debate about what a "crisis" is and how to define it, which we cannot discuss in detail in this book (see, for example, Gourevitch 1992; Habermas 1973; Laffan 2016; Preunkert 2015; Runciman 2016). Some authors see the danger that "crisis" becomes a catchword for every disrupting event (Dinan 2017). However, amongst authors there seems to be agreement that "crisis" is an unexpected, existential threat for society and its institutions, but as an "open moment" it also offers new choices; therefore, threat and choice must come together in a crisis.

in the French and Dutch voters' rejection of the Constitutional Treaty in 2005, "the EU is no stranger to crisis" (Webber 2017: 337).

One could, however, argue that the current crisis period is different compared to the past signifying an exceptional situation in which the EU must take decisions. The EU faces a multidimensional crisis in terms of issue areas (cf. economy and finance, migration, society, democracy), origins (cf. legitimacy issues; failure of EU policies and governance; a high variety of member states' interests and citizens' ideas and values; a number of external factors, such as a global financial breakdown, regional conflicts, and terrorism), and implications (cf. both centralisation and signs of disintegration; tensioned relations between member states due to growing mistrust and lack of perceived solidarity; damaging effects on core EU principles, such as the free movement of persons within the Schengen Area; damaging of the EU's international standing). In economic terms the recent crises have widened the economic gap both within countries (growing inequalities) and between member states (for example, donor countries vs. bail-out countries). In political terms the crises have destroyed trust mainly between Northern creditor countries and Southern debtor countries and between "asylum-seeker-takers" and "asylum-seeker-refusers". Moreover, anti-EU sentiment has gained weight not only amongst citizens, but even more so within political parties entering more frequently member states' governments.

The crises since the 1990s also reflect the EU's evolution from a market-creating project, which had (almost) uncontested and broad support among member states and met the "permissive consensus" of European citizens, towards an integration project that focuses more on policies of public concern (for example, migration, employment, security). A lack of problem-solving capacity in these areas contributed to the erosion of the "permissive consensus" in favour of a "constraining dissensus" (Hooghe/Marks 2009; Scharpf 2003; Schmidt 2013), a situation in which national policy-makers cannot take any more for granted that domestic public opinions support their EU strategies. This also holds when it comes to negotiations on a new MFF mirrored through specific narratives, such as "European added-value", "fairness", and "solidarity" as the criteria for building a long-term EU budget, intending to show political responsiveness to the electorates' concerns.

These broader developments on European integration – i.e. its growing politicisation (De Wilde/Zürn 2012; Grande/Kriesi 2015) – have divisive effects in the MFF context. The end of the simple dichotomy between net-payers and net-receivers as the core cleavage in budget negotiations is most striking. These traditional cleavages between net-contributors and net-recipients emerged during the negotiations on the Delors-II-package (1993-1999). A net-contributors-club, led by Germany, was unwilling to keep its paymaster's role, arguing with the high costs of unification. Additionally, the Netherlands became a net-contributor during the 1990s and EU newcomers Austria and Sweden were also concerned about the growing financial burden of the EU budget (Laffan 2000: 739). This cleavage had been intensified due to two enlargement rounds in 2004 and 2007.

While this "old" cleavage will certainly continue to exist, a diversification of intertwined new cleavages increases the complexity of the negotiations and the predictability of its outcome. During the negotiations of the MFF 2014-2020 the main frictions between net-payers and net-recipients became again apparent. The two most visible groups were the "Friends of Better Spending"[20] and the "Friends of Cohesion"[21] (see Stenbaeck/Jensen 2016). While the "Friends of Better Spending" advocated a freeze of the overall expenditure, the "Friends of Cohesion" consisted of net-receiver countries. In 2009, a group of member states (Germany, United Kingdom, France, the Netherlands, Sweden and Austria) expressed their will to cap the EU budget at 1% of the Gross Domestic Product (GDP) – marking the launch of the "1%-paradigm", that is well beneath the maximum ceiling agreed by member states (see also Kaiser/Prange-Gstöhl 2017: 17ff). The negotiations of the 2014-2020 MFF clearly took place in a delicate context due to the tense economic situation in many member states (ibid.: 16).[22]

New front lines run, first, between those Eurozone members that were under the various economic and financial stabilisation programmes, were forced to apply substantial austerity measures, and still suffer from the long-term effects of the economic crisis (all of these are net-receivers), and those Eurozone members that enabled massive financial payments and guarantees (mainly net-payers, but also net-receivers, such as Spain and Portugal, which had to provide their share to the Greek rescue package). A second new front line exists between "asylum-seeker-takers" and "asylum-seeker-refusers" ("migration-cleavage"), with new and old member states and net-payers and net-receivers in both camps. Thirdly, a new "rule of law-cleavage" has been opened, partly overlapping with the "migration-cleavage", between some Eastern EU member states (foremost Hungary

20 Austria, Finland, France, Germany, Italy, the Netherlands, and Sweden.

21 Bulgaria, Czech Republic, Estonia, Greece, Hungary, Latvia, Lithuania, Malta, Poland, Romania, Slovakia, Slovenia, and Spain.

22 We expand on the economic and financial crisis and its effects in Chapter 3.

and Poland) that stretch the Treaty provisions on European values and some Western/Northern member states prompting these countries to strictly comply with these rules; and, fourthly, one can observe the establishment of a "Brexit-cleavage", with a couple of net-payers claiming that "a smaller EU requires a smaller budget", and a coalition of both net-payers and net-receivers asking for "balancing the Brexit gap".

In sum, the net-contributor/net-receiver camps are not as clearly defined anymore as they have been in the negotiations for the two previous long-term EU budgets. Additionally, there is a group of countries that is not likely to align either with the group of net-contributors nor with the group of the net-receivers. These member states (inter alia, Belgium, Cyprus, Ireland, Italy and Spain) are situated on the brink of the two camps at least in terms of their per capita share to the EU budget. Elsewhere we have argued that their negotiation focus could be more on the financial resources delegated to individual programmes instead of the overall ceiling of the MFF (cf. Kaiser/Prange-Gstöhl 2017: 33).

The focus on the debate about the overall MFF ceiling, i.e. about the "1%-paradigm", masks the real underlying national interests of both the net-payers and the net-receivers – the more so as usually no member state's national contribution reaches 1% of its GNI. For example, in 2016, national contributions varied between 0.55% of GNI for the UK and 0.89% for Hungary. Net-contributors like the Netherlands (0.63%), Sweden (0.71%), Germany (0.73%), Denmark (0.77%), Austria (0.79%), Italy (0.83%), Finland (0.85%), France (0.86%), and Luxembourg (0.88%) landed well below 1%.[23]

Instead, the EU budget has a huge income effect for all net-receivers being a massive source for public investments. While in 2015 the share of EU funding in public investment was below 10% for the whole EU, it reached up to 84% in Portugal (see Chapter 7).

For net-payers the burden is rather reflected in their contributions in relation to their national budgets than in relation to their GNI. Germany as the biggest net-payer may serve as an example. In 2017, the German gross contribution to the EU budget was about €29.45 billion, which was equal to 0.9% of the national GNI, but 9% of the federal budget. The amount of net-contributions was €17.72 billion or 0.5% of the German GNI or 5.3% of the federal budget. This means that the German net-contributions to the

23 For all figures see http://ec.europa.eu/budget/figures/interactive/index_en.cfm (accessed 18 May 2018).

EU budget were as high as the country's investments in its education and research system.[24]

These figures might illustrate why so much attention is usually devoted to the negotiations on the overall MFF ceiling, although a budget of 1% of the EU's GNI looks small for a neutral observer: in national contexts it's simply significant provoking fierce defence of core interests.

### *1.3 Approach, findings and book structure*

Against this background, we aim at a comprehensive analysis of the conditions and potential outcomes of the post-2020 MFF negotiations. It is based on theoretical assumptions which presume that the multiannual financial framework, as a complex institutional structure, has developed into strong change-resisting patterns. This does not preclude successful reforms, the scope and the most likely areas of reform have to be, however, evaluated against the peculiarities of the long-term development of the EU budget as well as against the current challenges for European integration. That is why the analytical part of this book seeks to inform not only about current problem constellations, but also about the previous performance of the MFF structure in terms of adapting to new conditions.

The subsequent Chapter presents the conceptual framework of our analysis. It seeks to integrate different strands of institutional theory in order to make assumptions about why the MFF has become resistant to change and what this could mean for the 2021-2027 budget. We argue that the MFF's path-dependent characteristics should not primarily be considered as a problem. Rather, over the last decades it has sufficiently provided security and reliability of expectations for the key political actors and it has still been able to proceed with the needed adjustments and adaption. Challenges and problem constellations may, however, change. That is why Chapter 2 also makes the attempt to conceptualize the current crises phenomena in Europe as a process of European disintegration.

Chapters 3 and 4 turn towards these crises' phenomena. We state that the financial and economic crisis (Chapter 3) still plays a considerable role, not because of the immediate economic consequences. It rather provoked convictions and expectations about an urgent need for substantial reforms of the European Union which peaked in 2016/17 but have become

24 For all figures see Deutscher Bundestag (2017), here "Einzelplan 60", "Anlage 1".

silent again very soon. We, therefore, assume that the negotiations for the post-2020 MFF will not be significantly affected by comprehensive reform agendas. In Chapter 4, we analyse the impact of the most recent areas of conflict, namely the Brexit, the migration policy crisis and the challenge of defining a new security and defence policy. After its prolongation, the Brexit certainly has a special importance as it puts into question not only the time schedule towards a decision on the new MFF, but also the course of negotiations. As long as the UK has not left the European Union, many aspects of the MFF cannot be finally determined (esp. the overall budget ceiling and the question of rebates and correction mechanisms).

In Chapter 5, we discuss the potential for change that exists in terms of the financing of the post-2020 MFF. There has been a lively debate in the run-up to the negotiations about the introduction of new own resources for the European Union which would allow to limit the importance of the member states' financial contributions to the budget and, thus, the logic of "juste retour" during the negotiation phase. Interestingly, however, the new own resources that have been proposed hardly differ from those that were under consideration already for the 2007-2013 MFF. More importantly, it was also shown that most of those own resources would come with enormous political transaction costs especially for the member states. We, therefore, do not expect significant changes to the current financing structure.

Chapters 6-8 deal with the future of the EU's large expenditure programmes which are always addressed as targets for change and reforms. In this respect it is highly relevant that negotiations on these programmes start from different positions. The EU's Common Agricultural Policy was subject to substantial reform between 1992 and 2003 and afterwards developed in a very incremental way. The regional and cohesion policies have less reform potential as they managed to cope with the main challenge – the integration of the Central and Eastern European countries – through institutional adjustments already made under the two preceding financial frameworks. The research and innovation policies have a special role as they are always in danger of becoming a victim of budget decisions.

In Chapter 9, we develop scenarios for stability and change in terms of assumptions both for the structural and instrumental levels of the next multiannual financial framework. These scenarios take into account a number of conditions, such as the sequence and order of events, the existence/use of windows of opportunities, the probability of external shocks, the leadership capabilities and the actors' abilities to build coalitions, the cleavage structure, as well as specific developments in national and European politics.

Chapter 10 concludes on the impediments and potentials for reform of the post-2020 MFF in terms of European disintegration. Although we do not expect significant changes to the overall budget, we still pretend that certain elements of the next MFF are adequate to save the European Union from lasting disintegration.

# 2. Path-dependency and path-breaking reforms: the institutional conditions for the post-2020 EU budget

## *2.1 The institutional complexity of the multiannual financial framework*

The European long-term financial perspective is a complex institutional structure. It does not only determine the financial resources available for all EU policies over a period of seven years, it also defines what member states can expect in terms of their contributions to the European Union and the returns they will obtain from its various expenditure programmes. Technically, the MFF is thus a budget policy instrument that regulates the distribution of money among the EU member states by providing financial resources to the European polity and its policies. Politically, however, it is much more.

Firstly, it is an expression of a common understanding of the EU institutions and the member states about the problems that should be solved at the European level. Secondly, the MFF is a manifestation of the degree of solidarity among EU member states that they consider appropriate to support coherence and stability of the common integration project. And thirdly, and most importantly, the financial framework is a tool aimed at reducing political conflicts especially among member states' governments as it provides planning security about the burdens and benefits each EU member state can expect in a medium-term perspective.

Nevertheless, because of its complexity, negotiating a new multiannual financial framework is not a trivial undertaking. The complexity emerges from very different aspects. There is the relatively long duration of the MFF that – on the one hand – produces reliability of expectations for the actors involved, but – on the other hand – always evokes discussions about the necessity of initiating urgently needed reforms. As a result, conflicts over objectives are likely to emerge especially at the beginning of the negotiation process primarily about changes within the established institutional structure. A certain amount of complexity also exists because of the large variety of actors involved. In this respect, it is useful to differentiate between those actors who participate in the negotiations on the basis of EU treaty provisions (i.e. the Commission, the Council and the Parliament) and a much broader population of actors who can exert influence on the negotiations, because they may act either as "institutional" or "partisan" veto players (Tsebelis 2002), thus limiting the freedom of action especially for national governments. Institutional veto players have a role primarily in federalized or regionalized EU member states where central governments often have to act in agreement with subnational governments or second chambers. Partisan veto players, such as interest groups, political parties, companies, etc. vary significantly in their importance across different member states, but we can at least assume a relevant role for them a) in policy areas in which large EU expenditure programmes exist (esp. in agricultural policies) as well as b) in countries in which populist parties with anti-EU agendas put a lot of political pressure on national governments to protect domestic interests vis-à-vis European ambitions. And finally, budget negotiations may gain complexity because of the duration of the bargaining process which always implies the risk that unexpected events impact on the negotiations in an unforeseeable way.

In this chapter, we look at the MFF from an institutionalist perspective that allows to grasp the complexity of the phenomenon. We aim at providing a conceptual framework that does not only help to understand the logic of agreements on prior financial perspectives, but which also guides our analysis of the current negotiation process for the post-2020 budget.

Basically, as an institutional structure, the MFF's main role is to reduce uncertainty by establishing a stable, but not necessarily efficient, framework for the actors involved in EU politics (North 1990: 6). Therefore, we start from the assumption that a multiannual financial framework is not only – and probably not even primarily – deployed to solve problems, rather it is established to set reliable rules for political interactions. This does not mean that the next MFF, nor the ones in the past, (will be) were not specifically addressed to the various challenges the European Union faced (such as economic crises, the different enlargement rounds or global problems like climate change, terrorism or migration). However, from an institutional perspective we can presume an approach towards incremental alignment to new problems that does not strictly put into question the sources of funds for European policies or the programmes that have been conducted (in most cases) already for decades. Given that, we need institutional accounts that offer plausible explanations both for stability and change, which consider the particular constellation of actors and arenas in the European multi-level polity as well as the role of timing and sequency during the negotiation process.

### 2.2 *Stability and change – explanations for the limits of reforming a complex institutional structure*

To understand and explain stability and change in the post-2020 MFF, we employ a three-level institutionalist analysis (see also De Feo 2017; Lindner 2006). At the first level of this analysis, we focus on the structural dimension of the multiannual financial framework by conceptualizing conditions that exist for institutional stability and change.

The structural dimension of the MFF is defined by rules about how to organize the investments into European policies and the transfer of financial resources across EU member states. They concern the regulation of the negotiation process (especially the requirement of unanimous decision in the Council)[25], the duration of the multiannual framework, the strong link between budget headings and large expenditure programmes, the regulations about the revenue side as well as rules established for the review and evaluation of the MFF during its operational life. These institutional rules are mainly defined by the EU treaty (Art. 312 TFEU). It holds for the maximum amount of expenditures within the limits of the EU's own resources, the decision-making rules for the Parliament and the Council, the involvement of the European Council, the minimum duration of the MFF of five years, the MFF's determination of the annual ceilings of commitment and payment appropriations as well as the definition of expenditure categories that have to correspond with the EU's main sectors of activity. Consequently, the structural dimension of the MFF is a priori outside the focus of MFF negotiations as long as there is no consensus among EU member states on a treaty amendment.

From an institutionalist perspective, it is an important fact that the "constitutional" definition of the structural dimension of the MFF has taken place only with the Lisbon Treaty. By transforming the MFF from an inter-institutional agreement between the respective EU institutions into a legally binding act, the EU member states, acting as the "masters of the treaty", made sure that there is a high amount of security on the rules of interaction which largely eliminates conflicts about the MFF's structural dimension during the negotiation process. In theoretical terms, the Lisbon Treaty provided for a "lock-in" (Liebowitz/Margolis 1995) to a specific

25 According to Art. 312(2) TFEU, the Council may decide by qualified majority if the European Council authorizes the Council to do so by unanimous decision. The logic of decision-making on the MFF therefore is not changed, since all member states maintain a veto position.

institutional solution established to solve EU budgetary problems. This solution makes it difficult to change the structural dimension in the future, because the barriers for EU treaty revision are obviously much higher than those that existed before for changing an inter-institutional agreement between the Commission, the Council and the Parliament. The institutional trajectory that was established in 1988 with the "invention" of the MFF has further consolidated, thus limiting significantly the reform options for the future. We have to ask why the structural dimension of the MFF became more and more path-dependent?

Historical institutionalism provides for the assumption that a complex institutional structure (once it has become established as an institutional compromise of elites) tends to develop along a specific path as long as it produces positive feedbacks. The path-dependency argument has three important elements.

First of all, we need to define a critical juncture, a specific moment in time at which a new institutional path was established. Since the late 1970s, severe conflicts over the European budget posed a risk not only to what had already been achieved in the process of European integration, but also to the further development of the European Communities (EC) in general. The institutional conditions for solving the situation became more and more difficult, because of the existence of two separate lines of conflict: a first one between the member states and the European Parliament that acted increasingly self-confident after its first direct election in 1979; and a second one between the "old" and "new" members of the European Communities. Their growing divide was bridged in June 1984 only after Margaret Thatcher received the British rebate on the country's contribution to the EU budget. The critical juncture at which the institutional path of the MFF was taken was thus characterized by three distinct conditions:

1. An institutional conflict over political influence and decision-making power on the European budget between the Parliament and the Council,
2. An increasing level of insecurity about the resources that would be delegated in the future to long-established funding programmes especially in agricultural policy,
3. An obviously inadequate general financial endowment of the European level in light of the imminent deepening of European integration (i.e. the Single European Act of 1986) and the "Southern" enlargement of the EC regarding Greece (1981) as well as Portugal and Spain (1986).

We have already argued that the multidimensional crisis of European integration is a most recent development that differs from various critical situations in the past. However, the concept of path-dependency does not necessarily consider the size or the degree of the crisis as the crucial factor. Pierson (2000: 75) has rightly pointed out that:

> "'Small' events early on may have a big impact, while 'large' events at later stages may be less consequential. To put this another way, outcomes of early events or processes in the sequence are amplified, while later events or processes are dampened. Thus, when a particular event in a sequence occurs will make a big difference. In politics, the crucial implication of path dependence arguments is that early stages in a sequence can place particular aspects of political systems onto distinct tracks, which are then reinforced through time."

The critical juncture that emerged in the mid-1980s did not exist because of a "big" event or crisis, but as a result of a coincidence of time of constitutional and political conflicts. Each of the individual conflict dimensions would probably not have initiated an alternative institutional path. At least we can say that under the MFF structure that was established in 1988, the European Union managed a number of institutional reforms and several rounds of enlargement without putting into question the continuation of the institutional solution found for the long-term financial perspective.

Secondly, we have to provide plausible reasons for the re-enforcing of the institutional path over time. In this respect, increasing returns for the actors involved is the key point. Increasing returns can be of very different kind.[26] For the purpose of our analysis, the following three aspects are the most crucial ones:

1. The established institutional structure reduces the costs of negotiations and agreements in the future: this holds both for the duration of negotiations as well as for the level of conflict. The far-reaching predetermination of the MFF's structure facilitates the balancing of interests, because proposed changes can be quite easily evaluated by actors in terms of their consequences for themselves, but also for the members of the different coalitions and interest representations.
2. It allows for learning effects: actors become aware of the potential conflicts and diverging preferences that will most likely play a role in

26 The concept of "increasing returns" was developed in economic theory in order to explain why a particular technology stays successful on the market although alternative and even more efficient ones are available (cf. Arthur 1994; David 1985). The concept was later on adapted to the explanation of institutional stability (see especially Pierson 2000).

future negotiations. This is especially important if external factors (such as the economic development, the consequences of trade agreements, etc.) promote a dynamic under which certain member states cannot be clearly classified anymore as net-payers/net-recipients in terms of the overall budget or as contributors/beneficiaries of large-scale expenditure programmes.

3. It produces positive coordination effects: the MFF structure has certainly reinforced "juste retour" as the dominant logic of negotiations while existing cleavages among actors have further consolidated. Under the condition of unanimous agreement on the budget, coordination among actors is facilitated, because there is – from the beginning – a relatively clear understanding about what coalitions or compromises could support a final agreement. This holds especially if there is already a broad consensus about the degree to which reforms of the MFF are needed.

If these conditions (or at least some of them) are met, actors have hardly any incentive to change the institutional rules established for the solution of a political problem. They will most likely opt for change within the given structure, which means for institutional adjustment and adaption. This requires, however, that the given structure is sufficiently flexible to handle different degrees of sub-structural change.

And thirdly, we have to evaluate whether or not the current crises phenomena in Europe do qualify for another critical juncture at which an alternative path could be taken. This is one important objective of the book. The concept of path-dependency does not reject the possibility of institutional change. Rather it provides an explanation for structural stability and changes that follow the logic of the established institutional path. The MFF's structural dimension became largely immunized against rapid institutional change while in terms of the instrumental level we find sufficient empirical evidence for the assumption that the MFF is designed in a way that allows for institutional adaption and adjustments. We are thus in need of a conceptual understanding of the different forms and causes of change within a largely stable structure.

In his analysis of macroeconomic policies in Britain, Peter Hall (1993) has differentiated three degrees of policy change showing that there are at least two types of change that alter the instruments and techniques of public policies without putting into question existing paradigmatic objectives and convictions that exist in a policy domain. Hall relates policy change to learning processes which are taking place among key agents active in a policy field, such as state officials or experts with a privileged access to political decision-making at the interface between bureaucracy and society. The important aspect is that state interventions in a given field of action takes place within the limits of certain ideas and standards which are "comprehensible and plausible to the actors involved" (Anderson 1978: 23). Or, in the words of Hall (1993: 279), "normal policy-making" proceeds under a specific and stable policy paradigm:

> "More precisely, policymakers customarily work within a framework of ideas and standards that specifies not only the goals of policy and the kind of instruments that can be used to attain them, but also the very nature of the problems they are meant to be addressing. Like a Gestalt, this framework is embedded in the very terminology through which policymakers communicate about their work, and it is influential precisely because so much of it is taken for granted and unamenable to scrutiny as a whole. I am going to call this interpretive framework a policy paradigm."

This is especially true for European budget policies. As said before, in preparing the Commission's proposal for a new multiannual financial framework, there is already, long before the political bargaining begins, a comprehensive coordination with representatives from member states assembled in working groups of the Council. These representatives originate from administrative levels; thus, it is plausible to assume, that they consider necessary reforms as challenges of institutional adjustment and less as a political opportunity to change the structure. In more concrete terms, we can conceptualize three different levels of change.

At the *first level*, there is only limited adjustment of the existing instruments and administrative techniques as well as minor change in terms of the resources devoted to the different European policies. This type of policy change is likely in the absence of significant conflicts over the main objectives of European integration and in times in which the actors are not confronted with major crises phenomena. Institutional adjustment is the result of policy learning and of experiences made during the time of operation of the previous MFF (which is still running for years when the preparations for the new financial framework already starts).

At the *second level* we would expect that new challenges to European integration lead to a more substantial change especially at the instrumental level. Here changes are most likely in form of the establishment of new funding lines and/or in form of re-allocations across budget headings. This second order change would still adhere to the established framework of ideas and standards. However, such a policy shift goes beyond institutional adjustment as it requires certain adaptions to phenomena that have occurred only recently, or which have changed in their nature compared to the situation that existed when the previous MFF was agreed. Institutional adaption is certainly more demanding as it requires a consensus about the problems and possible solutions between the Commission, the Parliament and the Council as well as with relevant stakeholders.

At the *third level* we would anticipate that the policy change constitutes a paradigmatic shift in EU budget policies. Such a third-order change would comprehensively re-align the budget to relatively few policy areas. This would require a substantial re-allocation of funds across existing budget lines as well as a refocusing of investments on relatively few strategic areas in which the EU can provide an uncontested added value. It could also imply new rules for the financing of the European Union. At this level we assume that the member states would have to be the key agenda-setters, since paradigmatic change would require amendments of the EU treaty.

### *2.3 Actors and arenas – explanations for the particular pattern of budget negotiations in the European Union*

At the second level of institutional analysis we look at actors and arenas. Across the different strands of neo-institutionalism, it is generally accepted that actors' behaviour and interactions are influenced by the institutional setting in which they operate.

Rational choice institutionalists acknowledge the institutional environment as a source of restrictions and incentives which impact on their strategies that are based on stable preferences. Therefore, different institutional structures produce different actor strategies and different outcomes of their interactions. Proponents of sociological institutionalism focus more on shared norms and values that guide actors' behaviour. For them, it's the logic of appropriateness and not (as in RC institutionalism) the logic of consequentiality that mainly explains the actors' interaction. Under the logic of appropriateness, actors pursue politics following rules that are seen as "natural, rightful, expected, and legitimate" (March/Olson 1995: 1).

Mayntz and Scharpf (1995) have to some extent integrated the assumptions of rational choice and sociological institutionalism into their heuristic concept of actor-centred institutionalism. They consider the institutional environment that exists for a specific problem-solving process as the main variable (apart from the many non-institutional factors) that impacts on the actors involved, in terms of their orientations and capabilities, the actor constellations and the action situation. These three factors can later on provide an explanation for the interactions in which actors are engage in to solve the political problem. The institutional context, defined by a system of formal (often legal) regulations as well as informal (social) norms, is therefore crucial to understand how processes of political bargaining proceed and what outcomes they produce. In this respect, the institutional environment that structures European policy processes in general and EU budget negotiations in particular, is highly peculiar one.

Since the early 1990s, it has become widely accepted that the European Union has developed into a system of multi-level governance that consists of three distinct features (Grande 2000; Hooghe/Marks 2001; Marks et al. 1996; Peters/Pierre 2002):

1. decision-making competencies are shared by actors at different levels (i.e. a "dynamic" dispersion of authority);
2. actors and arenas are not ordered hierarchically as in traditional intergovernmental relationships (i.e. non-hierarchical institutional design);
3. consensual or non-majoritarian decision-making among states, which requires a continuous wide-ranging negotiation process (i.e. non-majoritarian negotiation system).

According to the first feature, decision-making competencies are dispersed across territorial levels, i.e. across supranational, national, and regional or local actors, or allocated sideways, to quasi-autonomous agencies or to non-public implementation bodies (Majone 1996; Thatcher/Stone Sweet 2002). It is precisely this dispersion of authority that makes the European multi-level governance system a highly dynamic one, in which "the competencies and functions of the different levels have not been fixed precisely yet … and cannot be fixed precisely at all" (Grande 2001: 9). What follows is that European governance is not a stable pattern, "but varies over time and across policy areas" (Kohler-Koch 1999: 32). With regard to aspects of authority relocation it is of special importance that in contrast to federal systems, in a multi-level governance system the interactions between the different levels are not "disciplined" by constitutional norms. As a consequence, the European system of multi-level governance is characterized by a considerable competition for competencies between the different territorial levels (Grande 2001; Mayntz 1999; Peters/Pierre 2002).

The idea of the second feature is that actors and arenas are not ordered hierarchically, so that "supranational institutions are not hierarchically superimposed upon the member states; and the member states and their regions are not subordinated to the supranational powers" (Grande 2001: 7). Rather, "political arenas are interconnected rather than nested" (Marks et al. 1996: 346f), which means that subnational actors not only operate at the national, but also at the supranational level. The consequences of this constellation are two-fold: firstly, in the European system of multi-level governance, actors at different territorial levels form "integrated systems of joint decision-making" (Scharpf 1988), leading to a growing demand for policy coordination; and secondly, regional and local actors "by-pass" the national level to pursue their interests at the supranational level (Beauregard/Pierre 2000; Peters/Pierre 2002), so that national governments could no longer monopolize the contacts to the European level.

The third point stresses that the European system of multi-level governance is characterized by a non-majoritarian mode of decision-making (Grande 2000: 8f; Moravcsik 2001: 173f). A non-majoritarian mode of decision-making is still considered necessary at least in matters of high importance to represent territorial interests. Both the non-hierarchical nature of the system and the still important role of national governments at the supranational level turn the European multi-level governance system into a negotiation system, in which bargaining capacities and skills – and not hierarchical power – determine the outcomes (Grande 2001).

For that reason, the agenda-setting capability of the different EU institutions is much more contested than we would expect on the basis of the treaty law. In general, the European Commission is the prime initiator of EU legislation and the "guardian of the treaty" and thus responsible for ensuring compliance of the member states with EU law.

In public policy research, the concept of policy entrepreneurship aims at providing explanations for the existence and the (sometimes unexpected) outcome of agenda-setting processes in which a political actor (i.e. the policy entrepreneur) succeeds in proposing and pushing through his problem solution strategy even against the anticipated resistance of other political actors whose agreement is needed for the implementation of this solution.

To do so, a policy entrepreneur must have some specific actor qualities as well as the capacity to make use of them. According to Kingdon (1984: 189f.), there are three main actor qualities: (1) the actor's status as a recognized expert and a serious leader who acts in the interests of others or has an authoritative decision-making position, (2) the actor's negotiation and networking capabilities which are mainly based on the combination of technical expertise and political savvy, and (3) the actor's persistence in the political arena which provides him with the opportunity to wait for a policy window and to make use of it when it opens. Based on these qualities the policy entrepreneur can initiate change through the coupling of at least two of three separate and independent streams within a political system which "carry" descriptions of problems, several possible strategies for the solution of the problem and a political event which render the agreement on such a strategy more likely (such as a crisis, unexpected election results or interest group campaigns).

For the study of EU politics, Kingdon's concept of the policy entrepreneur is quite useful as it clearly allows for the characterization of the different EU institutions' potential to act as a policy entrepreneur. The European Commission's entrepreneurial capacity stems from the possession of the required information and its technical resources. It also has the prime role in formal agenda-setting procedures, and it has established a comprehensive system of standing and ad-hoc committees as well as expert groups, which allow for the early coordination of legislative proposals with representatives from the member states and with private actors.

Yet, the role of the European Commission as the "natural" agenda-setter is not uncontested, especially not in the process of budget negotiations. This is mainly because of the gradual transition of the European Council from an informal forum of the Heads of States and Governments to the EU's "control centre". With the Lisbon Treaty, the European Council gained the status of a formal institution of the European Union, which "shall provide the Union with the necessary impetus for its development," (Article 15 TEU). The treaty also foresees that the European Council shall meet twice every six months with the option to convene special meetings if "the situation so requires". Meanwhile, the number of European Council meetings has significantly increased, especially in phases of immediate crisis management. This reflects the growing coordination needs among the Heads of States and Governments especially in the context of the Euro crisis and, more recently, the Brexit. But it also indicates that member states only engage in strengthening the coordination of their national policies at the European level (e.g. the EU's new "economic government") under the condition of reinforcing the intergovernmental dimension of European integration.

### *2.4 Timing and sequency – explanations for the "external" susceptibility of the budget negotiation process*

We have already referred to the varying impact of "small" or "big" events in the process of establishing an institutional path. However, it is not only the "size" of the event that matters. In fact, historical institutionalism does not simply focus on the continuous effect of institutional solutions established in the past. Rather, the timing and the temporal order of events has a significant impact on the policy outcome (Pierson 2000). This means that it is also the sequence of events that decides about the ongoing effect of a positive feedback loop that stabilizes a path-dependent institutional structure.

In the European system of multi-level governance, the timing and sequency has a particular significance, because certain events could impact at different moments on national or European politics. In Chapter 1, we already discussed the conditions under which the 2010 budget review failed to initiate major changes for the MFF 2014-2020. This was because of the fact that European politics were still in a mode of "normal" politics while at the member states' level the consequences of the financial crisis had already forced governments into a mode of crisis politics.

The asynchronicity of different modes of policy seems to impact also on the negotiations of the post-2020 budget. European actors, especially the European Commission, called for a conclusion of the negotiation before the elections to the European Parliament in May 2019 apparently worried by the expectation that the long-established informal "grand coalition" between the conservative and the socialist party may lose its majority. Member states' governments were, in contrast, less enthusiastic about reaching an early deal, probably because the electoral success of anti-EU protest parties had already made it more difficult at the national level to form governing coalitions in at least some countries (for example in Germany, Denmark, the Netherlands, and Sweden) and thus to agree on a national position for the budget negotiations.

In principle, various factors, such as the Brexit, the significant support anti-European populist parties receive across Europe, but also the disagreement among member states over migration policies, or the "isolationistic" agenda of the new U.S. administration, may open a window of opportunity for fundamental reforms in Europe. However, whether or not there actually is a window of opportunity and – more importantly – whether or not it can be utilized for initiating reforms depends on timing and sequence. We have argued elsewhere (Kaiser/Prange-Gstöhl 2017) that a policy window for substantial reforms could have existed between October 2017 (after the German elections) and spring 2018 when the European Commission drafted the MFF proposal. In the end, it did not materialize, mainly because of the lengthy negotiations for a new coalition government in Germany. The prolongation of the Brexit could again provide for such a policy window, especially if the UK does not manage to leave the Union by 31 October 2019. We assume that because of the prolongation of the Brexit the negotiations on the post-2020 MFF will not enter into a decisive phase before the end of 2019.

### *2.5 Integrating "disintegration" into an institutionalist perspective on the MFF*

The manifold crisis phenomena confronting the European Union for at least a decade have sparked a debate in the discipline of political science about possible tendencies of disintegration in Europe. Causes of disintegration have been found in increasingly greater heterogeneity of national interests which evoke the danger of a re-nationalization of certain policies in which the European Union lacks problem-solving capacity (Tassinari 2016), or as reactions to an expansive judicial development of law by the European Court of Justice (ECJ) to which member states reacted by opting-out from certain policies or by restricting the possibility to request preliminary ruling from the ECJ to national courts of last resort only (Arnull 2007). Rosamond has even identified a much more fundamental structural phenomenon that he describes as a crisis of the "democratic-capitalist agreement" (2016), in which the process of European integration is historically embedded. According to him, European integration initially profited from a de-coupling of the logics of capitalism and democracy, because it was at first the member states' level that has become confronted with low growth rates, post-industrial transition, increasing fiscal burdens, growing inequality and the decline of political parties. Therefore, supranational integration appeared to be an institutional solution for the collective problems at the national level. With the financial and the sovereign debt crises, however, Europe was increasingly considered as part of the problem and not the solution. The "permissive consensus" on integration – meaning the possibility to legitimize European integration mainly through positive policy outcomes and less through the democratic quality of its institutions and procedures – weakened (Rosamond 2016: 869). This shows that an asynchronicity of different policy modes (normal policies vs. crisis policies) within the European system of multi-level governance may not only be an element of explanation for a lack of reforms or an impediment for further integration, it can also provide indication for causes of disintegration.

In order to understand the drivers of disintegration, several attempts have also been made to evaluate established theories of integration and international relations to see if they can provide explanations for the opposing process.

In this context, Schmitter and Lefkofridi (2016) have argued that some of the components of neo-functional integration theory assume the possibility of "spill-backs" (as opposed to the traditional "spill-overs") within the integration process. In their words, a spill-back emerges "when member states no longer wish to deal with a policy at supranational level" (Schmitter/Lefkofridi 2016: 3). The key question is then, why European institutions should agree or be forced to withdraw a competence that exists for supranational policy-making. We can assume at least two motivations. Firstly, supranational policy-making in a given field does not produce sufficient results anymore or, secondly, resources that are bound in this policy area are needed to provide funding for more urgent or new challenges. In both cases, the withdrawal from a policy area (or parts of it) could be a reasonable strategy to stabilize the integration project. Technically, such a withdrawal would find expression first in the process of medium-term financial planning in form of changes of budget lines or the reallocation of funds across them.

One could argue that a collapse of the European Union seems to be not very likely or that even substantial steps towards disintegration are implausible. Vollaard (2018) has rightly observed that the disintegration of political systems is, from a historical perspective, per se not an unusual process. He argues that the process of European disintegration is thus fundamentally open to comparative and empirical scrutiny. Furthermore, from a conceptual perspective, it can be seen that disintegration is a multidimensional process that can take place at the political, economic, territorial, institutional, socio-cultural or legal level, without the need for disintegrative tendencies to exist simultaneously on several of these levels (Vollaard 2018: 120). To scrutinize what reasons may initiate even a limited or sectoral form of disintegration integration theory provides at least two explanations.

In neo-functionalistic terms, disintegration could emerge from exceptional shocks, integrative overstretch, a diminishing demand for European regulation, changing interest coalitions, or a declining desire for European solutions at the member states' level. (Lindberg/Scheingold 1971: 121; Vollaard 2018: 18). Liberal intergovernmentalism would conceive disintegration mainly as a decrease of policy coordination at EU level. This does not necessarily mean that there is less coordination in Europe, because it could take place in arenas outside the European Union or in form of bilateral or plurilateral coordination among member states. This could happen if relevant actors consider the costs of supranational integration as too high in terms of resources not available anymore at the national level, but also in view of political costs arising from negative impact on national identity, sovereignty or electoral results (Hooghe/Marks 2009; Vollaard 2018: 51). There are already some indications for a "repositioning" of processes of political coordination, both inside the EU's political system, but also away from the EU to the member states. We have already discussed the growing importance of the European Council as the new Union's ("secret") control centre at the expense of the supranational institutions. There are also cases in which European solutions have not much to do with European policy coordination. The most prominent case certainly is the EU-Turkey deal negotiated in the heyday of the refugee crisis. In fall 2015, EU-Commission Vice-President Frans Timmermans and the President of the European Council, Donald Tusk, had started negotiations with the Turkish government on financial compensations for Turkey if the country would hinder refugees from travelling to Greece. The German government, under enormous political pressure because of the large number of refugees entering the country, engaged in bilateral talks with Turkey that led in the end (with some support from the Dutch prime minister Mark Rutte) to an agreement between the EU and Turkey that was concluded by the European Council on 7/8 March 2016. The "Merkel deal" had some implications for other EU countries, especially because of the amount of money Merkel had promised to Turkey. It was considerably higher than foreseen in the Timmermans/Tusk initiative.

A disintegration of the European Union does not arrive as an unexpected stroke of fate. On the contrary, it can (and probably will) be the result of strategic action. In a series of "reflection papers" in 2017, the European Commission presented scenarios for the future of the EU (esp. European Commission 2017a, 2017b) that exposed the shape and the consequences of different levels of integration. The alternatives went from a "disintegration" towards the integration core of the single market, via differentiated integration to a much deeper political integration. Accordingly, alternative scenarios for the development of the EU's financial basis ranged from "significantly lower", via "broadly stable" to "significantly increased" (European Commission 2017b). Up to now, these "reflections" did not gain any importance for the reform debate. This confirms our theoretical consideration in so far as we currently do not see sufficient reason which could move the European Union beyond incremental change. However, they at least indicate that a certain limited form of "controlled" disintegration might be a reasonable strategy to stabilize the main achievements of European integration.

### *2.6 Conclusions*

The aim of this chapter has been to demonstrate what theoretical considerations guide our analysis of the post-2020 MFF negotiations and the scenarios for the budget bargaining output. We have explained the reasons that justify the assumption for institutional stability at the structural level of the MFF. We have also outlined the conditions and the potential degrees of change that exist within the given institutional context. Furthermore, we have argued that in an era of multidimensional crises the MFF's main function lies in the stabilization of the integrative core of the European Union while it should also find sufficient answers to certain aspects of disintegration.

More than any other policy process in the European Union, the negotiations for a new multiannual financial framework are determined by experiences the relevant actors made in the earlier funding period, by preferences on how the European Union should develop in a medium-term perspective, by assumptions about problem constellations in the near future and by specific interests concerning the impact of the post-2020 budget on political competition in the respective actors' arenas. On top of this, the negotiations – simply because of the length of the bargaining process – may always become subject to unforeseen developments.

# 3. The Union in a state of emergency: the financial and economic crisis and its repercussions

## *3.1 Introduction*

As described in Chapter 1, the various major challenges – or crises – the EU faces simultaneously, such as Brexit, the significant support anti-European populist parties receive across Europe, but also the disagreement among member states over migration and asylum policies, and the "isolationistic" agenda of the new U.S. administration, could – under certain conditions – open a window of opportunity for fundamental reforms in Europe. The economic and financial crisis, which is looming since a decade now, has triggered some of those crises, while their origins may be found further back in European integration history.

In this and the following chapter we will illustrate the multi-dimensional character of EU crises since the mid-2000s to demonstrate the new challenges and new demands framing decision-making on the next EU financial framework. In the following we will first focus on the financial and economic crisis, before Chapter 4 will address Brexit, international migration and asylum policies, as well as new security and defence concerns.

Against the background that among EU political leaders and institutions a broad consensus has emerged that the European Union needs substantial reforms (Council of the European Union 2017b; European Commission 2017a; European Council 2016a) and that leaders even committed themselves to make the Union within the next decade "stronger and more resilient, through even greater unity and solidarity amongst us and the respect of common rules" (Council of the European Union 2017c) one could assume that the next multiannual financial framework for the post-2020 period will become the key operational tool providing the financial means to meet the challenges and to achieve the objectives (also European Commission 2017b).

### 3.2 The origins and consequences of the crisis

Called by some authors "Europe`s first true existential crisis" (Copsey 2015: 15) the financial and economic crisis went in fact through various phases (see, for example, Overbeek 2012). Starting from a global financial and banking crisis triggered by the crash of Lehman Brothers in the USA – the fourth largest bank in America – in September 2008, it became a European sovereign debt and banking crisis soon afterwards. In May 2010, the narrative turned towards the Eurozone crisis when first Greece ran out of money and German Chancellor Angela Merkel prominently stated that "If the Euro Fails, Europe fails"[27]. The crisis finally headed into a socio-economic crisis particularly hitting hard Southern European member states, which faced sharply shrinking economies, high unemployment rates, and a decline of their welfare states (see, for example, Matthijs 2014).

The European sovereign debt crisis was provoked by the fallout from the global recession, which had its origins in the above-mentioned banking crisis. Globally acting banks were holding bad loans of creditors that were not able anymore to pay their mortgages, a situation that worsened when house prices began to fall, first in the USA, and banks could not sell on the property to recoup their investments. As a consequence, US mortgages lost their value, banks were not willing anymore to lend money to each other, and inter-bank lending seized leading to a liquidity crisis of banks. In several cases this development led to massive government interventions to provide liquidity or nationalise private banks.

At the same time, the global recession created a need on the part of European governments to borrow money in response to falling tax revenues and rising welfare payments during 2008-2010 bringing fairly balanced national accounts out of shape (Copsey 2015: 18). Particularly Ireland and Spain profited from sound public finances and stable economic growth leading to a very low level of public debt of 24% and 36% of GDP, respectively, in 2007 (Angeloni et al. 2012: 19).

The economic downturn led to increased demand for fresh money. Eurozone governments were borrowing money by selling bonds in the Euro currency on the financial market. However, no central bank served as buyer-of-last resort, which would have been the guarantee for creditors that

27 The original quote, which Angela Merkel stated on 19 May 2010 in the German Bundestag, is "Das ist unsere historische Aufgabe; denn scheitert der Euro, dann scheitert Europa" (Deutscher Bundestag 2010: 4126).

debt obligations of governments are always paid back in full. The European Central Bank was not allowed to play that role. As debt in weak European economies, such as Greece, Cyprus and Portugal, grew, market actors lost confidence that these governments would be able to fully return the loans. Interest payments demanded by the market rose sharply as a consequence. Before that, the relatively low interest rates in the Eurozone provoked growing government spending in several EU member states, concealed for many years by "artificial" tax revenues stemming from a booming construction sector reliant on property bubbles.

In parallel, private debt, both in the corporate sector and in households, increased substantially after the introduction of the Euro, especially in Ireland, Spain and Portugal:

> "The increase in private indebtedness was fuelled by the unprecedentedly low borrowing costs that came with the single currency. The resulting boom became self-reinforcing as higher inflation rates reduced the real borrowing costs even further so that real interest rates became negative in some instances" (Angeloni et al. 2012: 19).

The Eurozone crisis was reinforced by the fact that to a large extent the sovereign debt of countries in economic and financial trouble were held by banks in creditor countries, thus requiring the latter to stabilise or bailout the banks in their jurisdictions not to risk a major banking crash. In turn, the doubts of market actors about a country's creditworthiness increased by rescuing institutions that were considered as "too big to fail" (Angeloni et al. 2012: 24). In fact, in the Eurozone each member state had to handle this situation on its own due to a missing single resolution system. Each member state was responsible for its domestic banking system, "with the cost of bank capitalisation and rescue packages remaining with the individual countries" (Angeloni et al. 2012: 25).

There is thus a strong nexus between the banking crisis and the sovereign debt crisis. As Correa and Sapriza (2014: 25) point out, "the close connection between banks and sovereigns leads to financial instability by amplifying any shocks that affect either sector", that is, to "negative feedback loops" between the sectors (Pisani-Ferry 2011: 102). "The close links between Eurozone banks and national governments provided the multiplier that made the crisis systemic" (Baldwin/Giavazzi 2017).

Besides these economic origins of the crisis, there are – according to Mourlon-Druol (2014) – historic institutional shortcomings when creating a single currency (discussed since the 1960s) that had not been resolved by the time the Euro had been introduced. These shortcomings included a not fully integrated market with far-reaching mobility of goods and labour preventing the enforcement of wage adjustments in line with productivity; a lack of coordination of economic policy that could have enabled strong anti-cyclical fiscal policies, in combination with a non-enforcement of the fiscal coordination framework in place (i.e. the failure of the Stability and Growth Pact[28]); no focus on the necessary economic reforms to remain competitive contributing to a lack of economic convergence; non-existence of a stabilising financial mechanism; non-existence of a common banking policy, including supervision and resolution.

In sum, the outbreak of the crisis in the EU can broadly be explained by excessive public and private debt borrowed from abroad, diverging competitiveness amongst Eurozone members, and a weak regulation of the financial sector (see also Haas/Gnath 2016). The economic and political consequences of these flaws will be explained in the following.

First, since 2008, Europe has suffered economically from the financial and economic crisis. The EU's gross domestic product (GDP) fell by 4.2% in 2009, industrial production dropped back to the levels of the 1990s, 23 million people – or 10% of the EU's active population – were unemployed and deficits reached 7% of GDP. Public debt levels increased by more than 20% from below 70% before the crisis to 92% of GDP on average in 2014 (European Commission 2017b: 9). The negative trends continued through 2011 to 2012 with a gradual recovery across the EU since 2013.

However, "the EU average expresses diverse growth trajectories and very different experiences during the crisis across member states" (European Commission 2014a: 5). The Baltic states had been hit hardest. In 2009, GDP fell by 17.7% in Latvia, by 14.8% in Lithuania (both non-Euro members at that time) and by 14.3% in Estonia. Other Eurozone countries such as Finland (-8,2%), Slovenia (-8.0%), and Ireland (-7.0%) also experienced sharp contractions of their GDP. Only non-Euro member Poland saw a GDP increase of 1.6% (European Commission 2011c: 206). In terms of unemployment, again the Baltic countries as well as Ireland and Spain suffered most from the crisis. Between 2007 and 2010 unemployment rates rose from 4.3% to 17.8% in Lithuania, from 4.7% to 16.9% in Estonia, from 6.0% to 18.7% in Latvia, from 4.6% to 13.7% in Ireland, and from 8.3% to 20.1% in Spain. Only in Germany – where the unemployment rate even fell from 8.7% to 7.1% –, in Austria and in Poland (in

28 For Frankel (2015) "the Stability and Growth Pact had no teeth and no credibility. In other words, the moral hazard problem, though correctly identified, had not been effectively addressed".

both countries the rates did not change) unemployment did not increase between 2007 and 2011 (ibid.: 217).

The economic and financial crisis resulted in a rising gap between southern and northern European economies. While GDP in the northern Eurozone countries (Germany, France, the Netherlands and Belgium) has been growing in 2011 and 2012 due to their strong competitiveness, the economies in southern Eurozone states have experienced further contradictions over the same period (with the notable exemption of Finland which recovered only in 2014; see European Commission 2014b: 1) resulting in the Eurozone becoming a "two-speed" economy. Since 2014 the Eurozone as whole is back on a modest growth track with a GDP increase of 1.2% in 2014, 2.0% in 2015, 1.8% in 2016, 2.2% in 2017 (forecast), 2.1% in 2018 (forecast), and 1.9% in 2019 (forecast) (see European Commission 2017c: 185). However, except for Ireland and Spain the growth rates of those member states that were hit by the crisis most are still not at a level to compensate for the huge contraction characterising the years before. With 9.5% in March 2017, unemployment on the EU has fallen to its lowest level since 2009 (European Commission 2017b: 11). However, unemployment rates still differ substantially across the Euro area, with very low levels of unemployment in Germany (3.9%), the Netherlands (5.1%), Estonia (5.5%), and Austria (5.9%), and very high levels in Spain (18.2%) and Greece (23.5%) (ibid.: 13). Faced with these figures, one could safely agree with the European Commission's assessment that "[T]the convergence trends of the single currency's first years have proven partly illusory" (ibid.: 12).

The political consequences of the crisis have been severe. Hix (2015) argues that democratic accountability matters more than ever. On the one hand, the re-distributional effects of the crisis are potentially massive, for example, through the new stabilization mechanisms that had been introduced. The amounts committed to the European Stability Mechanism (ESM) by member states are much higher than the commitments of these states to the International Monetary Fund (IMF). As taxpayers are liable for these commitments, parliaments and citizens need to be empowered to hold their governments accountable for such re-distributional decisions (even if this financial assistance consisted of non-concessional loans and not of grants). On the other hand, governments in debtor countries had to gain acceptance for austerity measures (such as spending cuts, tax increases, and the freezing of public sector employment) imposed by non-accountable actors from outside.

Government instabilities in all bailout countries and serious challenges for governments in creditor countries have been a second effect of the crisis. "Southern Europe faced the outbreak of an 'electoral epidemic'", as Bosco and Verney (2016: 383) argue, reflecting citizens' political discontent. Especially in Spain and Greece, the impact on the party systems was notable. "Parliamentary breakthroughs by new contenders, changes in the identity of the three main parties, a major decline of the socialist parties and rising fragmentation radically reshaped the competitive arenas in these two South European states" (Bosco/Verney 2016: 403).

In other words, the crisis triggered a rise of populist and anti-European protest parties, both right- and left-wing, and both in debtor and creditor countries: Golden Dawn and Syriza in Greece, Podemos in Spain, the 5-Star-Movement in Italy, the Alternative für Deutschland in Germany, the True Finns Party in Finland, and the Party of Freedom in the Netherlands are just the prominent examples of that development. The fragmentation of national party systems and the political polarization of societies are the ultimately fallouts of this process reflecting the feeling amongst a large part of the population that they are faced with so-called "TINA" ("There Is No Alternative") politics (for example, Gerodimos/Karyotis 2015).

Last but not least, solidarity and fairness in the EU was questioned, a "us versus them"-dynamic became more explicit. Southern European debtor countries demanded more solidarity from northern European creditor countries to overcome their economic and financial problems (for example, Auer 2014; Longo/Murray 2015; Newman 2015; Pantazatou 2015). In his State-of-the-Union speech in September 2017 Commission President Juncker (2017) pointed out that "solidarity is not yet equally shared across all our member states". However, solidarity is ambiguous and contested. In the EU solidarity is mainly executed either through "direct reciprocity" or "enlightened self-interest" (Fernandes/Rubio 2012). In the first case, EU countries commit themselves to reciprocal aid in face of a risk that is equally spread among member states, for example in case of a terrorist attack or natural or man-made disasters (cf. Art. 222 TFEU). In the second case, "solidarity is driven by the donor EU countries' conviction that helping the recipient countries ultimately benefits them" (Fernandes/Rubio 2012: 5) and in turn generates economic benefits for the donor countries themselves. This is the logic of the cohesion funds or the ESM. Solidarity through "enlightened self-interest" is characterized by the differences within a group – richer EU member states help poorer ones to secure the stability of the group. This "us versus them"-logic exacerbated during the crisis – as, on the one hand, several national electorates and parliaments in creditor countries had difficulties seeing the benefits from helping other countries, and on the other hand, national electorates and parliaments in debtor countries felt oppressed by northern governments and EU institutions – undermining the general solidarity principle of the Union.

## *3.3 EU responses to the crisis*

Responses to the financial and economic crisis have been manifold, which some authors led to the conclusion that the Eurozone was "governed by panic" (Woodruff 2014). In the following we distinguish between financial (economic stimulus and budgetary austerity, fiscal measures) and regulatory responses (EMU governance).

### 3.3.1 Two sides of the same coin: economic stimulus and budgetary austerity

In December 2008, the European Council reacted to the economic downturn in the Union by approving a European Economic Recovery Plan (EERP). The EERP was equivalent to about 1.5% of the EU GDP (around €200 billion, with €170 billion coming from national budgets and €30 billion from the EU budget and the European Investment Bank). The plan had set out a programme to steer action to "smart investments" in people's skills, in energy efficiency, in clean technologies to boost sectors such as construction and automobiles in the low-carbon markets, and in infrastructure and interconnection (see European Commission 2008). The EU's recovery plan was also supposed to reinforce the Lisbon Strategy[29] by increasing investments in research, technological development and innovation through joining public and private forces.

During 2009/2010 EU member states launched stimulus packages marking the switch into a "crisis management mode".[30] In terms of the re-

29 In March 2000, the Heads of State and Government agreed making the EU "the most competitive and dynamic knowledge-based economy in the world, capable of sustainable economic growth with more and better jobs and greater social cohesion" (European Council 2000).

30 We have chosen a variation of net-payer/net-receiver and Eurogroup members/non-Eurogroup members: Germany, the Netherlands, Portugal, Poland, Sweden, and Spain.

spective national GDP the size of the German stimulus packages was 1.6% in 2009 and 2.4% in 2010 while the Swedish ones amounted to 0.6% in 2009 and 1.7% of the country's GDP in 2010. Spain reached a GDP equivalent of 0.8% (2009) and 0.5% in 2010. The Netherlands and Poland reached 0.8% and 0.9% in 2009 with hardly any changes in 2010 (0.8% respectively). The Portuguese government provided by far the lowest resources for fiscal stimulus. The national measures reached roughly 0.2% in 2009 and 0.1% in 2010 (Roeger/in't Veld 2010). The crucial point here is that, based on national measures which were also accounted for the EU Recovery Plan, the member states provided quite different national contributions to the EU initiative which called upon member states to make allowances of at least 1.2% of the EU's GDP.

Considerable differences also existed in terms of national austerity measures. While the Swedish government decided to increase public expenditures in the years following the crisis, the German government agreed on a budget cut of about €80 billion until 2014 (an equivalent of 0.4% of the GDP for 2011). In Spain, the budget cut amounted to 2.9% of the GDP in 2011 while the Dutch liberal party, which won the national election in June 2010, immediately announced to reduce the country's budget by about €45 billion (or 1.7% of the annual GDP) until 2014. The Polish government refrained from direct budget cuts. Rather it aimed at increasing public revenues through a 1% increase of the VAT and through further privatizations. In terms of austerity measures, Portugal is a special case as the country had to apply for coverage under the European Financial Stability Facility (EFSF) in 2011.

In terms of national spending on research and development (R&D) for 2009 we observe that the innovative performance of the six countries had no immediate impact on their policies. The governments of all the countries planned to increase public R&D investments. For 2010, however, the situation had changed significantly. The Spanish government announced a 4% reduction of the country's R&D budget in December 2009. In Sweden, investments in R&D remained largely the same. The share of the total budget was 3.6% in 2010, only 0.1% lower than in 2009. This is due to increased overall public expenditures. The German federal R&D budget for 2010 included a 6.5% increase for research and innovation. In Poland, the government aimed at a reduction of the budget for higher education and research of about six to seven percent. Despite considerable budget consolidation needs, the Portuguese government was able to avoid a reduction of public R&D investments. Rather, in 2009 related expenditures increased by €205 million (European Commission 2011d). All in all, the crisis consolidated the gap between strong innovation performers and weak one in the Eurozone. The European Commission (2016c: 33) concludes that "the most striking – and worrying – trend is that some member states which already had a public R&D intensity well below the EU average [...] have experienced budget cuts in their public R&D in recent years instead of building R&I capacities through more investments". Poland's research and innovation performance has marginally improved over the last decade (European Commission 2017c: 70), while Portugal R&D intensity fell from 1.58% of GDP in 2009 to 1.28% in 2015 (ibid: 73). Spain's innovation performance continues to decline relative to the EU average (ibid: 84).

These budget cuts and stimulus packages, which follow the logics of national concernment, were accompanied by several member states signalling that they were not willing (or more likely, not able) to achieve the old Barcelona 3%-target for investments in R&D that had been preserved in the Europe 2020 Strategy. The National Reform Programmes verified that only eleven member states planned to achieve the three percent target by 2020. Moreover, member states wanted the Commission to prioritise and focus its activities arguing with significant public budget constraints (Council of the European Union 2010a). Likewise, the European Parliament reminded the Commission that the Europe 2020 Strategy sets the EU's main orientations and priorities, and that therefore the EU budget must play a key role in achieving the strategy's objectives (European Parliament 2016b: point 7).

### 3.3.2 An investment plan for Europe[31]

The Eurozone crisis has consolidated and fundamentally intensified a divide between the stronger northern economies and the weaker southern ones. While the rhetoric about European growth policies and strategies have been strong, "growth remains anaemic" (Diamond et al. 2015: 62). With launching the new EU Investment Plan the Juncker-Commission swung towards the member states side, more explicitly following a "crisis" mode by setting up a public stimulus package at EU level promising an additional investment of initially €315 billion until 2017 (European

31 This section strongly builds on Kaiser/Prange-Gstöhl (2017).

Commission 2014c). The plan should serve three related policy objectives (ibid.: 5):

> "reverse downward investment trends and help boost job creation and economic recovery, without weighing on national public finances or creating new debt;
>
> take a decisive step towards meeting the long-term needs of our economy and increase our competitiveness;
>
> strengthen the European dimension of our human capital, productive capacity, knowledge and physical infrastructure, with a special focus on the interconnections vital to our Single Market."

At the core of the Investment Plan the EU created a European Fund for Strategic Investment (EFSI) based on the five pillars:

1. a guarantee provided through the EU budget of maximum €16 billion;
2. a guarantee provided by the European Investment Bank (EIB) of €5 billion;
3. member states, directly or through their National Promotion Banks or similar bodies, will have the opportunity to contribute to the Fund in the form of capital;
4. private investors can also join the Fund;
5. a pipeline of projects suitable for funding through the EFSI will be established at EU level.

The Commission estimates that the Fund could reach an overall multiplier effect of 1:15 in real investment in the economy, i.e. the initial contribution of €21 billions of public funds at EU level should yield approximately €315 billions of additional finance over three years (2015-2017). To achieve the above-mentioned objectives the Fund shall "support development of infrastructure; or investment in education, health, research, development, information and communications technology and innovation; or expansion of renewable energy and energy efficiency; or infrastructure projects in the environmental, natural resources, urban development and social fields; or SMEs and mid cap companies including by providing working capital risk financing" (European Commission 2015a: 4).

However, the leverage effect of 1:15 might be contested. The Risk Sharing Finance Facility (RSFF) under the EU's R&I funding programme Horizon 2020, an instrument with the same purpose, has a leverage effect of approximately1:6 (Euro2030 2014: 8). Unfortunately, the selection criteria for projects remain unclear and there is no guarantee that projects will be selected that anyhow would have been funded ("windfall gains"). Additionally, EFSI does not mobilise fresh money at EU level as mainly funds from Horizon 2020 and the Connecting Europe Facility (CEF) have been redeployed.

When the three Institutions finally politically agreed on the EFSI regulation at the end of May 2015 the results were not far away from the original Commission proposal. Neither the Council nor the EP questioned the establishment of the Fund as such. In terms of funding the EFSI Guarantee the Commission had proposed to redeploy €2.7 billion from Horizon 2020, €3.3 billion from the CEF and €2 billion from unused funds (margins) under heading 1A. While the main concern of the Council was that under no circumstances the Fund should lead to an increase of the EU budget[32], the EP completely rejected the idea of using funds from Horizon 2020 and the CEF. The European Parliament wanted the Fund to be gradually filled via the annual budgetary procedure until it reaches €8 billion by 2022.[33] The compromise finally foresaw a cut of Horizon 2020 of €2.2 billion, a cut of the CEF of €2.8 billion and the use of the MFF margins of €3 billion. As regards Horizon 2020 it should be noted that some actions, such as the European Research Council and the Marie Curie actions, were excluded from contributing to EFSI on the request of the EP.

In setting up EFSI, member states, both net-payers and net-receivers, accepted a cut of major instruments in support of more future-oriented policies, i.e. Horizon 2020 and the Connect Europe Facility. In this they were in line with the Commission and – in the end – with the European Parliament. One EFSI objective is to support investment in research, development and innovation. According to the EIB, the bank approved €30.2 billion under the EFSI in 2016, of which €21.5 billion has been signed.[34] In terms of research, development and innovation operations, EFSI financing by the EIB has reached €2.9 billion[35] amounting to a total investment of €8.6 billion[36] as of February 2017 (in 48 projects), reflecting a leverage effect of 1:3.[37]

---

32 See Agence Europe, "Juncker plan - political agreement at Council on EFSI", 11 March 2015.

33 See Report on the proposal for a regulation of the European Parliament and of the Council on the European Fund for Strategic Investments and amending Regulations (EU) No 1291/2013 and (EU) No 1316/2013, EP Committee on Budgets/EP Committee on Economic and Monetary Affairs, 20 April 2015.

34 See http://www.eib.org/infocentre/publications/all/european-fund-for-strategic-investments-in-2016.htm (accessed on 24 February 2017).

35 Note that for eight projects no financial figures have been disclosed.

36 Note that for ten projects no financial figures have been disclosed.

37 Own calculations (signed projects and approved projects) based on the EIB EFSI project list on http://www.eib.org/efsi/efsi-projects.

EFSI signals a continuation of "crisis" politics. For member states the baseline for their agreement to establish the Fund was to abstain from increasing the EU budget. Instead, funds have been redeployed within the "Competitiveness"-heading of the MFF. This move – i.e. shifting money away from Horizon 2020 and the CEF – was hardly debated amongst member states, and the extension of EFSI until 2020 as part of the 2017 MFF revision reached consensus easily and without any request to the Commission for an impact assessment of EFSI first. Member states might see control gains over backflows from the EU budget by being offered the opportunity to propose their "own" projects to be funded through the EFSI project pipeline. However, this does not guarantee automatic funding as the final decision over funding will be taken by an Investment Committee of eight independent experts. On the other hand, redeploying funds away from the Framework Programme for Research and Innovation could be detrimental for particularly the net-receiver countries as for most of them the gross domestic R&D investments depend to a large extend on the EU programme.[38] Nevertheless, in the end, the setting-up of EFSI illustrates how easily funding instruments can be adapted to crisis situations if the political will exists and if it is in the putative interest of member states.

### 3.3.3 Fiscal measures

Ireland, Greece, Spain, Cyprus, Latvia, Hungary, Portugal and Romania received financial support from the EU at certain times between 2008 and 2016. EU countries outside the Euro area that have experienced difficulties regarding their balance of payments have been supported by the Balance of Payments (BoP) assistance (cf. Art. 143 TFEU; Council of the European Union 2002). BoP is one of three EU loan programmes managed by the European Commission. It has the authority to raise up to €35 billion (European Commission 2010b: 4). Hungary, Latvia, and Romania have received €13.4 billion between 2008 and 2012.[39] BoP assistance takes the

---

38 Share of Gross Domestic Expenditure on Research and Development (GERD) funded by Framework Programme Seven 2007-2014: Cyprus 80%; Bulgaria 44%; Malta 43%; Latvia 35%; Estonia 29%; Romania and Hungary 21% (Commission calculation based on Corda database and Eurostat analysis).

39 See https://ec.europa.eu/info/business-economy-euro/economic-and-fiscal-policy-coordination/eu-financial-assistance/loan-programmes/balance-payments-bop-assistance_en#overview-of-balance-of-payments-assistance-programmes (accessed 14 November 2017).

form of medium-term loans (usually up to three years) that are conditional upon an economic reform programme. After the end of a programme debtor countries are monitored under post-programme surveillance until at least 75% of the financial assistance received has been repaid.

Between 2011 and 2014 Ireland and Portugal have received financial support under the second EU loan programme, the European Financial Stability Mechanism (EFSM), which is only available for Euro area countries. The EFSM was created by a Council Regulation (Council of the European Union 2010b) in May 2010 "to provide financial assistance to any EU country experiencing or threatened by severe financial difficulties using bonds issued on behalf of the European Union".[40] The emergency funding programme is reliant upon funds raised on the financial markets and guaranteed by the European Commission using the budget of the European Union as collateral. The EFSM had the authority to raise up to €60 billion (European Commission 2010b: 4). Its activation is always pursued jointly with the support of the International Monetary Fund (IMF).

As with BoP, support under the EFSM is conditional upon the implementation of an adjustment programme and receiving countries are subject to post-programme surveillance. Ireland[41] received €22.5 billion from the EFSM and will be under post-programme surveillance by the European Commission and the European Central Bank at least until 2031. Portugal[42] exited its economic adjustment programme in June 2014. The EFSM contributed €24.3 billion to that programme. Portugal will be under post-programme surveillance until 2026.

In parallel with the EFSM, EU member states agreed in May 2010 to set up the EFSF as an intergovernmental and temporary agreement outside the EU Treaties. The EFSF had a lending capacity of €440 billion. It could "issue bonds or other debt instruments (via the German Finance Agency),

---

40 See https://ec.europa.eu/info/business-economy-euro/economic-and-fiscal-policy-coordination/eu-financial-assistance/loan-programmes/european-financial-stabilisation-mechanism-efsm_en (accessed 14 November 2017).

41 The overall financial need of Ireland summed up to €85 billion for 2010 to 2013. Further to the support from the EFSM, loans to included contributions from the European Financial Stability Facility (€17.7 billion) and bilateral lending support from the United Kingdom, Sweden, and Denmark (€4.8 billion in total). In addition, Ireland had requested a loan from the IMF of around €22.5 billion (Council of the European Union 2011a).

42 The overall financial need of Portugal summed up to €78 billion for 2011 to 2014. Further to the support from the EFSM, the European Financial Stability Facility contributed another €26 billion. In addition, Portugal has requested a loan of €26 billion from the IMF (Council of the European Union 2011b)

to raise funds to provide loans to governments, to recapitalise banks, or to buy sovereign debt directly" (Hix 2015: 181f). Ireland, Portugal and Greece[43] have been supported by the EFSF with €18.4 billion, €26 billion, and €130.9 billion respectively.[44] Ireland exited the EFSF programme without the need for any further assistance in December 2013, Portugal in June 2014. The Greek EFSF programme ended in June 2015, but in contrast to Ireland and Portugal Greece had to enter a new programme under the European Stability Mechanism (ESM) in August 2015.

In September 2012 the temporary bailout instruments supporting Eurozone members in trouble have been replaced by the permanent European Stability Mechanism. The ESM is an international organization under international law established by an intergovernmental treaty. Generally, the ESM uses the same instruments as the EFSF did. It can provide loans to countries experiencing or threatened by severe financing problems, make available financial assistance in the form of a credit line, offer loans to countries for the recapitalization of financial institutions, and engage in direct recapitalization of financial institutions.

Support from the ESM is subject to "active participation of the IMF": "A euro area member state requesting financial assistance from the ESM is expected to address, wherever possible, a similar request to the IMF" (ESM Treaty). In addition, as of 1 March 2013, financial assistance is conditional on the ratification of the Treaty on Stability, Coordination and Governance in the Economic and Monetary Union. The ESM has a maximum lending capacity of €500 billion, and a capital stock, which is the safety net in case of capital losses, of €700 billion.

In July 2012, Spain was the first Eurozone member to call upon the mechanism after it had entered a recession in 2011. Until December 2013, when Spain exited the programme, the country received €41.3 billion of financial support. Cyprus, having joined the Euro only in 2008, followed in March 2013 as it was not able anymore to borrow money on the market. The ESM disbursed €6.3 billion in loans to Cyprus until March 2016.[45] In August 2015, Greece entered a third rescue package, this time under the

43 Greece additionally profited from the Greek Loan Facility (GLF). The GLF was the first financial support programme for Greece, agreed in May 2010. It consisted of bilateral loans from 14 Euro area countries, amounting to €52.9 billion, as well as a €20.1 billion loan from the IMF.

44 For all figures see https://www.esm.europa.eu/financial-assistance (accessed 14 November 2017).

45 For all figures see https://www.esm.europa.eu/financial-assistance (accessed 14 November 2017).

ESM. In total, the programme had a volume of €86 billion. When Greece left the programme in August 2018, €61.9 billion had been approved for disbursement (European Commission 2018h: 43).

Regardless of the measures initiated by Eurozone members, the European Central Bank was the largest stabilizer during the Euro crisis (Enderlein et al. 2016). In 2012, Mario Draghi, the ECB president, declared that "within our mandate, the ECB is ready to do whatever it takes to preserve the euro. And believe me, it will be enough" (Draghi 2012). While the ECB technically cannot bailout a state, in response to the crisis it implemented a series of so-called "non-standard measures" to lower the country risks and support commercial institutions (Enderlein et al. 2016: 18). In 2010, the ECB established the Securities Markets Programme (SMP), through which it bought Eurozone member states' bonds on the secondary market. In 2012, the SMP was replaced by the Outright Monetary Transactions (OMTs), which had the same purpose but foresaw "no ex-ante quantitative limits" (European Central Bank 2012).

At its meeting on 22 January 2015 the Governing Council of the ECB decided to launch an expanded asset purchase programme (APP[46]), encompassing the existing purchase programmes in order to "provide a monetary stimulus" by "making access to finance cheaper" (European Central Bank 2015). Under this programme, the combined monthly purchases of public and private (known as "quantitative easing") sector securities and bonds by the ECB amounted to €60 billion until the end of 2017. From January to September 2018 the ECB reduced its monthly purchases to €30 billion (European Central Bank 2017).

In addition, since December 2011 the ECB supports bank lending and liquidity in the Eurozone through so-called (Targeted-) Long-Term Refinancing Operations (T-LTROs). These operations shall ease private sector credit conditions and stimulate bank lending to the real economy (European Central Bank 2014, 2016).

This number of measures and level of creativity in circumventing its original purpose, made Mourlon-Druol (2014: 1293) conclude that "far

46 The expanded asset purchase programme combines four single sub-programmes : 1) the third covered bond purchase programme (CBPP3) that started in October 2014 ; 2) the asset-backed securities purchase programme (ABSPP) that started in November 2014 ; 3) the public sector purchase programme (PSPP) that started in March 2015 ; 4) the corporate sector purchase programme (CSPP) that started in June 2016 (see https://www.ecb.europa.eu/mopo/implement/omt/html/ index.en.html#cbpp3, accessed 16 November 2017).

from being static and stubbornly concerned with anti-inflationary policy, incapable of devising any 'creative' measure in face of the urgency, the ECB has partly adapted itself to circumstances".

The mobilization of large sums to bailout Eurozone countries in financial and economic trouble have raised the question whether a "transfer union" has already been established. Although the ESM provides loans, which are raised on the financial market and which are eventually paid back by debtor countries, taxpayers may be held liable, in particular if debtors fail to meet their commitments. Moreover, both the EFSF and the ESM have – as intergovernmental organizations – undermined the no-bailout clause of the EU Treaty (Art. 125 TFEU). Being outside the EU Treaty raises legitimacy concerns as these organizations are beyond the control and scrutiny of democratic institutions. While for practical reasons it seemed more reasonable to create new institutions outside the EU Treaty (as was done with the Schengen agreement, for example) instead of amending the Treaty, for legitimacy reasons the intergovernmental treaties should be transferred into the EU legislative framework (for example, Hix 2015; Scharpf 2013; Schmidt 2015).

### 3.3.4 Reforming EMU governance

"Two-Pack", "Six-Pack", "Euro Plus-Pact", "Fiscal Compact", "Banking Union" – the Eurozone crisis has been perceived to a large extent as a regulatory or governance crisis. Long persisting flaws of the Economic and Monetary Union (EMU) have been brought to light and have been reinforced by the crisis (for example, Buti/Carnot 2012; Hall 2014; Mourlon-Druol 2014). The long-term problems included:

1. a not fully integrated market with far-reaching mobility of goods and labour which could have forced wage adjustments in line with productivity;
2. a lack of coordination of economic policies which could have enabled strong anti-cyclical fiscal policies (i.e. a weak Stability and Growth Pact);
3. no common financial mechanism that could have acted as an "automatic stabilizer" (as national budgets do at national level);
4. non-existence of an EU-wide banking supervision, which would be needed in a Capital Union to guarantee a functioning market.

In a relatively short period of time, i.e. between 2011 and 2013, European leaders sought to address these shortcomings by introducing new rules –

either through secondary legislation (cf. "Two-Pack", "Six-Pack", "Banking Union") or through creating new intergovernmental treaties (cf. "Euro Plus-Pact", "Fiscal Compact"). As the monetary part of EMU had already been supranationalized to the ECB, these measures were targeted at the economic part of EMU. These aspects of EMU are decentralized and characterized by strong policy coordination in areas of member states competence with the Stability and Growth Pact (SGP) as its core instrument (see, for example, Hodson 2015; Schuknecht et al. 2011; Seng/Biesenbender 2012)[47]. The SGP had been adopted in 1997 as the fiscal pillar of EMU. It aims to prevent fiscal policies from heading into potentially problematic directions and to correct excessive budget deficits or excessive public debt burdens since the EU Treaty "prohibits member states from posting budget deficits in excess of 3 per cent of GDP and government debt in excess of 60 per cent of GDP" (Hodson 2015: 184). To meet these targets, the SGP consists of a so-called "preventive arm" and a "corrective arm". The "preventive arm" aims to ensure sound budgetary policies over the medium term by setting parameters for member states' fiscal planning and policies.[48] The "corrective arm" ensures that member states adopt appropriate policy responses to correct excessive deficits (and/or debts) by implementing the Excessive Deficit Procedure (EDP).[49]

The SGP was a result of the cleavage between norther European countries, led by Germany, and Mediterranean countries, led by France and

47 For a complete overview of the SGP and its working modes and mechanisms see European Commission 2017d.

48 The "preventive arm" works with the following elements: a) under the Medium-Term Budgetary Objectives (MTOs) all EU member states are expected to either reach their medium-term budgetary objectives, or to be heading towards them by adjusting their structural budgetary positions at a rate of 0.5% of GDP per year as a benchmark. MTOs take into account the need to achieve sustainable debt levels. MTOs are updated every 3 years; b) Stability and Convergence Programmes and Draft Budgetary Plans: Euro area countries outline how they intend to reach their MTOs in their Stability Programmes, while the other EU member states do so in Convergence Programmes. EU Member States sharing the Euro currency must also submit each year (by 15 October) Draft Budgetary Plans; c) under the Expenditure Benchmark, spending increases which go beyond a country's medium-term potential economic growth rate must be matched by additional discretionary revenue measures. It, therefore, sets an upper limit for the net growth of government expenditure.

49 The legal basis for the SGP are Articles 121 (multilateral surveillance), 126 (Excessive Deficit Procedure), and 136 (the possibility of financial sanctions for member states whose currency is the Euro) of the TFEU.

Spain. Member states with strong currencies, like Germany, were concerned about maintaining price stability, while countries such as France and Spain were more concerned about growth than price stability. Hence, the Stability and Growth Pact was a compromise between the German proposal for the creation of a Stability Pact – which would maintain convergence obligations after member states joined the Euro area – and the French, Spanish and Italian concerns that excessive focus on budgetary discipline would be at the expense of growth.

The governance reforms adopted since 2011 took mainly three directions: first, tightening economic policy coordination and fostering fiscal discipline by introducing stricter surveillance and compliance rules ("Six-Pack"; "Fiscal Compact"; "Two-Pack"); second, strengthening banking supervision ("Banking Union"); third, stronger coordination with non-Eurozone countries ("Euro Plus-Pact").

As concerns the first direction, the "Six-Pack" (five Regulations and one Directive) of December 2011 sought to reinforce the "preventive arm" of the SGP. The reform added a system of financial sanctions as enforcement mechanisms, the Macroeconomic Imbalance Procedure (MIP) – an alert mechanism to monitor and prevent economic developments that could jeopardise macroeconomic stability[50] – as well as the new principle of reverse qualified majority voting (i.e. a Commission recommendation for corrective actions under the EDP is carried unless a qualified majority in the Council rejects it).

The intergovernmental Treaty on Stability, Coordination and Governance in the Economic and Monetary Union (TSCG), usually known as "Fiscal Compact", entered into force in January 2013. It complements the "Six-Pack" in terms of budgetary surveillance. Formally, the "Fiscal Compact" is one section of the TSCG (Title III of the TSCG).[51] It contains the requirement to have a balanced budget rule in domestic legal orders (Article 3 TSCG)[52], applies reverse qualified majority voting to all steps

50 To assess an imbalance the procedure uses a set of 14 macroeconomic indicators such as export market share, labour costs, private sector debt, public administration debt, unemployment, property prices.

51 Title I is on "Purpose and Scope", Title II on "Consistency and Relationship with the Law of the Union", Title IV on "Economic Policy Coordination and Convergence", Title V on "Governance of the Euro Area", and Title VI "General and Final Provisions".

52 According to an analysis by the Commission "the substance of the Fiscal Compact has been introduced in the national fiscal frameworks of all Contracting Parties" (European Commission 2017e).

of the EDP (Article 7 TSCG), and requests budgetary and economic partnership programmes, detailing structural reforms, from Treaty members that are under the EDP (Article 5 TSCG). Out of the 25 Contracting Parties to the TSCG (all EU members except Croatia, the Czech Republic, and the UK), 22 are formally bound by the "Fiscal Compact" (i.e. the 19 Eurozone member states plus Bulgaria, Denmark and Romania). The TSCG has also established the Euro summit meetings (Article 12 TSCG).

As the TSCG is an intergovernmental Treaty it is not part of the Union legal order. However, the TSCG includes safeguards to ensure consistency with Union law. An incorporation clause foresees to include the TSCG into Union law, and to this end take the necessary within five years from its entry into force (that is, by 1 January 2018).[53] Moreover, the TSCG must be applied and interpreted in conformity with the EU Treaties, and non-compliance of Treaty obligations will be subject to the judgment of the European Court of Justice, including the imposition of financial sanctions. Several provisions of the TSCG, such as the budgetary and economic partnership programmes or the public debt issuance plans, will be implemented through EU institutions (see Articles 5 and 6 TSCG) and "the content and format of such programmes shall be defined in European Union law" (Article 5 TSCG).

To further deepen budgetary surveillance and coordination in the Euro area the Union adopted the so-called "Two-Pack" in March 2013. This regulation integrates some elements of the "Fiscal Compact" into EU law, including the requirement for member states in EDP to prepare economic partnership programmes and the requirement for ex-ante coordination of member states' debt issuance plans. It also introduces a common budgetary timeline and common budgetary rules for the Eurozone. Within this new procedure the Commission will examine and give an opinion on Euro area members draft budgets before annual budgets are adopted by national parliaments. Most importantly, the Commission is empowered to ask for a revised draft budget if it detects severe non-compliance with the obligations under the SGP.

The second direction of governance reforms relates to the common management and supervision of banks in the Eurozone, i.e. the so-called "Banking Union" (Council of the European Union 2016; European Commission 2012, 2015c).

53 On 6 December 2017, the Commission published a proposal for a Council directive incorporating the Fiscal Compact (European Commission 2017f).

The plan for completing the Banking Union consists of three pillars. First, under the Single Supervisory Mechanism (SSM[54]) the European Central Bank is the central supervisor of financial institutions in the Euro area and in non-euro EU countries that choose to join the SSM. The SSM is in effect since 4 November 2014. The Single Resolution Mechanism (SRM[55]) is the second pillar. Since 1 January 2013 it is the central mechanism for bank resolution in the EU. The SRM guarantees the orderly restructuring of a bank in case a bank is failing or likely to fail. The SRM consists of the Single Resolution Board (SRB) and the Single Resolution Fund (SRF). The SRB is an independent EU Agency enforcing the SRM and managing the SRF. The SRF may be used to ensure the exercise of the resolution powers conferred to the SRB (for example, to guarantee the assets or liabilities of the institution under resolution; to make loans to, or to purchase assets of, the institution under resolution). It shall only be used as a last resort, i.e. if other measures do not work. The SRF is composed of contributions from credit institutions and certain investment firms in the 19 participating member states within the Banking Union.[56] It will be built up in steps between 2016 and 2023 until reaching the target level of at least 1% of covered deposits of all credit institutions authorized in the participating member states.[57] To be fully operational during the build-up phase, Eurozone member states endorsed the setting up of Loan Facility Agreements (LFA) in December 2015 (Council of the European Union 2015a). This intergovernmental agreement acknowledges that "most notably during the transitional period when the SRF has not yet reached its target level, situations may exist where the means available in the SRF are

54 Council Regulation (EU) No 1024/2013 of 15 October 2013 conferring specific tasks on the European Central Bank concerning policies relating to the prudential supervision of credit institutions, OJ L 287, 29 October 2013, pp. 63-89.

55 Regulation (EU) No 806/2014 of the European Parliament and of the Council of 15 July 2014 establishing uniform rules and a uniform procedure for the resolution of credit institutions and certain investment firms in the framework of a Single Resolution Mechanism and a Single Resolution Fund and amending Regulation (EU) No 1093/2010, OJ L 225, 30 July 2014, pp. 1-90.

56 See https://srb.europa.eu/en/content/single-resolution-fund (accessed 21 November 2017). More than 3.500 institutions have to contribute to the Fund (Single Resolution Board 2017).

57 See https://srb.europa.eu/sites/srbsite/files/_def_srb_fund-web.pdf (accessed 21 November 2017).

not sufficient to undertake a particular resolution action".[58] To this end, each participating member state has entered into a LFA with the SRB, "providing a national individual credit line to the SRB to back its national compartment in the SRF in case of possible funding shortfalls following resolution cases of banks of the member state concerned" (ibid.).

The third pillar of the Banking Union has been more difficult to agree upon amongst Euro area members and within the European Parliament and is not implemented yet. In November 2015, the Commission has tabled a legislative proposal for a European Deposit Insurance Scheme (EDIS). The EDIS proposal (European Commission 2015b) builds on the system of national deposit guarantee schemes, which are in force since 2014. EDIS would apply to deposits below €100.000 of all banks in the Banking Union. When one of these banks is placed into insolvency or in resolution and it is necessary to pay out deposits or to finance their transfer to another bank, the national deposit guarantee schemes together with the EDIS would intervene. The Commission proposal suggested that EDIS would turn into a fully mutualized insurance scheme – thus replacing national schemes – by July 2024. The scheme would be financially covered by a European Deposit Insurance Fund filled by ex-ante contributions that are owed and paid by banks. This Fund would be administered by the SRB.

After the initial proposal had been stuck with the co-legislators for two years, the Commission tried to give new impetus to the negotiations in October 2017 by laying out options on how to end deadlock in the Council and the Parliament (European Commission 2017g). The Commission expressed its expectation that the Banking Union is completed by 2019.

Last but not least, the third direction of governance reforms focussed on relations with non-Eurozone countries. The so-called "Euro Plus Pact" (European Council 2011) of March 2011 strives for stronger economic coordination between Eurozone and non-Eurozone (at that time: Bulgaria, Denmark, Latvia, Lithuania, Poland and Romania) states. It seeks to encourage growth and greater economic convergence between the countries concerned, thereby addressing underlying factors of the economic and financial crisis, such as competitiveness, employment, sustainability of public finances, and financial stability (EPSC 2015: 3). The Pact was also conceived "as an intergovernmental solution to increase fiscal and eco-

---

58 See https://srb.europa.eu/sites/srbsite/files/_def_srb_fund-web.pdf (accessed 21 November 2017).

nomic discipline in the Member States" (EPSC 2015: 1). As like other economic policy tools also the "Euro Plus-Pact" is to encourage member states "to undertake reforms in areas that fall under their national competence" (EPSC 2015: 3). While some concrete goals were agreed and are to be reviewed on a yearly basis by the heads of state or government, the Pact is not sufficiently linked to or embedded in the European Semester cycle, and as a non-binding declaration by the Heads of States and Governments its implementation takes place on a voluntary basis.

These EU level governance reforms, however, ignore a major underlying factor of the crisis, i.e. the crisis having been shaped by varieties of capitalism within the Eurozone. Hall (2014: 1226) argues in relation to the Eurozone that "serious problems were created by institutional asymmetries in the political economies of its member states". With entry into the Economic and Monetary Union northern European coordinated market economies, such as Germany, the Netherlands, Belgium, Finland, and Austria (Hall/Soskice 2001), were able to continue "to pursue export-led growth strategies in a more favourable context in which their principal trading partners could no longer devalue in order to increase the competitiveness of their own products against those exports" (Hall 2014. 1228). On the other hand, for southern European mixed-market economies (Hancké 2013), such as Greece, Portugal and Spain, "entry into monetary union [...] called into question the viability of the demand-led growth strategies on which these countries had long relied, because they could no longer devalue to offset the accompanying inflation" (Hall 2014: 1228). In parallel, confidence effects generated by the Monetary Union lowered the cost of capital in southern Europe nurturing a growth model based on a credit-fuelled consumption and construction boom (Copsey 2015: 38).

These observations on national idiosyncrasies can have important implications for future EU finances as persistent or even greater divergence between member states, in terms of institutions, policies and economies, increases the likelihood that well-established cleavages continue to exist, or new ones emerge.

### *3.4 Conclusions*

The European Union has reacted to the financial and economic crisis through regulatory, policy, and budgetary means – often in combination. A plethora of activities after the outbreak of the crisis shows a turn from "normal" to "crisis" politics while being stuck in path-dependent structures (Schimmelfennig 2014; Verdun 2015).

As regards the preparations of the MFF 2014-2020, these "crisis" politics reinforced classical change-resisting factors as the main frictions between net contributors and net recipients continued to exist. The two most visible groups were the "Friends of Better Spending" and the "'Friends of Cohesion" – labels that were used by these groups themselves (see Stenbaeck/Jensen 2016). In contrast to earlier budget negotiations, the "Friends of Better Spending" were from the beginning solid against any increase of the EU budget. As early as 2009, a group of member states (Germany, United Kingdom, France, the Netherlands, Sweden and Austria) voiced their demand to cap the EU budget at 1% of the GDP. In November 2010, the European Council affirmed that the member states' strengthening of fiscal discipline resulting from the crisis must be reflected in the annual Union budget and the new MFF (2014-2020). In view of the MFF negotiations and following the European Council declaration of November 2010, the leaders of net contributor countries France, Germany, the Netherlands and Finland in December 2010 signed a letter written by then UK Prime Minister Cameron to cap growth in the new MFF to the rate of inflation. According to that group of member states EU spending should be in line with the efforts national governments were making to make savings and cut public deficits as a reaction to the economic crisis.

Due to the Euro crisis, the group of the "Friends of Cohesion" was clearly less united. The group consisted of Euro- and non-Euro countries that were differently affected by the crisis. Three member states (Spain, Greece and Portugal) received support from the different Euro stabilization mechanisms. Although being beneficiaries of that support, Portugal and Spain had to provide their share to the Greek rescue package. The same holds for a number of Euro countries that had to overcome severe economic problems even though they did not receive direct support from the Euro group. This holds especially for the Baltic countries that were already members of the Euro zone (Estonia) or prepared for their accession (Latvia, Lithuania). In that situation, the "Friends of Cohesion" were not in a very strong position to argue in favour of a bigger budget. As part of that group received stabilization funds, they were dependent on the "solidarity" of the contributors to these instruments which were all members of the "Friends of Better Spending" group. The non-Euro countries of the "Friends of Cohesion" group had to accept that the net payers were already significantly burdened by their contributions to stabilize the common currency. Consequently, new change-resisting factors appeared in form of a cleavage between members and non-members of the Eurogroup.

In view of plans to deepen the Economic and Monetary Union and the related Commission proposals of December 2017 (European Commission 2017h), it is not unlikely that these cleavages will continue to exist in the next round of MFF negotiations. The proposals on EMU reform could have ample financial impact as the Commission itself seems to admit by promising that "the Commission will continue to assess the further implications for the EU budget in the context of the preparation of the post-2020 multiannual financial framework and will make the necessary proposals" (ibid.: 16).

A first proposal could be construed as a concession to non-Euro member countries. The Commission suggests setting up a dedicated "convergence facility" under the post-2020 MFF for EU member states on their way to joining the Euro. The aim is to support those countries in fulfilling the four convergence criteria listed in Article 140 TFEU and in Protocol No 13 annexed to the Union Treaties. While not being explicit about what function such a "convergence facility" would have, indications could be drawn from the "pilot" facility the Commission proposes already for 2018-2020. This pilot, which will be realised by increasing the budget under the Structural Reform Support Programme, should offer "technical support" to member states covering "all policies that can help achieve a high degree of convergence, such as support for reforms in the areas of public financial management, the business environment, the financial sector, labour and product markets, and the public administration" (ibid.: 11). No co-financing from member states is required.

Secondly, the Commission proposes for the post-2020 MFF a new "reform delivery tool" for member states striving for reforms agreed with the Commission in so-called "reform commitments". Notably, this programme would have its own budget, "separate from and in addition to the European Structural and Investment Funds" (European Commission 2017i: 1). It seems clear that the Commission wants to get a better grip on the structural reform in member states under the European Semester by providing financial incentives. It remains, however, foggy what the exact difference to the Structural Funds would be leaving doubts concerning potential inconsistencies and double-spending. As under the "convergence facility" pilot, no co-financing from member states is foreseen.

Thirdly, the Commission presents elements of a "stabilization function" for Euro area members "as a way of preserving investment levels in the event of large asymmetric shocks" (European Commission 2017h: 5).

Managed by the Commission and subject to strict eligibility criteria (which would still be to be defined), the member state facing a large asymmetric shock would automatically be entitled for financial support through the "stabilization function" (i.e. a mix of loans and grants from the EU budget and the still-to-be-created European Monetary Fund or the ESM). The Commission suggests that a "limited borrowing capacity could be constructed in the post-2020 Multiannual Financial Framework" for which "an increase of the own resources ceiling could be necessary" (ibid.: 15, footnote 28). According to the ideas of the Commission, the "stabilization function" would be completed by "an insurance mechanism based on voluntary member states' contributions", which could be either a dedicated fund outside the EU budget (which would obviously again violate the principle of budget unity) or a budget line under the MFF (ibid.: 15).

Fourthly, the Commission presents a proposal to set-up a new Union body, i.e. the European Monetary Fund (EMF). The EMF should act as an upgraded successor of the European Stability Mechanism (ESM). That means, the "EMF should provide stability support to its members when their regular access to market financing is impaired or is at risk of being impaired" (European Commission 2017j: 22). Integrating the ESM into the Union legal framework enhances the democratic control by the European Parliament. Moreover, national parliaments will also have the right to obtain information about the EMF activities, and to engage in a dialogue with the new body (ibid.: 18). The lending capacity of the EMF will be no less than €500 billion, and the capital stock of the EMF should amount to €700 billion. In contrast to the ESM, the future EMF will be able to develop new financial instruments in addition to other EU financial instruments and programmes (ibid.: 6)

In sum, these plans hint at macroeconomic stabilization being an explicit objective of the future EU budget. This objective should be underpinned by financial incentives (for convergence and reform) and correction tools (in case a member state faces severe stability problems). The Commission proposal for the post-2020 MFF incorporates these new instruments. The Reform Support Programme subsumes the "Reform Delivery Tool" and the "Convergence Facility" with an amount of €22 billion for the seven-year period. For the so-called "European Investment Stabilization Function" it is proposed that "the EU budget will guarantee back-to-back loans of up to €30 billion" (European Commission 2018c: 11) with the option to complement the Stabilization Function with additional sources outside the MFF.

Another option to create a "fiscal capacity" has been proposed by French President Emmanuel Macron – i.e. a dedicated Eurozone budget (Macron 2017). While he did not make explicit how such a separate budget could work, what volume it should have, how it could be financed or whether it would be established in addition or at the expense of the MFF, there does not seem to be much appetite amongst EU leaders for such a radical solution reforming the Eurozone.[59] Similarly, European institutions seem to be at least lukewarm vis-à-vis, if not against, such far-reaching plans. The Commission positioned itself with the above discussed proposals, and the European Parliament is sceptical about any suggestion than could potentially violate the unity of the budget (European Parliament 2017a: 28).

A focus on new Eurozone tools and programmes for the post-2020 MFF could harden the front between Eurozone members and non-Eurozone members if the latter realize that the additional funding comes in particular at the expense of traditional programmes, such as structural and cohesion policies, and no appropriate compensation mechanisms are foreseen or conditionality would undermine national leeways in an unacceptable manner.

59 A principle political agreement on a new Eurozone budget reached between French President Macron and German Chancellor Merkel on 19 June 2018 was immediately rejected, for example, by Dutch Prime Minister Rutte, who also opposed the European Commission proposal for a new investment programme for Euro member countries within the next MFF (available at: https://www.euractiv.com/section/economy-jobs/news/rutte-rejects-commissions-new-funds-for-monetary-union; accessed 26 June 2018). In a letter to Donald Tusk, President of the Euro Summit, on 25 June 2018 the Eurogroup President, Mario Centeno, confirmed the persisting differences between the member states "on the need for and possible features of a Eurozone budget" (available at: http://www.consilium.europa.eu/media/35798/2018-06-25-letter-president-centeno-to-president-tusk.pdf; accessed 1 July 2018).

# 4. Brexit, migration and defence: new challenges as a reform opener for the EU's future budget?

## *4.1 Brexit: a net-payer leaving the Union*

On 23 June 2016 a majority of the people of the United Kingdom (UK) voted for leaving the European Union. On a turnout of 72.2%, 48.1% of votes were cast in favour of "remain" (i.e. Scotland, Northern Ireland, Gibraltar) and 51.9% of votes were cast in favour of "leave" (i.e. England, Wales). Prime Minister Cameron resigned the day later, on 29 March 2017 the UK government triggered Article 50 TEU, which rules withdrawal from the EU, and on 19 June 2017 withdrawal negotiation between the UK and the EU started. The UK government decided to leave the EU on 29 March 2019. This date is derived from Article 50(3) TEU, which states that "the Treaties shall cease to apply to the State in question from the date of entry into force of the withdrawal agreement or, failing that, two years after the notification" that a member state wants to exit the EU. This two-year period could only be extended if the European Council, in agreement with the member state concerned, unanimously decides to do so. Once the withdrawal takes effect the UK will become a third state vis-à-vis the EU. The UK's withdrawal from the EU means unravelling all the rights and obligations – from access to the Internal Market, to structural funds, to joint external action – that the UK has acquired both during the accession to the EU and over then 46 years of membership.

Throughout these years, since 1973, euroscepticism is a continued characteristic of UK membership (McGowan/Phinnemore 2017). The Union tried to balance this scepticism through granting the UK "opt-outs" (for example, no need to adopt the single currency, no need to participate in the Schengen acquis, no application of the Charter of Rights for Workers) or "opt-ins" (for example, in the area of freedom, security, and justice). A highlight of that exceptionalism is Margaret Thatcher's five-year endeavour to reduce the British contribution to the Community budget. At the Fontainebleau European Council in June 1984, Heads of States and Governments agreed to accept a rebate on the UK payments (European Council 1984). According to the Fontainebleau agreement in 1984 the UK received a lump-sum compensation of ECU 1 billion for the budgetary year 1984. From 1985 onwards, it received two thirds of the difference between what it paid in Value-Added Tax (VAT) and what it received from the Community, respective Union, budget. To lower the compensation burden for the biggest net-payer, it was also agreed that Germany shoulders only two thirds of its normal share ("German correction"). Calculation of the difference or "gap" has been based only on the UK's VAT payments and not on customs duties and agricultural levies. This system has remained more or less unchanged throughout the years, although the conditions under which the rebate had been granted in 1984 (i.e. a low UK share in Community agricultural expenditure on which the Community budget was concentrated in parallel with a high share of the UK VAT base in relation to its GNP) fundamentally evolved (Cipriani 2014: 45). All member states finance the UK rebate. Since 2002, Germany, the Netherlands, Austria and Sweden pay only 25% of their normal financing share of the UK correction leaving the highest financial burden on France and Italy (Council of the European Union 2014).[60]

Pressure on the governing Conservatives rose when the right-wing, anti-EU UK Independent Party (UKIP) gained 16.5% in the 2009 European Parliament elections. UKIP even became the largest UK party in the following 2014 European Parliament elections increasing further the internal pressure on Prime Minister David Cameron and his Conservative-Liberal Democratic coalition government to seek reform of the EU and the UK-EU relationship. Embedded into that anti-EU climate, in January 2013, Cameron committed himself – if the Conservatives would win the 2015 elections – to re-negotiate EU membership and put this "new settlement" to voters in an "in-out" referendum "within the first half of the next parliament" (i.e. until the end of 2017).[61] Immediately after winning the general elections in May 2015 by an absolute majority of seats in the House of Commons, Cameron stated to put his promises into practice.

Between November 2015 and February 2016 the "new settlement" was negotiated between the UK and the EU touching upon four areas: economic governance (i.e. the relation between Eurozone- and non-Eurozone-

60 Additionally, "for the period 2014-2020 only, Denmark, the Netherlands and Sweden shall benefit from gross reductions in their annual GNI-based contribution of €130 million, €695 million and €185 million respectively. Austria shall benefit from a gross reduction in its annual GNI-based contribution of €30 million in 2014, €20 million in 2015 and €10 million in 2016" (Council of the European Union 2014: 107).

61 See speech of Prime Minister David Cameron on 23 January 2013 (available at: https://www.gov.uk/government/speeches/eu-speech-at-bloomberg; accessed 23 November 2017).

members), competitiveness (i.e. less "red tape" for enterprises in the Internal Market and the commitment to an ambitious trade policy), sovereignty (i.e. the respect for UK's "opt-outs" and more power for national parliaments in relation to EU legislation), and migration within in EU (i.e. limiting social benefits for EU migrants and their children).

On 19 February 2016, the Heads of States and Governments of the EU adopted a Decision "concerning a new settlement for the United Kingdom within the European Union", which would have taken effect in all member states if the UK voted to remain in the EU (cf. European Council 2016b).

In fact, the new settlement mainly reiterated existing laws and agreements between the UK and the Union and remained rather vague on several issues, such as competitiveness. In substance, the agreement foresaw the amendment of two Regulations related to social benefits, but no change of primary law.[62] Although the deal did not make essential changes to the position of the UK in the EU, it nevertheless allowed Cameron to proclaim that the new status would give the UK "the best of both worlds" (HM Government 2016).

As the UK has finally chosen to leave the "new settlement" never came into force. Instead, the UK and the EU negotiated on the UK's withdrawal between June 2017 and November 2018. Citizens' rights (of both, EU citizens in the UK and UK citizens in the EU), peace, stability and reconciliation on the island of Ireland (full commitment to the Good Friday Agreement[63] and the Common Travel Area[64]), as well as the financial settlement

---

62 In relation to primary law the Decision only referred to future enlargements: "With regard to future enlargements of the European Union, it is noted that appropriate transitional measures concerning free movement of persons will be provided for in the relevant Acts of Accession to be agreed by all Member States, in accordance with the Treaties. In this context, the position expressed by the United Kingdom in favour of such transitional measures is noted" (European Council 2016b: 9)

63 The Good Friday Agreement (GFA) of 10 April 1998 "is the overarching framework for deepening peace, political stability and reconciliation in Northern Ireland and on the island of Ireland. It is the foundation of the Peace Process and was resoundingly endorsed by referendum on both parts of the island of Ireland in 1998" (Council of the European Union 2017d). The GFA was concluded between the political parties in Northern Ireland and the Governments of Ireland and the UK. It established several joint governing bodies and regulates important citizenship rights of the people of Northern Ireland.

64 The Common Travel Area is a long-standing arrangement between Ireland and the United Kingdom which enables Irish and UK citizens to travel and reside in either jurisdiction without restriction and provides for associated rights and entitlements in both jurisdictions (see Council of the European Union 2017e).

(or "UK exit bill") have become the three core topics during the first negotiation phase (Council of the European Union 2017f; HM Government 2017; May 2017). Profound disagreement rose about the sequencing of the negotiations. While the EU insisted on a "phased approach to negotiations" with, first, orderly negotiations on the UK's withdrawal, and, second, talking about the framework for the future relationship, the UK preferred parallel negotiations on withdrawal and future relationships. In the end, both parties followed a phased approach, first concentrating on the orderly withdrawal of the UK. In December 2017, the European Council decided that sufficient progress had been made on the withdrawal arrangements and that the second phase, addressing transitional arrangements as well as the overall understanding on the framework for the future relationship, could be launched (European Council 2017a). As, in fact, none of the issues for an orderly withdrawal of the UK had been solved definitely by the end of 2017, both processes ran in parallel. In February 2018, the European Council initiated the second negotiation phase.

As regards citizens' rights, the main aim of the EU was to secure – after Brexit – the same level of protection that EU-27 citizens in the UK, and UK citizens in the EU-27, enjoy under EU law prior to the withdrawal date. This included rights that will materialize only at a later stage, such as pensions, as well as rights which are in the process of being obtained, such as the right to permanent residence or the right to join family members at any time. The jurisdiction of the Court of Justice of the EU should continue to apply. The UK particularly wanted to limit family reunification and the exportation of social benefits in case an EU citizen leaves the UK.

Concerning the special situation of the island of Ireland, both parties in principle agreed on the need to protect "the peace process and of the Good Friday Agreement ("Belfast Agreement") in all its parts, the maintenance of existing bilateral agreements and arrangements between the United Kingdom and Ireland including the Common Travel Area, and specific issues arising from Ireland's unique geographic situation, including the aim of avoiding a hard border between Ireland and Northern Ireland" (European Commission 2017k: 2). However, since the UK general election on 8 June 2017, in which the Conservative Party lost its absolute majority, the May government needed to be backed by the Northern Irish Democratic Unionist Party (DUP).[65] DUP is a pro-Brexit party rejecting any possi-

65 The terms of cooperation are settled in the "Confidence and Supply Agreement between the Conservative and Unionist Party and the Democratic Unionist Party" (UK Prime Minister's Office 2017).

ble exceptions for Northern Ireland (for example, the part of the UK staying in the Customs Union and the Internal Market as a way of achieving an invisible border) in the withdrawal agreement.[66] On the EU side, the government of the Republic of Ireland had attached tight strings to the negotiations. In November 2017, it threatened to block the move to phase two of the talks if the UK did not provide written commitment to five Irish "red lines" relating to the avoidance of a hard border, maintaining the Common Travel Area, and respecting the Good Friday Agreement.[67]

The third core negotiation issue, the UK's financial settlement, was linked to the current and future EU budget. The so-called "exit bill" was expected to cover outstanding bills from previous MFFs ("reste à liquider"), the financial programming for the period between the date of withdrawal of the United Kingdom and the end of the MFF 2014-2020, future outstanding spending allocations, i.e. spending promises the EU undertakes before Brexit, but that will only be paid after the UK has left the EU ("future reste à liquider" related in particular to the European Strategic Investment Funds), as well as other liabilities, such as pensions of EU officials or commitments made outside the MFF (for example, European Development Fund, Trust Funds). These obligations could partly be offset by flows of money back to the UK from its share of assets, budget receipts and the payment of the UK rebate (Barker 2017: 3). Nevertheless, such a bill could have easily been summed up to €60 billion for the UK (Barker 2017).

In her "Florence speech"[68] in September 2017 Theresa May confirmed that the UK will fulfil its commitments until 2020, i.e. for the MFF 2014-2020. However, the calculations, and the principles behind them, are tremendously contested, and the UK was not able to quantify these commitments or at least propose a methodology how to calculate them, which led the Commission to speak of a deadlock after five rounds of negotiations in October 2017 (Barnier 2017). In December 2017, agreement was reached on the UK's settlement, however, without mentioning a concrete figure

66 See "The Thorniest of Brexit Issues: The Northern Ireland Border", Bloomberg.com, 3 October 2017 (accessed 29 November 2017).

67 See "Dublin's 5 Brexit demands show path to sufficient progress", Politico.eu, 29 November 2017 (accessed 30 November 2017).

68 See "PM's Florence speech: a new era of cooperation and partnership between the UK and the EU" of 22 September 2017 (available at: https://www.gov.uk/government/speeches/pms-florence-speech-a-new-era-of-cooperation-and-partnership-between-the-uk-and-the-eu; accessed 24 November 2017).

(European Commission 2017l). Table 1 provides an overview of the actual gross financial contribution of the UK between 2001 and 2016.

*Table 4.1: UK's gross, final and net national contributions to the EU budget 2001-2016 (in EUR million)*[69]

| *Year* | *Gross National Contribution*[70] *(A)* | *UK rebate* | *Rebate as % of (A)* | *Final National Contribution* | *Net Contribution*[71] |
|---|---|---|---|---|---|
| *2001* | 11 977.0 | 7 342.5 | 61% | 4 634.4 | -1 229.2 |
| *2002* | 13 019.2 | 4 933.5 | 38% | 8 085.7 | 1 924.7 |
| *2003* | 13 056.7 | 5 184.9 | 40% | 7 872.1 | 1 697.6 |
| *2004* | 14 650.9 | 5 272.1 | 36% | 9 378.9 | 2 248.7 |
| *2005* | 14 815.9 | 5 185.8 | 35% | 9 630.2 | 959.8 |
| *2006* | 15 052.3 | 5 221.4 | 35% | 9 830.2 | 1 536.0 |
| *2007* | 15 963.2 | 5 188.9 | 33% | 10 771.9 | 3 349.0 |
| *2008* | 13 870.9 | 6 252.0 | 45% | 7 613.8 | 303.9 |
| *2009* | 12 922.4 | 5 657.7 | 44% | 7 879.6 | 1 632.5 |
| *2010* | 15 626.8 | 3 562.7 | 23% | 12 145.8 | 5 400.2 |
| *2011* | 14 780.3 | 3 595.9 | 24% | 11 273.4 | 4 703.4 |
| *2012* | 17 185.8 | 3 803.6 | 22% | 13 461.1 | 6 527.2 |
| *2013* | 18 757.3 | 4 329.5 | 23% | 14 509.5 | 8 201.2 |
| *2014* | 17 457.5 | 6 066.3 | 35% | 11 341.6 | 4 356.9 |
| *2015* | 24 337.2 | 6 083.6 | 25% | 18 209.4 | 10 751.8 |
| *2016* | 18 566.4 | 5 870.2 | 32% | 13 460.5 | 6 408.9 |

It is noticeable that the UK final national contribution and its net-payer position increases significantly with the beginning of the financial and economic crisis in the EU in 2009/2010. A net-payer leaving the Union will shake up the established balance amongst EU members, in particular amongst net-contributors. As Haas and Rubio (2017: 9) have shown, the net-contributors would be quite differently affected if the post-Brexit MFF maintained the level of current spending, reduced only by the amount of EU transfers from the UK. Austria, Germany, the Netherlands and Sweden

69 Sources: European Parliamentary Research Service 2016; European Commission 2016d, 2017m.

70 The gross national contribution is calculated as follows: VAT-based own resource + GNI based own resource (EPRS 2016: footnote 4).

71 Net payment is calculated by final national contribution minus receipt from the EU budget. For figures see http://ec.europa.eu/budget/library/figures/internet-tables-all.xls (accessed 24 November 2017).

would be confronted with an increase of their national contributions by 14% to 16% while the other two members of the "friends of better spending-group", i.e. France and Finland, would face a significantly lower increase of expenditures of about 7%.[72] Apart from that, the four countries with the highest burden are also the countries that profit from the 25% rebate on the British rebate. Therefore, these four countries might establish a coalition aimed at maintaining rebates even beyond 2020 as correction mechanisms for net contributor countries. Eliminating the rebates is not an automatism. Overall old cleavages might remain and new ones a likely to appear in relation to the financing of new challenges, such as international migration flows and defence concerns. Moreover, individual member states, such as Ireland, could try to politically link negotiations on Brexit and MFF negotiations to seek special financial support through the future EU budget to compensate for the potential re-instalment of a "hard" border (cf. Becker 2017: 15). Seeing Brexit as a "window of opportunity" (Enderlein et al. 2016; Fabbrini 2016) for a fundamental recast of the EU budget could, therefore, turn out as a fallacy.

Negotiations on the withdrawal agreement were concluded in November 2018. The agreement ensures citizens' rights on both sides, regulates the financial settlement, lays down governance arrangements to provide for consistent interpretation of the withdrawal agreement, defines provisions to respect the unique situation of Northern Ireland, includes a time-limited transition period, and includes so-called "separation provisions" that regulate the orderly conclusion of the EU legal order after the transition period (HM Government 2018).

The European Council endorsed the withdrawal agreement at a special meeting on 25 November 2018. At the same time the European Council approved the Political Declaration setting out the framework for the future relationship between the EU and the UK (Council of the European Union 2018a). The declaration sets out a number of principles and areas of interest for future relationships. In line with article 50 of the EU Treaty, the European Parliament is set to vote on the withdrawal agreement in early

72 In early reactions on this issue, representatives of Austria, Germany, and Sweden rejected any will to increase their contributions as an effect to Brexit; see "Austria won't increase contribution to EU budget after Brexit", Euractiv.com, 27 April 2017 (accessed 2 July 2018); "What the EU27 wants from the Brexit", Politico.eu, 29 March 2017 (accessed 2 July 2018); "Jens Spahn: EU Budget will not automatically remain the same once the UK leaves", Politico, 16 November 2016 (accessed 2 July 2018).

2019, before the final vote of the Council. On the UK side the House of Commons has rejected the Withdrawal Agreement three times on 15 January, 12 March, and 29 March 2019. As a consequence, and to avoid a "no deal" Brexit, the European Council agreed to postpone the Brexit a first time until 22 May 2019 and a second time until 31 October 2019.

### *4.2 International migration, refugees and asylum policy*

By the end of 2017, Frontex, the EU's border and coast guard agency, headlines that the overall level of migration flows into the Union remains low.[73] Within the first 10 months of 2017 irregular border crossings via the four main migratory routes into the EU (i.e. the Central, Western, and Eastern Mediterranean routes as well as the Western Balkans route) had fallen by 63% to around 173.000 persons compared to the same period in 2016. Figures suggest that the EU was able get the unprecedented inflow of asylum-seekers of the years 2015 and 2016 again under control. However, in his State-of-the-Union speech in September 2017, Commission President Juncker pointed out that "migration stays on our radar" (Juncker 2017). Implications for the long-term EU budget are therefore likely since the Commission points out that "the pressures driving migration will also multiply and flows will come from different parts of the world as the effects of population growth, widespread tensions and climate change take hold" (European Commission 2017a: 11).

The so-called refugee crisis saw the number of asylum-applicants peak in 2015 and 2016.[74] While in 2014, 626.000 persons sought asylum in the EU, the number rose to 1.32 million in 2015 and 1.26 million in 2016. The following table gives an overview of the distribution of asylum-seekers in 2015 and 2016 by major destination countries. The numbers for the EU as a whole dropped to 341.335 in the first half of 2017. Measured by applicants per million population, Malta (1.038) and Greece (1.021) received most asylum-seekers in 2017, followed by Luxemburg (929), Cyprus (894) and Austria (685). At the lower end are Poland (34), the Czech Republic (33), and Slovakia (5).

---

73 See http://frontex.europa.eu/news/migratory-flows-in-october-overall-levels-remain-low-spain-arrivals-soar-hcsz3c (accessed 30 November 2017).

74 All following figures on asylum applications are based on the Eurostat database at http://appsso.eurostat.ec.europa.eu/nui/submitViewTableAction.do.

*Table 4.2: Asylum applicants in 2015 and 2016 by EU destination*

| *Destination* | *2015* | | *2016* | | |
|---|---|---|---|---|---|
| | *Total* | *% of EU total** | *Total* | *% of EU total** | *Change 2016 to 2015* |
| *Germany* | 476.060 | 36.1 | 745.150 | 59.1 | +56.5%) |
| *Hungary* | 177.130 | 13.4 | 29.435 | 2.3 | -83.4% |
| *Sweden* | 162.455 | 12.3 | 28.790 | 2.3 | -82.3% |
| *Austria* | 88.160 | 6.7 | 42.245 | 3.4 | -52.1% |
| *Italy* | 83.535 | 6.3 | 122.960 | 9.8 | +47.2%) |
| *France* | 76.165 | 5.8 | 84.265 | 6.5 | +10.6% |
| *Greece* | 13.210 | 1.0 | 51.105 | 4.1 | +387% |

* EU total in 2015: 1.32 Million, in 2016: 1.26 Million.

While the EU started intergovernmental cooperation on home and migration affairs no later than in 1993 with the Maastricht Treaty[75], the massive, unauthorized inflow of refugees and asylum seekers in 2015/2016 has blown up its related policies and instruments putting the EU's area of freedom, security, and justice under stress (see Buananno 2017). With the Amsterdam Treaty, the European Communities gained competences in migration and asylum issues in 1999. The European Council, at its special meeting in Tampere on 15 and 16 October 1999, agreed to work towards establishing the Common European Asylum System (CEAS)[76], including a method for determining the member state responsible for the examination of an asylum application (i.e. the "Dublin Regulation"[77]). This method defines a hierarchy of criteria, running from family considerations, to recent possession of visa or residence permit in a member state, to whether

75 For a comprehensive overview of the evolution of EU migration and asylum policy see Faure et al. (2015).

76 The origins of this system have been established by the Dublin Convention (Dublin I), which was signed in Dublin on 15 June 1990. It came into force on 1 September 1997 for the twelve signatories Belgium, Denmark, France, Germany, Greece, Ireland, Italy, Luxembourg, the Netherlands, Portugal, Spain and the United Kingdom. Austria and Sweden joint the system 1 October 1997, Finland on 1 January 1998 (European Community 1997). Article 78 of the Treaty on the Functioning of the EU (TFEU) provides for the establishment of the CEAS.

77 See Council of the European Union 2003; European Parliament & Council of the European Union 2013a.

the applicant has entered EU irregularly, or regularly. If none of these criteria apply, the responsibility lies with the member state where the asylum-seeker arrived ("first arrival"-principle).

At the same time as the "Dublin Regulation" was suspended, the Schengen system partly collapsed. The Schengen Agreement – initially signed in 1985 between the governments of Belgium, the Federal Republic of Germany, France, Luxemburg, and the Netherlands – abolished internal borders between 22 of the 28 EU member states and those of the four EFTA countries Iceland, Norway, Liechtenstein, and Switzerland. It is key to the EU principle of the free movement of persons inside the Union. In December 2015, the European Commission acknowledged that "it is obvious that the refugee crisis has significant consequences for the situation at the EU's external borders and within the Schengen area" (European Commission 2015c: 3). Incoming refugees were travelling further to the member states of their preference instead of having their applications examined by the member states responsible under the Dublin rules. This situation led to temporary reintroduction of controls at the Austrian, Danish, German, Hungarian, Norwegian, Slovenian, and Swedish internal borders[78], a measure that is exceptionally foreseen as a last resort under the Schengen Borders Code (SBC) in the event of a serious threat to public policy and internal security (European Parliament & Council of the European Union 2016: Chapter 2). Such a temporary border control is limited to 30 days with the possibility of prolongation of up to two years. The respective country notifies the other member states and the Commission at least 10 days ahead of the measure providing the necessary justification and information. The Commission may issue an opinion with regard to the necessity of the measure and its proportionality but cannot veto the decision. In cases where the overall functioning of the Schengen area is put at risk by serious and persistent deficiencies at an EU external border, member states may only introduce temporary border controls based on a Council recommendation (cf. Article 29 SBC). As consequence of the crisis and the malfunction controls at the Greek external border, border controls have been reintroduced and prolonged 50 times since September 2015 as compared to 36 cases of reintroduced border controls in the period 2006-2015 (European Commission 2017n: 2).

---

78 Austria, Denmark, Germany, Norway, and Sweden continue border controls due to the "security situation in Europe and threats resulting from the continuous significant secondary movements" (i.e. based on Article 29 SBC).

In general, the EU's migration and asylum policies are a patchwork of measures being far from a "common policy". As a shared competence between the EU and its member states, this area consists of "a complex system of competences that shape the decision-making" (Faure et al. 2015: 15). These competences are either "shared between the Commission and the member states, with the member states pursuing their own policies in parallel to a common EU policy, or exclusive competences of the member states, with the Commission playing a coordinating role" (Faure et al. 2015: 15). The result is that the EU mainly regulates in the area of legal migration and integration, but less so in the area of illegal migration (apart from the fight against smuggling refugees and return policies).

In order to promote the management of migration and refugee flows the EU has several programmes in place, which are mainly funded through the EU's multiannual financial framework, both under heading 3 "Security and Citizenship" and heading 4 "Global Europe". During the financial period 2007-2013 the EU External Border Fund[79] (€1.82 billion), the European Return Fund[80] (€676 million), the European Integration Fund[81] (€825 million), and the European Refugee Fund[82] (€630 million) have been the main instruments.

Between 2014 and 2020 EU funding is mainly channelled through the Asylum, Migration and Integration Fund[83] (€3.14 billion) and the Internal Security Fund-Borders and Visa[84] (€2.76 billion). Additionally, the EU budget under humanitarian aid and development cooperation (i.e. the Global Public Goods and Challenges thematic programme under the Development Cooperation Instrument; €344 million), EU Trust Funds and the European Development Fund outside the EU budget contribute to migration and asylum issues (see den Hertog 2016).

The already existing fragmented landscape of funding instruments has been completed by additional crisis instruments, i.e. the so-called Trust Funds. These funds are established outside the MFF in an ad-hoc manner,

---

79 Support for the management of external borders and a common visa policy.

80 Support for initiatives seeking to improve return management.

81 Support of activities that facilitate the integration of non-EU immigrants into European societies.

82 Support for EU countries that face disproportionally large influxes of asylum seekers.

83 Measures to promote the efficient management of migration flows and the implementation, strengthening and development of a common Union approach to asylum and immigration.

84 Measures to support a common visa policy and control of the external borders.

legally based on the Financial Regulation, by pooling money from across the EU budget, the member states and other donors. They therefore do not necessarily provide fresh money.[85] Three Trust Funds have been set up as a crisis response: the EU Regional Trust Fund in Response to the Syrian Crisis (the so-called "Madad Fund"; €1 billion), the EU Emergency Trust Fund for stability and addressing the root causes of irregular migration and displaced persons in Africa (€3.6 billion), and the Facility for Refugees in Turkey (€3 billion) which is linked to the EU-Turkey Statement (European Council 2016c). In total, in 2015, 2016 and 2017 the Commission mobilized an EU budget of over €17 billion, i.e. the initial allocation to address the refugee crisis (which was €7.6 billion) was more than doubled (European Commission 2017o).

Besides additional funding, the EU initiated regulatory measures as crisis response.[86] In September 2015, a temporary internal emergency mechanism for the relocation of a total of 160.000 asylum-seekers from Italy and Greece to the rest of the member states was adopted by the Council at qualified majority, against the votes of Slovakia, the Czech Republic, Romania and Hungary (Council of the European Union 2015b, 2015c). The legal commitment was later reduced to 98.000 persons. Its implementation remained, nevertheless, rather poor, although the Commission claimed that almost all eligible persons registered for relocation in Greece and Italy have been successfully relocated, i.e. 31.500 (European Commission 2017p). The mechanism finally ceased on 26 September 2017. Facing the resistance of a number of member states to implement the Decision – Hungary and Slovakia have even challenged this process before the European Court of Justice – the idea of a permanent relocation mechanism, proposed by the Commission in September 2015, was dropped.

To prevent illegal entrance into the EU, working with third countries, i.e. countries of transit and origin of asylum seekers, becomes ever more important. The EU's global approach to migration and mobility (GAMM) provides the framework for the EU's relations with third countries in the area of migration. Since June 2016, the EU applies a migration partnership framework to tackle irregular migration and its root causes in cooperation with countries of origin and transit (European Council 2016d).

---

85 For example, the European Commission's contributions of up to €500 million for the "Madad Fund" draws from the European Neighbourhood Instrument, the Instrument for Pre-Accession and the Development Cooperation Instrument (Faure et al. 2015: 19).

86 For a comprehensive overview of measures, see Bendel (2017).

Other crucial initiatives towards third countries are EU readmission agreements to implement the EU's return policy as well as resettlement programmes. So far, the EU has concluded 17 readmission agreements with non-EU countries, for example, with Hong Kong since 2004, Ukraine, Bosnia & Herzegovina, Moldova, and Serbia since 2008, Azerbaijan and Turkey since 2014. Moreover, the Cotonou Agreement between the EU and African countries foresees readmission provisions. New readmission agreements are negotiated for example with Morocco (notably since 2003), Nigeria, Tunisia and Jordan. EU readmission agreements operate alongside but take precedence over bilateral readmission agreements between individual EU member states and non-EU countries. The agreements shall facilitate the return of people residing irregularly in an EU country, either to their home country or to a transit country.

Resettlement is the process of bringing asylum-seekers in from outside the EU in a controlled, ordered, and legal way. The first EU-wide resettlement scheme was launched in July 2015. EU member states agreed to resettle 22.000 people in need of international protection. By September 2017, when the programme was to end, about 75% of the resettlement had been completed (European Commission 2017q). The EU-Turkey Statement also foresees a "One for One" resettlement mechanism. In July 2016, the Commission proposed a permanent Union Resettlement Framework (European Commission 2016e). This new mechanism would "complement the current ad-hoc multilateral and national resettlement programmes by providing common EU rules on the admission of third-country nationals, procedures of the resettlement process, types of status to be accorded by the member states, decision-making procedures for the implementation of the framework and the financial support for the member states' resettlement efforts".[87] Only in November 2017 the Council was ready to start negotiations with the European Parliament. Mid-2018 the Committee of Permanent Representatives postponed the negotiations for an undefined period.

In terms of funding, the European Fund for Sustainable Development (EFSD) supports this policy. The EU established the EFSD in September 2017 (European Parliament & Council of the European Union 2017) to support investment in Africa and the European Neighbourhood and fight the root causes of migration. As the core instrument of the External In-

87 See http://www.europarl.europa.eu/legislative-train/theme-towards-a-new-policy-on-migration/file-jd-eu-resettlement-framework (accessed 2 December 2018).

vestment Plan it will integrate financial instruments into more traditional forms of assistance such as grants – namely guarantees, risk sharing instruments, as well as the blending of existing grants and loans, i.e. it works exactly like the European Fund for Strategic Investments. The fund foresees a budget of €4.1 billion, of which €1.5 billion are guarantees, and €2.6 billion come from the blending facilities under the African Investment Facility and the Neighbourhood Investment Facility (European Commission 2016f). Member states are invited to pledge additional contributions to the instrument. The EFSD is expected to mobilise total investments of up to €44 billion until 2020 (ibid.: 11).

In view of the measures taken to fight the "refugee crisis" den Hertog (2016: 28) concludes that "it is clear that the Commission considers funding to be one of its main responses to the 'refugee crisis'. As compared to the legal and operational responses that have sparked fierce public and political debate, such as the relocation mechanism, budgetary proposals have proven to be less politically charged and were adopted with less scrutiny".

Similar to the financial and economic crisis, the "refugee crisis" was followed by a plethora of measures, both in regulatory and budgetary terms. The unusual fast budgetary amendments undertaken by the Union in 2015, 2016 and 2017 show that the original foreseen commitments for that policy (headings 3 and partly 4 of the MFF) were insufficient in order to react to the crisis and to further handle the new situation both within the Union and at its external borders. The crisis required the Union to fully exhaust its budgetary flexibility instruments (European Parliament 2016c). Moreover, Articles 67 and 80 TFEU require the European Union to frame and implement a common policy on asylum, immigration and external borders based on solidarity and fair sharing of responsibility between the member states. The EU budget is likely to be used to "ease" such solidarity through a higher share of the overall MFF, in particular by bolstering the protection and surveillance of the EU's external border and fostering the cooperation with third countries (see also European Council 2017b).

### *4.3 New dynamics in security and defence policies*

More than 60 years after the Treaty on establishing the European Defence Community failed to be ratified in the French National Assembly, the idea of creating a European Defence Union gained new momentum particularly since 2016. The possibility for a common defence policy is codified in Article 42(2) TEU, which allows for a "progressive framing of a common

Union defence policy". The destabilization of the EU's nearer abroad and wider neighbourhood (which includes sub-Saharan conflicts), Russia´s expansionist policies, Brexit, uncertainty in the transatlantic partnership as well as intensified terrorist threat were important drivers behind the new dynamics (see, for example, European Commission 2017r). In parallel, the EU realised that member states treated defence policy rather stepmotherly. Between 2005 and 2015, defence spending of the EU decreased by nearly 11% reaching an overall amount of €200 billion. The GDP share of defence expenditure has also dropped to the lowest recorded level of 1.4% in 2015. In 2016, four out of 28 EU member states reached the NATO spending target of 2% of GDP (i.e. Estonia, Greece, Poland, and the United Kingdom) (European Commission 2016g: 4).

The European Council has already placed emphasis on defence in December 2013 when it adopted three major objectives: (a) to increase the effectiveness, visibility and impact of Common Security and Defence Policy (CSDP); (b) to enhance the development of EU member state capabilities; and (c) to strengthen the European defence industry (European Council 2013). Moreover, then European Commission President-candidate Jean-Claude Juncker announced in July 2014 that:

> "I also believe that we need to work on a stronger Europe when it comes to security and defence matters. Yes, Europe is chiefly a 'soft power'. But even the strongest soft powers cannot make do in the long run without at least some integrated defence capacities." (Juncker 2014)

The political umbrella for the EU's new security and defence ambitions is the 2016 "EU Global Strategy for the European Union's foreign and security policy" (EUGS). The revamped strategy – which has been described as a "correction" of the 2003 European Security Strategy (Biscop 2016) – has been presented by the High Representative of the Union for Foreign Affairs and Security Policy and Vice President of the European Commission (HR/VP), Federica Mogherini, to the European Council on 28 June 2016. It focuses the EU's external action on five areas: security and defence; resilience in the Southern and Eastern neighbourhood; an integrated approach to conflicts and crises; cooperative regional orders; and global governance (European Union 2016).

In implementing these goals, the strategy acknowledges the nexus between policies that are usually perceived and "internal" and policies that are usually perceived as "external". The Council specifically identified the linkages between EU external policy, including CSDP, and the European

Agenda on Security (European Commission 2015d)[88] as important targets for building better policy coherence, which will include "countering hybrid threats, cyber security, strategic communication, preventing and countering terrorism and violent extremism, and enhancing the security of critical infrastructure" (Council of the European Union 2017g: 4). Improved shared risk analysis at country and regional level and monitoring of external pressures are core measures for the EU to fulfil its new approach calling for enhanced funding of external actions. The EU is therefore setting up a "menu of funding instruments" (European Union 2017: 27), amongst which are the Trust Funds as well as the European External Investment Plan.

Under the MFF 2014-2020 the heading "Global Europe" covers all EU external action. "Global Europe" has a total budget of €58.7 billion, i.e. 6.5% of the overall MFF (payments in 2011 prices).

It includes development assistance (through the Development Cooperation Instrument; about one-fourth of the overall heading), enlargement policies (through the Instrument for Pre-Accession; about one-fifth of the overall heading), the ENP (through the European Neighbourhood Instrument; about one-fourth of the overall heading), humanitarian aid and response to crises (several instruments; about one-fifth of the overall heading), and CFSP (about 4% of the overall heading).

In his State-of-the-Union speech in September 2016, Commission President Jean-Claude Juncker proposed a number of initiatives in the area of defence, including the creation of a European Defence Fund (EDF), the creation of a single headquarters for operations, the implementation of permanent structured cooperation and a move towards common military assets (Juncker 2016). Following that, the European Council endorsed a defence package consisting of the implementation of the EU Global Strategy in the areas of security and defence, the European Defence Action Plan and cooperation with NATO in December 2016. The European Defence Action Plan had been proposed by the Commission in November 2016 paving the way for preparatory actions in view of the EDF, mobilising additional investments for SMEs, opening up EFSI for defence purposes, enhancing the skills for the defence sector, launching initiatives to create synergies with other EU policies (such as space policy), and com-

88 The European Agenda on Security already highlighted the strong relationship between internal and external policies and the need for better coherence.

pleting the Single Market in the area of defence (European Commission 2016g: 13ff).

With launching the European Defence Fund, the Union for the first time in its history will financially support military research (European Commission 2017s). Following the European Council of December 2013, which called for the creation of a so-called preparatory action to test the new approach of defence research outside the research and innovation Framework Programme Horizon 2020, the Industry Commissioner, Elżbieta Bieńkowska, on 30 March 2015 launched a high level group of politicians, academics, business representatives to advise on how the EU can support research related to the Common Security and Defence Policy. The EDF – with a total proposed budget of €13 billion for the MFF 2021-2027 (European Commission 2018i) – will consist of a "research window" to finance collaborative research in innovative defence products and technologies at EU level and a "capability window" to support the joint development and the joint acquisition of key defence capabilities. Between 2017 and 2020 the preparatory action funded already joint research projects with a proposed amount of €90 million for the whole period. For the post-2020 MFF, the Commission proposes a dedicated "defence research window" with a budget of €4.1 billion (). Under the "capability window" the Commission had tabled a proposal for a new European Defence Industrial Development Programme (European Commission 2017t). The programme foresaw an EU budget of €500 million for the years 2019 and 2020. In the post-2020 MFF, the amount for the development part of the EDF should increase to €8.9 billion for the whole seven-year-period. The Commission proposed that "the Programme could [...] support the spin-in of commercial innovation into future defence projects, such as artificial intelligence, big data, cyber defence, robotics and super-computing" (European Commission 2017s: 9). To fund the new programme under the 2014-2020 MFF the envelopes of the Connecting Europe Facility (i.e. internal energy market, energy security, environmental protection), the European Satellite Navigation Programmes (Galileo), the European Earth Observation Programme (Copernicus), the ITER Programme and the unallocated margin have to be reduced (European Commission 2017t: 25), meaning a shift of expenditure within "Competitiveness"-heading of the MFF.

On 11 December 2017, the Council adopted a decision establishing Permanent Structured Cooperation (PESCO), a specific flexibility tool in the area of security and defence policy (Council of the European Union 2017h). Articles 42(6) and 46 TEU and Protocol 10 of the Treaties foresee the possibility that a number of EU member states work together more closely in well-defined areas and towards joint targets as defined in Protocol 10. All EU member states, except Denmark, Malta, and the UK, participate in PESCO. They have agreed to 20 commitments of a binding nature, amongst which a number are directly expenditure-relevant:

> "- Regularly increasing defence budgets in real terms, in order to reach agreed objectives.
>
> - Successive medium-term increase in defence investment expenditure to 20 % of total defence spending (collective benchmark) in order to fill strategic capability gaps by participating in defence capabilities projects.
>
> - Increasing joint and "collaborative" strategic defence capabilities projects. Such joint and collaborative projects should be supported through the European Defence Fund if required and as appropriate.
>
> - Increasing the share of expenditure allocated to defence research and technology with a view to nearing the 2 % of total defence spending (collective benchmark).
>
> - Commitment to the intensive involvement of a future European Defence Fund in multinational procurement with identified EU added value.
>
> - Participating Member States will strive for an ambitious approach to common funding of military CSDP operations and missions, beyond what will be defined as common cost according to the Athena council decision." (Council of the European Union 2017h)

National contributions to PESCO will be defined in and assessed through National Implementation Plans. To fill PESCO with life, the Council also adopted a declaration announcing the launch of initially 17 projects under PESCO. The projects cover areas such as training, capability development and operational readiness in the field of defence. These initial projects were formally adopted by the Council o("PESCO-format") on 6 March 2018 and will primarily financed by the participating member states. Co-financing of up to 30% is foreseen through the European Defence Fund (Wolfstädter/Kreilinger 2017: 9). Upon invitation by participating member states, third states may take part in PESCO's individual projects.

In a speech on 13 December 2017, HR/VP Federica Mogherini announced, "a new European Peace Facility, financed and managed together with our member states" (Mogherini 2017). According to the plans of Mogherini this instrument – a fund of €10.5 billion outside the MFF – should increase the EU's capabilities to plan and deeply its military missions as well as "support our partners in dealing with our shared security challenges" (ibid.). The European Peace Facility will replace old instruments, such as the "Athena Mechanism"[89] and the "African Peace Facility" but aims at substantially increase the funding of the common costs of EU missions.

### *4.4 Conclusions*

This chapter has engaged in some of the new challenges the EU is facing. It has been shown that the migration and defence challenges already had some impact on the distribution of budgets within the current MFF, but also on the need to mobilise funding outside the financial framework (similar to some of the solutions found as a consequence of the financial and economic crisis).

The UK leaving the EU has usually been seen as a crucial issue in the negotiations for the next MFF. The reiterated concern is how to fill the budget gap – if at all – when a net-payer leaves the Union. However, before and until the UK has not completely exited the EU, one can actually not perfectly define how big a gap would be and which member states might need to stand in for closing it – if at all. First, a transition phase after Brexit (possibly until 31 December 2020 or even longer) would guarantee that the UK "will contribute to, and participate in, the implementation of the Union annual budgets for the years 2019 and 2020 as if it had remained in the Union" (TF50 2017: 9). This includes the UK's share of the financing of the budgetary commitments outstanding on 31 December 2020 (so-called "reste à liquider"). Second, a judgment on the real financial gap must be falsified due to the complex system of rebates for net contributors. It is possible that the system will be abandoned or at least changed making forecasts on a future financial gap difficult. Current calculations are based on the assumption that the UK remains in the EU (see, for example, UK House of Commons 2017). Third, the UK leaving the Union will lower the average EU GDP per capita. Some of the current net-receivers that are at the edge of becoming net contributors (such as Spain, Ireland, the Baltic states, Croatia, Slovenia, Malta, Cyprus) might cross that line. In such a case the composition of member states that should fill the financial gap would change considerably. Fourth, it is not yet clear how the relationships between the EU and the UK will develop in the future. The UK might financially contribute to the EU budget for staying,

89 The "Athena Mechanism" is so far the funding arrangement outside the MFF for the financing of the common costs of military CSDP operations.

for example, in the Single Market or for participating in any other policies of the EU. While negotiations on the future relationship between the EU and the UK would determine these potential costs, it would mitigate the budget losses. Last but not least, the UK government has stated that "it may wish to participate in some Union budgetary programmes of the new MFF post-2020 as a non-Member State" (TF50 2017: 12). The UK's future participation in EU programmes and any related contributions would be another source of narrowing the future financial gap. Any estimation of future payments is rather unreliable, however, it is fair to say that the deeper the future relationship of the UK with the EU, the larger its payments will be, and the narrower the financial gap of a net-payer leaving the Union can be expected (UK House of Commons 2017).

Severe and multiple external crises have generated new enthusiasm amongst EU leaders for deeper European integration in the area of defence and security (see, for example, König/Walter-Franke 2017). The first EU foreign policy strategy of 2003 was triggered by the World Trade Center attacks of September 2001 and the following "war on terror" in Iraq. However, it lost some of its drive shortly after its adoption (Toje 2005) as EU member states were split on the US-led Iraq invasion, resources were scarce, and from an institutional perspective the EU still missed some of the competences and institutions it finally gained with the Lisbon Treaty. The so-called Arab Spring of 2011, which led to destabilization processes and violent conflicts in several countries around the EU and catalysed huge refugee flows, and the Ukraine crisis since 2014 revealed the weaknesses of the EU's neighbourhood policy (ENP). As a reaction to these crises, the EU has revised the ENP twice in 2011 and in 2015 (Gstöhl 2017), and at the latest since 2013 has put more emphasis on its policies towards the neighbours of the ENP countries (Gstöhl 2015). Since 2015, an increasing number of terrorist attacks, the isolationist international politics of the Trump administration as well as the prospects of the UK exiting the EU have provided some dynamics to EU defence policy integration, with the European Defence Fund and PESCO as its most visible results.

If EU member states are willing to build a European Security and Defence Union – as proposed by Commission President Juncker in his 2017 State-of-the-Union address (Juncker 2017) – a bigger budget for this area could be requested. In September 2017 French President Macron pointed out in his Sorbonne Speech that "at the beginning of the next decade, Europe needs to establish a common intervention force, a common defence budget and a common doctrine for action" (Macron 2017). The likelihood of a "common defence budget" – which can be assumed should even be larger than the envisioned €13 billion for the European Defence Fund under the post-2020 MFF – will certainly depend on a number of conditions – independent of whether it will be "a new and separate budget" or "a budget line under the MFF": first, the net-benefits or net-losses to be experienced by member states under the forthcoming European Defence Fund (i.e. "juste retour"-principle); second, the extent to which the financing of other policy areas might suffer – and therefore those member states that profited from those sacrificed funding – from a shift of policy priorities; third, the leadership capabilities of the French-German axis to convince others to follow (provided, of course, that France and Germany want the same); fourth, the necessary level of trust by member states that their interests are best preserved by EU institutions.

For the EU and its budget migration and asylum policy seem to be the most controversial of the new challenges. While on the one hand, the massive influx of refugees in 2015 and 2016 has split member states on how to respond, it has on the other hand, mostly stretched the MFF and its capabilities to handle the crisis. In the future the EU might need more resources for border controls and new partnerships with countries of origin as well as with transit countries. The Commission is certainly keen to avoid the constant annual search for additional funds and to amend a running MFF, while member states' governments need to make sure that the number of protection-seekers remains low as they fear that otherwise they will further lose confidence of their national electorate. Moreover, in the context of the reform of the European Common Asylum System the EU might need additional funds to incentivise the solidarity of those member states that are not willing to take refugees or support those that are at the forefront of receiving most refugees.

The discussed new challenges certainly influence the post-2020 MFF negotiations. However, the still unknown ultimate (financial) consequences of the Brexit and the existence of varying positions of member states in policy areas of mainly national competence and high societal sensitivity, such as defence and immigration, indicate that there is no automatism leading from the identification of new – in principle EU-wide – challenges to substantial changes in the EU's budget layout. The proposal of the European Commission for the post-2020 MFF reflects the perceived need for additional activities in the areas of migration and defence as follows[90]:

90 All figures European Commission (2018j : 30; commitments in constant 2018 prices).

1. a formal separation of the migration and defence budget lines by creating two new headings called “Migration and Border Management” and “Security and Defence”;
2. creating a new “Integrated Border Management Fund” worth €8.2 billion, serving, for example, to reinforce the member states’ capacities to control their borders, to exchange border guards between member states or between a member state and a third country, and to co-share border control equipment;
3. increasing the “Asylum and Migration Fund” to almost €10 billion (compared to €3.4 billion under the MFF 2014-2020);
4. reinforcing FRONTEX by increasing its staff from about 1.300 to 10.000 until 2021 (the relevant budget line should be pumped-up from €3 billion under the 2014-2020 MFF to €10.5 billion under the post-2020 MFF);
5. equipping the new European Defence Fund with a budget of €11.4 billion, of which two-thirds for “capability development” and one-third for “research”;
6. a new activity labelled as “strategic transport infrastructure” for “military mobility” under the Connecting Europe Facility worth almost €6 billion.

In sum, according to the Commission proposal the “Migration and Border Management” activities amount to 2.7% and the “Security and Defence” activities to 2.1% of the post-2020 MFF budget, which would not signal a turnaround in budgetary priorities.

# 5. Reforming the own resources: perspectives on the revenue-side of the EU budget

## 5.1 *Own resources! – Own resources?*

Over the last three decades, the system of the EU's own resources has been extraordinary stable in terms of the main sources of income, but highly dynamic in view of the evolution of the share the different sources provided for the budget. Basically, the own resources stem from customs duties that are directly delegated to the EU budget after a deduction of 20% that the member states retain for their administrative efforts.[91] The second source is a levy of 0.3% of the value-added tax that is collected at the member states' level and then transferred to the EU budget. The third – and by far the most important – source is a levy the member states hand over to the European Union on the basis of their respective Gross National Income (GNI).

With some variations, this system is in place since 1988. Some adjustments have been made for the 2000-2006 MFF when member states' levies that were till then based on their Gross National Product (GNP) were started to be calculated on GNI basis. After 2000, the subsequent four multiannual financial frameworks largely maintained this own resource structure. Given that the EU has almost doubled the number of member states after 2000 the further adjustments to that structure were quite limited:

- The overall ceiling for GNI based payments was increased from 1.07% in 2000 to 1.23 for the MFF 2014-2020,
- The VAT-based resources were reduced from 1% in 2000 to 0.30% after 2007.
- Since 2001, rebates and correction both in GNI and VAT-based levies apply to Austria, Denmark, Germany, the Netherlands, Sweden and the UK.

91 The customs duties are a traditional own resource that exist since the establishment of the customs union in 1968. Until 2018, a second traditional own resource existed with a levy on sugar production which, however, always provided a very limited share to the budget.

Accordingly, the GNI contributions of the member states became the most important source for the EU budget. The respective share increased from 41% in 1998 to 71% in 2018. In a strict sense, the most important own resource of the European Union is not an own resource, but a mandatory levy provided by the member states. It can be considered an own resource, because national parliaments have no say about it anymore once they have ratified a Decision of the Council on Own Resources which is part of the legislative package for each MFF.

The stability of the own resource structure contrast with constantly recurring demands for reforming the system. It is, however, noticeable that neither the justifications for changes nor the envisaged new financing instruments have changed significantly over time. The European Commission argued already in 2004 that although the "current financing system performs relatively well from a fiscal point of view" and despite the fact that "it has ensured a smooth financing and kept administrative costs of the system quite low", the system "has been criticized for insufficient transparency for EU citizens, and limited financial autonomy, as well as for its complexity and opacity" (European Commission 2004: 36). Already at that time, the proposed new own resources were a tax on corporate income, a genuine VAT resource, and an energy tax. And already at that time the main justification was that the new own resources could partially replace financial means provided by the member states on the basis of their GNI (ibid.: 36-37).

This indicates that the main motivation for the "invention" of new own resources is to dial back the trend that led to a domination of the GNI-based levies provided by the member states. If true, we would expect the European Parliament and the Commission being in the reform's driver seat while member states' governments should be keen to slow down the discourse. And this is what has actually happened during the last two decades. The importance of GNI-based contributions helps member states to keep the EU finances under control while they also provide a significant amount of certainty about the impact a new multiannual financial framework will have on national budgets. Moreover, and this is often neglected in the debate, the decision on own resources has a strong democratic legitimacy, because it requires ratification through national parliaments while the European Parliament has only a right to be heard (Art. 311(2) TFEU).

Beyond political rhetoric, the two main problems with the current system of own resources its complexity (especially in terms of the various correction mechanisms) as well as its main effect, namely the consolidation of the "juste retour" logic of budget negotiations.

Rebates and correction mechanisms increase complexity. However, the even larger problem is that they are difficult to remove even if the reasons for awarding them do not persist anymore. The famous British rebate, introduced in 1984 in order to compensate for Britain's low agricultural expenditures and an unfair VAT-based burden in relation to the country's GDP, was rational at that time since the country was one of the poorest EU member states. It still exists although Britain is today one of the richest members of the Union. As long as decisions on own resources require unanimity in the Council the obstacles for change are extremely high. That is why the Brexit could open up a window of opportunity to phase-out some rebates and correction mechanisms, but they will certainly not fully disappear.

The "juste retour" logic could be considered as a significant problem if the EU budget would be just a financial instrument aimed at financing common European policies in a most efficient and effective way. But this is not the case. Critics of the current own resource system tend to overlook that it is also (and this is at least equally important) the only instrument available to organise the financial transfers among member states which are an expression of European solidarity. As a consequence, it is vital for a compromise on a new European budget that member state governments have sufficient certainty about the payments to and the revenues from the European level. If this would not be provided anymore, the European Union would be in need of a formal financial correction mechanism as it exists in federal and regionalized countries.

Núñez Ferrer et al. (2016) have therefore rightly stated that there are a number of structural conditions that render EU budget reforms in general and changes of the own resource system in particular difficult. A first key aspect is the fiscal heterogeneity of the member states in terms of the size, the development and the degree of specialization of their economies that produce different government tax revenues as a share of GDP. A second aspect concerns societal fragmentation and the level of domestic conflicts which have an impact on budget choices and the provision of public goods. And there are enormous institutional variations across the member states' political systems (centralized vs. decentralized, consensus vs. majoritarian style of decision-making, number of veto players in the system, etc.) that influence the overall level of spending, but also impact on whether or not there is vertical and horizontal competition among political actors (ibid.: 48-49). These variations are extraordinary stable and therefore limit considerably national government's room for manoeuvre in EU budget negotiations.

Moreover, as already described in Chapter 2, one should not underestimate the importance of political actors' learning effects. Under the current, largely unchanged, structure the EU has managed to incorporate 13 new member states that have – compared to the former EU-15 countries – a considerably lower level of economic performance and social welfare. The EU even managed to overcome the most serious economic consequences of the 2008 financial crisis even though productivity did not yet increase in all countries beyond the pre-crisis level. Therefore, the conditions that existed for an agreement on the MFF's 2007-2013 and 2014-2020 were certainly not better compared to the current situation in which the Brexit is the only challenge for which political actors cannot draw on experience.

## *5.2 The revenue-side of the MFF 2014-2020*

In terms of the revenue-side, the MFF 2014-2020 is not much different from its predecessor. The three types of own resources remained the same while only small changes exist in terms of rebates and correction mechanisms:

- Germany, the Netherlands and Sweden profit from a reduced VAT call rate of 0.15% instead of 0.3%,
- Austria, Denmark, the Netherlands and Sweden benefit from a reduction of their GNI-based contributions. Denmark receives a deduction of €130 million, the Netherlands of €695 million, Sweden of €185 million. The Austrian deduction amounts to €30 million in 2014, to €20 million in 2015 and to €10 million in 2016.
- Germany, the Netherlands, Sweden and Austria maintain their "rebate on the rebate". This means that these countries contribute less than they would have to pay for the compensation of the British rebate. As for Germany, this correction amounted to roughly one billion Euro for 2014-2018.

As such, the MFF 2014-2020 is a paragon of institutional stability. There were, however, three developments that may have an impact on the negotiations for the post-2020 budget.

A first trend concerns the further increase of the importance of the GNI-based contributions of the member states for the overall budget. The respective call rate increased to 0.7% of GNI for the period 2012-2016 after it had been quite stable at around 0.6% of GNI for the last two decades (European Commission 2018u: 8). To some extent, the increase can be explained by the method that is applied to measure the amount of GNI contributions. Given the requirement for a balanced EU budget, the GNI-based levies are calculated always after taking into account the other revenues. This means that GNI contributions always have to cover the EU annual payment appropriations.

A second trend refers to the fact that there are some dynamics in the position of member states as net-payers or net-recipients. Table 5.1 gives an overview of the respective situation in 2016/17.

*Table 5.1: Net-payer and net-recipients member states in the EU and their net-payments/net-receipts 2016/17 in percent of GDP (Wirtschaftskammer Österreich 2017)*

| Member State | Net contributions in percent of GDP (2016) | Net receipts in percent of GDP (2017) |
|---|---|---|
| | | |
| Germany | 0.4 | - |
| France | 0.36 | - |
| Sweden | 0.33 | - |
| Netherlands | 0.3 | - |
| Denmark | 0.28 | - |
| Belgium | 0.28 | - |
| United Kingdom | 0.24 | - |
| Austria | 0.23 | - |
| Italy | 0.14 | - |
| Finland | 0.14 | - |
| Bulgaria | - | 4.17 |
| Romania | - | 3.64 |
| Hungary | - | 3.34 |
| Lithuania | - | 3.12 |
| Slovakia | - | 2.53 |
| Greece | - | 2.47 |
| Czech Republic | - | 2.04 |
| Latvia | - | 2.04 |
| Poland | - | 1.75 |
| Malta | - | 1.3 |
| Croatia | - | 1.2 |
| Portugal | - | 0.99 |
| Slovenia | - | 0.51 |
| Spain | - | 0.19 |
| Cyprus | - | 0.18 |
| Ireland | - | 0.16 |
| Luxembourg | - | 0.03 |

The important message behind the figures is that we have at least four net-recipients that are close to become net-payers, namely Spain, Cyprus, Ireland and Luxembourg. Even if they stay as net-recipients, their overall ratio of burdens and benefits is almost equal. This could have consequences for the negotiations for the post-2020 budget as the camp of the net-recipients might become smaller while the camp of the net-payers becomes more heterogeneous.

A third trend which also could impact on these negotiations consists of a continuation of the efforts to reform the EU own resource system. We have already shown that the issue never disappeared from the agenda although hardly any changes were made. Nevertheless, when the European Parliament, the Council and the European Commission concluded the final agreement of the MFF 2014-2020 in December 2013 they also decided to establish a High-Level Group of Experts that was mandated to evaluate reform options for the establishment of new own resources.

### *5.3 Future financing of the EU – the report of the High-Level Group on Own Resources*

On 25 February 2014, the Presidents of the European Commission, the Council and the European Parliament established an inter-institutional group of experts ("The High-Level Group on Own Resources") that was chaired by the former Italian Prime Minister and EU Commissioner Mario Monti. The group was mandated in a quite unspecific way in the sense that it had been asked to explore ways to make the current system of income to the EU budget "simpler, fairer, more transparent, and more democratically accountable".[92] The expert group worked for two years and published its final report in December 2016 (High Level Group on Own Resources 2016).

The experts made recommendations for the reform of the revenue side system by evaluating options for new own resources against eight indicators:

1. the equity and fairness in terms of the effects on the member states,
2. the efficiency in terms of the level of revenues and administrative costs,

92 Cf. "Q&A: The EU's high-level Group on own resources", MEMO of the European Commission, Strasbourg, 25 February 2014.

3. the sufficiency and stability in terms of reliability of revenues for the EU budget,
4. the transparency and simplicity in terms of the capability of EU citizens to acknowledge their contribution to EU finances,
5. the democratic accountability and the budgetary discipline in terms of the EU's parliament's capacity to pursue democratic control,
6. the European added-value in terms of linkages to existing EU policies,
7. the protection of the principle of subsidiarity in terms of the question of the level of governance responsible for collecting the tax, and
8. the political transaction costs in terms of resistance from political or societal actors.

We do not neglect the importance of all these indicators for a political decision on new own resources. Nevertheless, we argue that two of them, the fairness in terms of their effects on the member states and the political transaction costs associated with their implementation, are certainly the most crucial ones, because they are directly related to the "juste retour" logic that dominates budget negotiations.

In this respect, the key message, the High-Level Group had for political actors at member states' and European levels was (in a way hidden) in the report's annex (High Level Group on Own Resources 2016: 87). Compared to the existing own resources, all alternatives that were proposed by the group (with the exemption of a reformed VAT-based system) scored poorer in terms of political transaction costs that would arise if implemented. These political transaction costs would accumulate primarily at the level of the member states. Moreover, apart from the EU-wide corporate income tax, all other alternatives do not perform better than the existing own resources with respect to a fair treatment of the member states.

As for the carbon tax, it is assumed that it would meet considerable resistance from transport and fuel industries. Since member states' industries differ significantly in view of their $CO_2$ intensity, a European carbon tax could not exist either without strong re-distributional effects or the application of new compensation rules.

The main problem with the delegation of revenues from the European Emission Trading System (ETS) to the MFF arises from the fact that it currently fuels national budgets. It is also – similar to the carbon tax – confronted with the large differences that exist across member states' industrial capacities. In contrast to the carbon tax, however, the ETS revenues would be stronger linked to an already existing European policy framework and they could disburden above-average net-payers with a strong industrial basis as GNI-based payments could be reduced.

Few incentives for political actors also exist to opt for a European motor fuel tax. It would be difficult to implement as may member states have varying exemptions in this field while the amount of revenues generated from the fuel tax is relevant for national budgets. Apart from that, some member states have regulated that the use of revenues from this tax is limited to public investments in the road infrastructure. That is why the group considers the political transaction costs significant.

The same holds, more or less, also for the proposed electricity tax. Member states differ significantly on how consumption of electricity is taxed. In some countries, this tax is also directly linked with public initiatives for energy transition as it is especially the case with the German "Energiewende" (the strategy to abolish both nuclear and coal-based power generation, see Chapter 1). Due to the fact that some member states have very low electricity tax rates, the need for harmonization would be high, so too were the political costs.

The main advantage of an EU-wide corporate tax would be that it is closely related to activities (and benefits) of companies within the single market. The share of the tax revenues that would be delegated to the European budget could be determined taking into account national peculiarities. The problem is, however, that there are still member states in the European Union that apply generous exemptions to multinational companies. Therefore, political transaction costs to implement a European corporate tax would be high.

A financial transaction tax (FTT) looks, at first sight, more promising. There is broad public support for it. The FTT is closely linked with an integrated European financial market. The administrative costs are relatively low. It has, however, a significant problem in terms of fairness and equity, because the market is highly concentrated in only few financial centres in a small number of member states. Apart from that, there are doubts about how much revenues the FTT would generate and how stable the level of revenues would be.

Stable revenues for the EU budget could be generated by a reformed system of own resources from the value-added tax (VAT). Under the current regulation, the VAT-based own resources have a share of around 12% of the total revenues, but they are collected under an enormous administrative effort and they come only with various correction mechanisms in order to provide an acceptable level of fairness among member states. The High-Level Group's proposal aims at reforming this own resource in a way that would focus on fairness among EU citizens, not member states. It would derive from a direct application of a fixed EU rate on the net value of products and services. The experts consider the political transaction costs for the implementation of a reformed VAT-based own resource to be low, because of the fact that there is already for a considerable time a European harmonized legal basis in place. This assessment is, however, not well justified. A harmonized VAT basis is needed to prevent distortion of competition and barriers to free movement of goods and services in the single market. It therefore mainly addresses the interests of companies. Under the proposed new VAT-based own resource it would be mainly citizens who would consider parts of the costs of their consumption as an individual contribution to the European Union. Unsurprisingly, this proposal immediately received strong criticism especially from net-payer governments. In a position paper on the new MFF, the German government called for the complete abolishment of the VAT-based own resource.[93] The French position is generally more open to new EU own resources, but is mainly supports new common European taxes (such as the FTT) and not necessarily a strengthening of the VAT base.

### *5.4 Perspectives on the revenue side post-2020*

In preparing the legal proposals for the post-2020 MFF, the European Commission reacted in a quite defensive way to the proposals of the High-Level Group. A first reaction can be found in the "Reflection Paper on the Future of EU Finances" presented in June 2017. In terms of the new own resources that were under discussion, the paper states that

> "[…] none could by itself fit all the criteria identified as necessary for an own resource. Some can bring in stable and significant revenues and lead to real reshaping of the revenue side. Others would bring in more modest revenues, but could be more politically relevant or acceptable, in particular if they accompanied priority policy objectives, such as the decarbonization of the European economy, the deepening of the single market and of economic and monetary union or the financing of new priorities" (European Commission 2017b: 27-28).

This shows the whole dilemma of the debate on new own resources. Those that have a plausible rationality in terms of a strong linkage with EU prior-

93 "Positionen der Bundesregierung zum Mehrjährigen Finanzrahmen der Europäischen Union (MFR) post-2020," Bundesregierung der Bundesrepublik Deutschland, Berlin, 25. Januar 2018 (see https://www.bundeskanzlerin.de/resource/blob/656734/317304/803e6efc4233cca62a460bb8ec97336a/2018-02-22-mehrjaehriger-eu-finanzrahmen-data.pdf, accessed 1 June 2018).

ities and policies do not provide sufficient and reliable revenues. Those that would keep the current level of EU finances stable meet strong political resistance or they do not perform better in terms of fairness and equality among member states.

Accordingly, the Commission's proposal for a new Council decision on the system of Own Resources of the European Union (European Commission 2018b) is quite cautious in terms of new own resources. It proposes the introduction of:

1. "a share of the relaunched Common Consolidated Corporate Tax base to be phased in once the necessary legislation has been adopted"
2. "a share of the auctioning revenue of the European Emission Trading System", and
3. "a national contribution calculated on the amount of non-recycled plastic packaging waste" (European Commission 2018b: 4)

All in all, the European Commission estimates that if member states agree on these new own resources, they could have a share of 12% of the total 2021-2027 budget. Most financial resources would, however, be generated from the Corporate Tax (around 12 billion Euro per year) while revenues from the Emission Trading System would amount to 1.2 to 3 billion Euro per year, from the levy on plastic package waste around 7 billion Euro per year (European Commission 2018b: 7-8). This means that more than 50% of the revenues from the new own resources would stem from a tax that has yet not even sufficient political support from the member states.

Given that, the political bargaining will certainly concentrate on reforming the "old" own resources. In this respect, the Commission has proposed to cut the collection costs for customs duties that member states are allowed to retain back to 10% (which was already the rule between 1970 and 2000), to reduce the share of the GNI-based resources by the level of revenues originating from the new own revenues, and to "simplify" the VAT-based own resources primarily by phasing-out the existing rebates for some net-payer member states. Tables 5.1 provides an overview of the Commission's proposal on own resources. It shows that the most significant change would occur in terms of the weight of the GNI-based payments of the member states. This is, however, obviously only true under the assumption that the final agreement comes at least close to the overall budget ceiling that was proposed by the Commission.

*Table 5.2: EU Commission's proposal on Own Resources – estimated evolution and structure of EU financing (European Commission 2018b: 9)*

| | *Budget 2018* | | *Estimated Average 2021-2027* | |
|---|---|---|---|---|
| | *EUR billion* | *% of total revenue* | *EUR billion* | *% of total revenue* |
| *Traditional Own Resources* | 23 | 15.8 | 26 | 15 |
| *Existing national contributions of which* | 120 | 82.9 | 128 | 72 |
| *Reformed VAT-based Own Resources* | 17 | 11.9 | 25 | 14 |
| *GNI-based Own Resources* | 103 | 71 | 103 | 58 |
| | | | | |
| *New Own Resources of which* | - | - | 22 | 12 |
| *Corporate Tax Base* | - | - | 12 | 6 |
| *Emission Trading System* | - | - | 3 | 2 |
| *Plastic packaging waste* | - | - | 7 | 4 |
| | | | | |
| *Total Own Resources* | 143 | 98.7 | 176 | 99 |
| *Revenue other than Own Resources* | 2 | 1.3 | 2 | 1 |
| *Total Revenue* | 145 | 100 | 178 | 100 |

Compared to the European Commission, the reaction from the European Parliament on the High-Level Group's report was much more enthusiastic. In a resolution of 14 March 2018 (European Parliament 2018a), the Parliament did not even welcome and support the new own resources mentioned in the report. In went even further proposing an EU-wide tax for companies in the digital sector. Considerations on the political transaction costs associated with these taxes and levies are largely missing in the resolution.

As for the member states we have initial evidence of very reserved attitudes towards a substantial reform of the own resource system. This reservation exists in two ways. On the one hand, member states' governments have not been very eager to reveal their positions on the topic. They are more concerned with the impact of the Brexit on the overall budget ceiling. There is, however, at least an indication that the German and the Dutch government are against an increase of the "tax burden" for European citizens. On the other hand, the question of introducing new own resources is very closely linked with the death or survival of the different rebates that exist for most net-payer member states. It is therefore not a surprise that governments that want to maintain their national rebate are not very eager to let other actors have a look in their cards. We can at least state that no powerful coalition of member states has already been established that has clearly formulated a common position on new own resources.

### *5.5 Conclusions*

There are convincing reasons to assume that the debate over new own resources will (again) not become the chief subject of the MFF negotiations. The recommendations of the High-Level Group already indicate that changes on the revenue side may be sensible, but only under very specific conditions.

First, changes on the revenue side have to come along with reforms on the expenditure side. The introduction of a European tax raises awareness of citizens about the financial means they contribute to EU policies and thus generates expectations regarding the achievement of a European added value. As a consequence, those taxes must have a clear link to policies that are regarded as situated best at the European level. Under this premise, there are only few plausible candidates especially if taxation targets an issue for which no national levies exist.

Second, in terms of efficiency, the current system of own resources has its merits. It might not be the most transparent way to finance European policies, but it provides the necessary resources in a stable and reliable way. The High-Level Group on Own Resources considered the need for reliability only with respect to the European level. This is incomprehensible, because stability and reliability of payments to the European Union is obviously a factor that plays an important role in member states' negotiation strategies.

Third, the potential of reform options for new own resources should not be overestimated. Only few options exist that have a realistic chance of becoming implemented and implementation should, as the group concludes, be done gradually in a phase-in process (High Level Group on Own Resources 2016: 12). That is why it was probably not a good idea that the European Commission incorporated a "Trojan Horse" into its proposal for a decision on own resources. The Commission proposes that all future revenues that arise from EU policies should be immediately delegated to the EU budget (European Commission 2018b: 5).

And fourth, it is probably simply not the time for a comprehensive reform of the own resource system. Net-payer member states will already be under enormous pressure to compensate for the loss of the British contribution to the EU budget. They also have to find a solution for some kind of phasing-out of their rebates which will be difficult to defend after Brexit. Under these circumstances it is not very likely that there will be also a compromise on new own resources. On the contrary, the needed solutions are much easier to find using a reformed GNI model. Given that not even net receiver member states are strongly in favour of a reform of the own resource system it is mainly the European Parliament that opts for comprehensive change. This will most probably result in an introduction of a very limited number of new "European taxes" which offer a symbolic entry into a broader approach after 2027. As for now, the environmental taxes (related to the emission trading system and to plastic packaging waste) are the most likely candidates.

# 6. On shaky ground: perspectives on the EU's agricultural policy

## *6.1 The Common Agricultural Policy (CAP) – six decades of incremental institutional reforms*

The Common Agricultural Policy became fully operational in 1962. It is thus the oldest supranationalized policy in the European Union. Over the last six decades, it has always consumed the largest share of the budget, although this share has been decreasing constantly due to a number of reforms that have changed the objectives and instruments of the policy. Since the 1980s, the share of the CAP expenditures of the total EU budget decreased from more than 70% to around 40%. This does, however, not mean that the EU spent less on agriculture. The total expenditures have increased from about 20 billion Euro per year to slightly below 50 billion Euro. In terms of the overall European GDP, the expenditures decreased from 0.66% in the 1990s to 0.36% in 2017.[94] One has to take into account, however, that the EU's GDP has increased considerably during the same period through the acceptance of 16 new member states.

The CAP has been running through various reforms that were apparently not primarily aimed at reducing costs, but at eliminating negative policy outcomes. Basically, there were two main drivers for reform, an internal one, emerging, since the end of the 1960s, from a massive overproduction in certain sectors of agricultural production, and an external one arising from increasing political pressure when agricultural trade became subject to transnational regulation under the authority of the GATT and later on the World Trade Organization (WTO) in the 1990s. More recently, agricultural mass production came into view because of its negative impact on climate change.

Institutional change in this policy area took place in three distinct phases. Until the early 1990s, reforms were made in form of institutional adjustment. They were limited to instrumental change primarily aimed at

94 Data obtained from the European Union's website information on the development of CAP expenditures, see: https://ec.europa.eu/agriculture/sites/agriculture/files/cap-post-2013/graphs/graph2_en.pdf (accessed 31 March 2019).

gaining control of overproduction. What followed was a decade of institutional adaption (1992-2003) characterized by reforms that altered not only instruments, but also some of the objectives of the policy. Afterwards, reforms were again more focussed on the instrumental level and mainly targeted at stabilizing the changes that were initiated during the "decade of reforms".

A first attempt to get the costs and production in the agricultural sector under control was taken with the Mansholt-Plan in 1968. It was based on an approach to reduce guaranteed payments to farmers for certain product categories and to oust small family farm businesses from the market in favour of industrial farm sizes. Mansholt considered radical intervention into the market structure necessary in order to limit the sprawling overproduction. This overproduction was indeed significant: 1.2 million tons of sugar, six million tons of crops, and 300.000 tons of frozen butter were stored in Europe in 1968. Mansholt argued that without a drastic change, "butter will flow in the streets by 1970".[95] The Mansholt-Plan was never implemented, because of massive political resistance especially in Germany where family-owned small farm businesses dominated the market. Nevertheless, that plan had some importance as it already included the central aspect of later reforms, namely the rejection of political market intervention in favour of the strengthening of market forces.

The "decade of reforms" was then initiated by the MacSharry reform in 1992. While internal pressure was still high because of the overproduction, this reform was conducted also under growing external pressure. Since 1987, global trade negotiations were going on under the GATT's Uruguay Round (1987-1994) and it became evident that an agreement on agricultural trade would be a pre-condition for the successful conclusion of the negotiation round. From the perspective of the European Union, the most critical aspect concerned its export subsidies which were used to keep overproduction within limits through the provision of financial support for the export of agricultural products to third countries. The key change that emerged from the MacSharry reform was the shift from a system of guaranteed market prices for agricultural products to a guaranteed income for farmers. The reform also established an entry point for future instrumental changes in terms of new requirements for farmers aimed at stipulating environmental goals and demand for product diversification.

95 "Butter auf die Straße", Der Spiegel 51/1968, 16 December 1968, p. 109.

The Agenda 2000 of 1999 became a perfect example of institutional adaption as it changed the key instruments and particular objectives of the policy field. In terms of objectives, it "officially" introduced market-orientation and competitiveness, the integration of environmental concerns and the development of the rural areas. The reform, however, maintained the aim of stabilizing agricultural incomes and thus did not constitute a paradigmatic change in the policy field. At the instrumental level, it led to the establishment of the two pillars of funding that still structure the distribution of public financial resources to the farming industry. Direct payments to farmers were comprised in pillar I while pillar II provided funding for the protection of the environment and the developing of rural areas. In contrast to pillar I, which is solely financed by the European Union, pillar II receives co-funding from the member states. In addition, member states were authorized to shift to a certain extent funds between the two pillars. Funds that are shifted from pillar I to pillar II (limited to a maximum of 15%) do not need to be co-financed by the member states. The reform also introduced the concept of "cross-compliance" through which direct payments became conditional to the observance of environmental standards that were defined at the national level.

In a third step, the changes achieved by the Agenda 2000 were further developed with the Fischler reform in 2003. It led to a further de-coupling of agricultural production and payments for farmers by introducing the concepts of the Single Payment Scheme (SPS) and the Single Area Payment Scheme (SAPS). Farmers now received their income on the basis of the land they use independent of what they produced. It also added food safety standards to the cross-compliance requirements, and it determined the further reduction of direct payments and the shift of the respective funds to the second pillar (called "modulation").

Over time, the CAP certainly assumed a path-dependent logic. There has been some institutional adaption to objectives and instruments, but no radical policy shift. This comes not as a surprise. Being the largest expenditure programme within the multiannual financial framework, the CAP funding has a bigger role to play than just organizing food production in Europe. It is, as we will see in the next section, a key institution for the balancing of payments and receipts for a significant number of member states. Apart from that, there was one main condition for the success of institutional reforms in the field of the Common Agricultural Policy: the stability of farmer's businesses and income. The changes in the CAP have certainly altered the occupational profile in farming, they have to a much lesser extent led to structural changes in the sector. The share of farming business with less than five hectares (which is by far the largest group of farming businesses in Europe) increased between 1999 and 2013 from 58% (EU-15) to 66% (EU-28). After 2009, the salary increase in the agricultural industry was at least even if not higher compared to the construction, manufacturing or service industries, albeit the much lower average of farmers' income compares to other industrial sectors (European Communities 2003, European Commission 2018v). How can this level of stability be explained? We suggest that the most convincing rationale lies in the preference of the clear majority of member states' governments to leave the expenditures of the Common Agricultural Policy largely untouched. A study prepared by the European Commission in 2015 gave a good indication in so far as it summarized the positions of the member states on the CAP in the negotiation phase for the 2014-2020 MFF. Apart from Sweden and the UK, none of the member states expressed a preference to reduce the budget level. Estonia, Finland, Luxembourg, and the Netherlands did not express a clear position while the remaining member states opted in favour of maintaining the budget level (European Union 2015: 37-38). We can therefore assume, that the "classical" net-payer/net-recipient cleavage is not a sufficient explanatory factor for the development of the agriculture budget. Rather, it is the camp of the net-payer countries that is strategically weakened by the fact that some of the net-payer countries "need" the CAP much more than others for balancing their net-contribution to the EU. Moreover, due to the Brexit, the number of net-payers that profit less from CAP revenues gets even smaller.

### *6.2 Agriculture under the MFF 2014-2020*

In the period 2014-2020, the CAP did not change much compared to the previous MFF. This holds both for the overall funding as well as for the main structural components. The total CAP budget amounted to 426 billion Euro, including the co-financing resources provided by the member states. The share of national co-funding was 14% (OECD 2017: 22). The distribution of resources between the main budget lines also remained extraordinary stable: 68% of the total budget were spent under pillar I, 27% under pillar II, the remaining 5% were used for the organization of the agricultural common market. This includes the financing of a crisis reserve. Given that a significant amount of financial means distributed under pillar II goes directly to farming companies, the share of agricultural expenditures directly transferred to farms was 90% (ibid.: 22-23). As in the previous funding period, the member states differed considerably in terms of net agricultural budget ratio. Table 6.1 presents the respective data for the budget year 2017.

*Table 6.1: Financing the CAP – contributions and receipts by member states, fiscal year 2017 in EUR million*[96]

| *Member State* | *Total national contribution to EU budget* | *Total receipts from heading 2: Sustainable Growth: Natural Resources* | *Thereof, receipts from Pillar I (EAGF)* |
|---|---|---|---|
| *Belgium* | 2 978 | 528 | 422 |
| *Bulgaria* | 379 | 1 015 | 812 |
| *Czech Republic* | 1 282 | 1 128 | 865 |
| *Denmark* | 1 927 | 1 036 | 864 |
| *Germany* | 19 587 | 6 069 | 5,051 |
| *Estonia* | 154 | 235 | 125 |
| *Ireland* | 1 777 | 1 508 | 1 230 |
| *Greece* | 1 248 | 2 850 | 2 111 |
| *Spain* | 8 080 | 5 894 | 5 086 |
| *France* | 16 234 | 9 151 | 7 338 |
| *Croatia* | 359 | 313 | 156 |
| *Italy* | 12 000 | 4 933 | 4 069 |
| *Cyprus* | 137 | 74 | 57 |
| *Latvia* | 184 | 394 | 219 |
| *Lithuania* | 274 | 715 | 450 |
| *Luxembourg* | 307 | 38 | 22 |
| *Hungary* | 821 | 1 517 | 1 313 |
| *Malta* | 82 | 14 | 6 |
| *Netherlands* | 3 384 | 902 | 818 |
| *Austria* | 2 429 | 1 207 | 722 |
| *Poland* | 3 048 | 4 078 | 3 483 |
| *Portugal* | 1 375 | 1 276 | 722 |
| *Romania* | 1 229 | 3 332 | 1 892 |
| *Slovenia* | 293 | 233 | 145 |
| *Slovakia* | 600 | 617 | 444 |
| *Finland* | 1 595 | 873 | 537 |
| *Sweden* | 2 629 | 751 | 633 |
| *United Kingdom* | 10 575 | 3 676 | 3 083 |

96 Data obtained from the European Union's website information on the 2014-2020 budget, see: http://ec.europa.eu/budget/graphs/revenue_expediture.html (accessed 31 March 2019).

Not surprisingly, Germany is by far the largest net-payer followed by Italy, France and the UK. More interestingly, the system produces a considerable number of member states that are able to generate more money from the CAP than they pay into the overall budget. This holds for Bulgaria, Estonia, Greece, Latvia, Lithuania, Hungary, Poland, Romania, and Slovakia. In terms of revenues, the CAP funding is much more important for France than for any other net-payer. More than 50% of the country's contribution to the overall budget were balanced by receipts from heading 2 of the MFF. Moreover, several member states' revenues from the CAP come close to their overall budget contributions. This is the case for the Czech Republic, Ireland, Croatia, Portugal, and Slovenia. Taken together, we find at least 15 out of 28 member states that are in an extraordinary favourable position and therefore hardly have any (fiscal) incentive to change the role agricultural expenditures play within the financial framework.

The institutional stability of the CAP is quite remarkable given that it was the first time (as for the whole MFF) that the funding of the agricultural policy had been defined under the new rules of the Lisbon Treaty. The co-decision process involving the European Parliament and the Council did not impact very much on the outcome. This can, however, not be taken for granted for the future. Compared to the member states representatives in the Council, the European Parliament got under significant pressure from environmental and food safety lobby groups who considered the full participation of the Parliament as a novel opportunity to table their proposals for the budget negotiations. On March 11, 2013, the chairman of the EP's agriculture committee, Paolo de Castro, publicly criticized NGOs for their campaigns which, in his opinion, halted a time-saving legislative manoeuvre that would have allowed the committee to decide which of the hundreds of CAP amendments would go before the Parliament for vote.[97] We can assume that the Parliament will learn from these experiences for the next round of negotiations for the 2021-2027 budget.

At the instrumental level, the CAP 2014-2020 continued with the "greening" of the EU's agricultural policy, both under pillar I and pillar II. In terms of direct payments, 30% of the total subsidies became subject to environmental requirements, such as the maintenance of permanent grass-

97 See: "CAP 2014-2020 – A long road to reform", Euractiv, 4 July 2013, https://www.euractiv.com/section/agriculture-food/linksdossier/cap-2014-2020-a-long-road-to-reform/ (accessed 25 March 2019).

land, crop diversification or the establishment of ecological focus areas (such as field margins, biotopes or hedges). Under pillar II, another 30% of the funds delegated to rural development are reserved for measures that are beneficial for the environment or climate change.

Apart from that, some provisions were established that were aimed at having a structuring effect on the farm industry. One of these provisions regulated that direct payments should be delegated only to "active" farmers thus making sure that large companies (airports, real estate services) that are not involved in farm production although they possess a considerable amount of land do not profit anymore from CAP funding. A "Young Farmers Scheme" was established in order to provide start-up financing for new farm businesses. This measure was aimed at facilitating the demographic change in the sector in which currently only 6% of the farmers are under 35.

## *6.3 Perspectives of the EU's agricultural policy 2021-2027*

On 2 May 2018, the European Commission adopted its proposal for the post-2020 MFF, in which the Common Agricultural Policy will have a total budget of €365.2 billion (European Commission 2018x). This is, compared to the 2014-2020 financing period, a 5% cut (on the basis of expenditures for the 2020 budget multiplied by 7 for the seven years of the MFF's operational duration). The decrease is foreseen with respect to direct payments to farmers which "would be streamlined and better targeted via capping or degressive payments" (European Commission 2018w: 5), but also for rural development. The CAP structure is – according to the Commission's proposal – likely to be maintained. Funding will further on take place within the two-pillar system, with €286.2 billion allocated to the European Agricultural Guarantee Fund (pillar I) and €78.8 billion allocated to the European Agricultural Fund for Rural Development (pillar II).

The European Commission considers a budget reduction necessary because of the Brexit. According to the Commission's calculation, the withdrawal of the UK would have required a cut of the CAP budget of 8.9%, meaning that the proposed cut of 5% is already based on the assumption that the remaining 27 member states will at least partially compensate for the UK contribution.

The data provided by the European Commission are, however, slightly misleading. As table 6.2 shows, the 5% reduction holds only in nominal terms. In real terms, meaning in current prices and under the assumption that the 2014-2027 budget would have been established for only 27 member states, the post-2020 CAP faces a reduction of only 3% while the CAP's share of the total MFF budget decreases from 35.3% to 28.5%. Under this calculation, the expenditures for direct payments to farmers would actually increase (even if only by 2%), meaning that the real victim of the Commission's proposal is the European Agricultural Fund for Rural Development which would suffer a decrease of 17%.

*Table 6.2: Post-2020 CAP sub-ceilings compared to the MFF 2014-2020 as commitments in EUR million, current prices (European Parliament 2018d: 4)*

| | *EU28, 2014-2020 A* | *EU27, 2000 (x7) B* | *EU27, 2014-2020 C* | *EU27, 2021-2027 D* | *Change in %, B/D* | *Change in %, C/D* |
|---|---|---|---|---|---|---|
| *EAGF (Pillar I)* | 302 797 | 284 803 | 280 351 | 286 195 | 0.5 | 2 |
| *EAFRD (Pillar II)* | 100 273 | 97 67 | 95 078 | 78 811 | -19 | -17 |
| *Total CAP* | 403 07 | 382 437 | 375 429 | 365 005 | -5 | -3 |
| *Total MFF* | 1 115 919 | 1 151 866 | 1 063 101 | 1 279 408 | 11 | 20 |
| *CAP as % of MFF* | 36.1 | 33.2 | 35.3 | 28.5 | - | - |

Given that, the European Commission certainly incentivizes the member states to shift funds from pillar I to pillar II, but it also relocates the political conflict over fewer direct payments to the member states level. This comes with an intention of the European Commission to cut also the EU's co-financing rate in pillar II by 10%, thus putting even more pressure on the member states to provide higher investments in order to keep the level of support for rural development at a comparable level. It remains to be seen whether or not the member states will finally accept this political manoeuvre. The situation becomes even more complex by the fact that the post-2020 CAP proposal would further diminish the level of coherence among member states. There is, on the one hand, a growing gap between "old" member states that profit mainly from direct payments and "new" member states that benefit primarily from the rural development funding. As table 6.3 indicates, the 13 member states that entered the EU after 2004 receive only 25% of the direct payments, but 38.1% from the pillar II budget. On the other hand, in terms of total CAP spending, 60% of all expenditures would be delegated to just five member states: France, Spain, Italy, Germany and Poland.

*Table 6.3: CAP allocations per member state 2021-2027, in EUR million, constant 2018 prices (European Parliament 2018d: 7)*

| *Member State* | *Pillar I – Direct Payments* | *Pillar I – Market Interventions* | *Pillar II* | *Total* | *Share of Total CAP* |
|---|---|---|---|---|---|
| | | | | | |
| *Belgium* | 3 020.8 | 2.6 | 417.9 | 3 441.3 | 1.1 |
| *Bulgaria* | 4 930.2 | 172.8 | 1 752.4 | 6 855.4 | 2.2 |
| *Czech Republic* | 5 218.2 | 44.0 | 1 609.7 | 6 871.9 | 2.2 |
| *Denmark* | 5 263.5 | 1.8 | 471.6 | 5 736.9 | 1.8 |
| *Germany* | 30 003.0 | 263.5 | 6 185.0 | 36 424.5 | 11.5 |
| *Estonia* | 1 102.4 | 0.9 | 546.6 | 1 650.0 | 0.5 |
| *Ireland* | 7 240.5 | 0.4 | 1 646.4 | 8 887.3 | 2.8 |
| *Greece* | 12 668.8 | 391.0 | 3 170.0 | 16 229.8 | 5.1 |
| *Spain* | 29 750.3 | 2 921.7 | 6 228.2 | 38 900.2 | 12.3 |
| *France* | 44 464.1 | 3 385.1 | 7 522.4 | 55 371.6 | 17.5 |
| *Croatia* | 2 207.7 | 76.7 | 1 750.1 | 4 034.5 | 1.3 |
| *Italy* | 22 146.8 | 2 262.1 | 7 902.2 | 32 311.1 | 10.2 |
| *Cyprus* | 290.8 | 28.8 | 99.5 | 419.1 | 0.1 |
| *Latvia* | 1 967.4 | 2.0 | 729.7 | 2 699.2 | 0.8 |
| *Lithuania* | 3 343.9 | 3.7 | 1 214.2 | 4 561.7 | 1.4 |
| *Luxembourg* | 199.9 | 0.2 | 76.5 | 276.5 | 0.1 |
| *Hungary* | 7 587.8 | 200.6 | 2 589.1 | 10 337.4 | 3.3 |
| *Malta* | 28.0 | 0.1 | 75.9 | 104.1 | 0.1 |
| *Netherlands* | 4 378.5 | 1.8 | 455.0 | 4 835.4 | 1.5 |
| *Austria* | 4 135.6 | 91.0 | 2 988.8 | 7 215.5 | 2.3 |
| *Poland* | 18 859.5 | 31.3 | 8 198.2 | 27 088.9 | 8.6 |
| *Portugal* | 3 741.0 | 1.038.6 | 3 068.1 | 7 847.7 | 2.5 |
| *Romania* | 11 869.7 | 323.0 | 6 006.1 | 18 198.8 | 5.8 |
| *Slovenia* | 802.8 | 34.2 | 636.1 | 1 473.1 | 0.5 |
| *Slovakia* | 2 444.5 | 36.6 | 1 416.3 | 3 897.5 | 1.2 |
| *Finland* | 3 169.0 | 1.2 | 1 816.6 | 4 986.8 | 1.6 |
| *Sweden* | 4 187.7 | 3.7 | 1 316.0 | 5 507.4 | 1.7 |
| *Total* | 235 022.0 | 11 319.4 | 69 861.7 | 316 203.3 | 100 |
| *% of total expenditures* | 74.3 | 3.6 | 22.1 | | |

This could, for two reasons, significantly impact on the negotiations in the Council. Firstly, the "new" member states, with the exemption of Poland and Romania which benefit above-average also from pillar I subsidies, could focus on harmonizing member states' position in terms of direct payments. Secondly, it could become more difficult to separate the debates on the funding of CAP and the cohesion policy. Given that there are strong linkages between pillar II of the CAP and regional development programmes funded under heading I of the MFF, the "new" member states could be less willing to accept cuts in both budget lines (see also Chapter 7). But even in the "old member states'" camp, France, Germany and Italy (with a combined share of almost 40% of the total CAP expenditures) seem to be increasingly captured by the existing financing structure and thus hardly open for compromise with other net-payer countries, if we take into account that Austria, Denmark, Finland, the Netherlands and Sweden have a combined share of just about 9% of the total CAP expenditures. Another burden for the MFF negotiations exists in terms of the second CAP pillar because there is hardly any support for the Commission's claim that the distribution of funds for rural development "is based on objective criteria linked to the policy objectives" (European Commission 2018x: 8). Apart from the fact that this statement is a repetition (in exactly the same wording) of a claim already made in the respective regulation for the current MFF[98], it is also quite astonishing that the proposed distribution can be calculated on the basis of a uniform percentage cut to the national allocations established already for the CAP 2014-2020 (Matthews 2018a: 310).

The post-2020 CAP will alter the relation between the European Union and its member states also in another respect. Member states will be required to develop national strategic plans in which conditions and measures have to be defined in relevance to the specific needs for the domestic agricultural industry. This allows, in principle, for a reduction of number and detail of rules of the common policy established at the European level, because national strategic plans will be checked by the Commission in terms of coherence and consistency with EU requirements. In member states in which strategic plans will be developed also at the regional level, the respective member state government has to ensure that

98 Exactly the same statement can be found in the proposal for a regulation of the European Parliament and the Council establishing rules for direct payment to farmers under support schemes within the framework of the common agricultural policy, COM(2011) 625 final, 12 October 2011, Brussels, p. 9.

they match with national rules and procedures. The effects of strategic planning at the member states' level seem, however, to be less clear. On the one hand, it obviously increases the administrative efforts at regional and national levels without a clear perspective on the degree to which country-specific regulations may differ from European norms. It is also unclear whether the Commission will have the institutional capabilities and the political will to monitor and sanction (if needed) the national implementation. If not, the stronger involvement of the member states appears to be a concession for the stronger involvement the European Commission expects from member states in financing especially the second pillar of the CAP.

The "greening" of the CAP continues on the basis of more specified rules for farmers. The CAP 2014-2020 cross-compliance environmental and climate change standards as well as the obligations defined for the greening of the agricultural policy have been transferred into an integrated "enhanced conditionality" scheme composed of 15 compulsory regulatory requirements which will be specified in the respective national strategic plans established by each member state (European Commission 2018w: 24-25). By proposing "enhanced conditionality", the European Commission certainly reacted to a report prepared in 2017 by the European Court of Auditors (ECA) which found that the "greening" as it had been implemented in the CAP 2014-2020 was "unlikely to provide significant benefits for the environment and climate" (European Court of Auditors 2017: 2). The ECA analysis concluded that only 4.5% of the total farm land in the EU was covered by a change of farming practices due to the new greening regulations (ibid.: 27). The explanation that was offered by the report indicates that the greening requirements were too soft in the sense that they "generally reflect normal farming practice" (ibid.: 30). Therefore, it remains to be seen whether the new conditionally rules will cause any qualitative change. They could be considered as "in substance a simplified version of the current framework" (European Parliament 2018d: 9), but also as a win in terms of bindingness, since all the exemptions that applied to the CAP 2014-2020 have been eliminated although it is not clear as to what extent the member states are still authorized to reintroduce them into their strategic plans (Matthews 2018b). Apart from that, the contribution the post-2020 CAP will make to the protection of the environment and the climate could simply be reduced by the lower level of funding reserved for pillar II. Of course, member states have various options to compensate for the loss with national funding (especially by increasing national co-financing and by shifting of resources between pillars), but they would probably be criticized by their farmers if they would link better funding with stricter rules for conditionality which would have a negative impact on farmer's competitiveness within the single agricultural market. Putting responsibility to the greening of the CAP mostly on the shoulders of the member states was also criticized by another report of the European Court of Auditors. The opinion published on 25 October 2018 notes:

> "Despite the Commission's ambitions and calls for a greener CAP, the proposal does not reflect a clear increase in environmental and climate ambition. We recognise that the proposal includes tools addressing environmental and climate- related objectives. However, Member States would be responsible for prioritising the types of interventions to finance in their CAP strategic plans. It is unclear how the Commission would check these plans to ensure environmental and climate ambition. The Commission's estimate of the CAPs contribution to related EU targets appears unrealistic" (European Court of Auditors 2018: 3).

The reactions, the European Commission received on the post-2020 CAP proposal by the European Parliament and the member states were very much in line with expectations that exist for the "theater season".

The EP's committee for agriculture issued an opinion for the budget committee on 10 October 2018 which argued that "a possible reduction of the CAP budget will have disastrous effects". It called for a budget "to be maintained in the 2021-2027 MFF at least at the level of the 2014-2020 budget for the EU-27 in real terms" (European Parliament 2018c: 3).

Member States' governments also offered the usual reflexes. In a meeting of the General Affairs Council on 18 September 2018, 18 member states opposed the MFF proposal's cuts both for agriculture and cohesion policies (France, Italy, Spain, Portugal, Poland, Belgium, Ireland, Estonia, Slovenia, Greece, Lithuania, the Czech Republic, Hungary, Slovakia, Finland, Croatia, Cyprus and Malta). Sweden, Denmark and the Netherlands showed willingness to support cuts in the main expenditure areas while Germany stressed the need to balance between new priorities and traditional policies.[99] Months later, the member states' positions were more differentiated, but they did not change in substance. On 9 April 2019, the debate in the General Affairs Council confirmed the rejection of budget cuts for the CAP 2021-2027 by France, Spain, Ireland and Italy. Germany specified its earlier position arguing that the CAP and the cohesion policy today represent 72% of the total budget and that these two policies "can-

99 "Uncertainty over timetable for Council's adoption of 2021-2027 multiannual financial framework", Agence Europe, 19 September 2018.

not remain as they are". Sweden, Denmark and the Netherlands stayed with their call for a reduction of the CAP expenditures with the Dutch government showing a preference for a gradual decrease of direct payments. Germany and Belgium opted for at least 40% of expenditures delegated to measures dealing with climate change while Poland requested an increase in appropriations for the second pillar.[100]

Reactions from NGOs and lobby groups were also not very supportive. Environmental groups, such as Greenpeace, called the CAP proposal "a disaster for the environment". BirdLife Europe argued that "the European Commission's claim that the new proposal will deliver a higher environmental and climate ambition has fallen flat" (Matthews 2018b). The two largest confederations of the European farming industry (COPA and COGECA) unsurprisingly vehemently oppose the cuts of the CAP budget, but they also raised concern about the effects the new rules of conditionality may have in practice.[101] Farm Europe, a European think tank specialized on agricultural policy, considered the proposal as a plan "for strong renationalization and bureaucratization"[102].

## *6.4 Conclusions*

The current debate on the EU Commission's proposal for the post-2020 Common Agricultural Policy shows the dilemma of reforming a path-dependent institutional structure in the absence of internal or external shocks. The Brexit certainly is a (financial) challenge, but it does not qualify for a path-breaking event. The loss of the British budget contribution causes cuts of the agricultural budget and a stronger financial involvement of the member states in terms of their co-financing expenditures primarily for the second CAP pillar. However, the UK has never been a member state that provoked a specific problem in view of the CAP's redistributional effects or the "juste retour" logic. If there was such a problem, it was solved with the British rebate and this will impact on the MFF negoti-

100 "Member states reiterate their differences on CAP and cohesion after 2020", Agence Europe, 10 April 2019.

101 "COPA and COGECA position on the CAP post 2020", Brussels, 18 September 2018.

102 "CAP Reform: A renationalization project that would cost 20% of farmers' income", Farm Europe Press Release, 01 June 2018, https://www.farm-europe.eu/news/reforme-de-la-pac-un-projet-de-renationalisation-qui-couterait-20-au-revenu-des-agriculteurs/ (accessed 12 April 2019).

ations in more general terms, but not particularly on the debate of the future CAP. That is why the Commission's proposal is sufficiently characterized as a plan with some institutional adjustments and very little institutional adaption.

Institutional adjustments have been made primarily with respect to the greening of the agricultural policy. They were not well received neither by other EU institutions (esp. the Court of Auditors) nor by environmental lobby groups. The criticism is, however, premature in the sense that the effectiveness of the new conditionality rules cannot be adequately evaluated on the basis of the legislative proposal. This is a matter of implementation and of coordination between the member states and the European Commission in dealing with the national strategic plans.

Even more difficult to assess is the potential impact of the growing importance of the member states (and in some cases of regions within member states) in implementing the post-2020 CAP. Claims that the strategic plans constitute a re-nationalization of the Common Agricultural Policy are not well justified. This is standard rhetoric of actors who tend to ignore that the European Union is in desperate need of certain forms of differentiated integration in order to stabilize the whole integration project. Agricultural markets across Europe are heterogeneous in many ways: in terms of size of farming companies, in terms of geographic conditions for farming, in view of customer preferences for ecological farming and regional production, with respect to technology and innovation as well as in light of export-orientation of the industry. Strengthening vertical policy coordination in the implementation of the future CAP is therefore not an abandonment of a common policy, but a necessity for a future-oriented policy framework (let alone that it would more strongly respect the EU's principle of subsidiarity).

The new role of the member states in implementing the agricultural policy is a form of institutional adaption that reacts to the lack of coherence in the European farming sector. In principle, it seems to be an appropriate approach, however, doubts remain whether it is the result of novel conceptual thinking or just a consequence of anticipated budgetary problems. Member states will be under certain pressure to compensate for the significant cuts proposed by the Commission for rural development. This holds especially for member states that profit most from a relatively stable financial endowment of the first pillar. It is therefore reasonable to assume that the European Commission has anticipated that member states would not be highly motivated to provide own financial resources for rural development without some voice and responsibility in planning and implementing the respective programmes. In this respect, it is worth noting that the new delivery model will also cut the direct link that currently exists in measuring compliance between the EU level and individual beneficiaries. This is certainly a win in terms of the CAP's democratic legitimacy, transparency and accountability.

# 7. Coherence and conditionality: perspectives on the EU's regional and cohesion policy

## *7.1 The EU's regional policy and the problem of economic, social and territorial disparities across the Union*

A comprehensive approach to regional development and cohesion was established in the European Union only in 1988. In the context of the accession of Greece (1981), Portugal and Spain (1986), the EU integrated already existing structural funds (the European Social Fund, ESF, established in 1958, and the European Regional Development Fund, ERDF, established in 1975) into a cohesion policy framework. Prior to 1988, support mechanisms for regional development at the European level were largely "intergovernmental" in the sense that the European Commission was mainly responsible for organizing the distribution of funds among member states that they provided on the basis of fixed national quotas. Those funds were delegated to existing regional development policies at the national level. Only with the 1984 reform of the ERDF, the European Commission received a budget share of 5% of the fund's resources to establish a specific European regional development programme (Commission of the European Communities 1985: VII).

Unlike the EU's agricultural policy in which a "decade of reforms" (see Chapter 6) led to a more comprehensive institutional adaption of policy objectives and instruments, the regional policy went through steady incremental reforms since it had been introduced. Constantly faced with stark criticism about its impact and effects, the EU regional policy was in need of a "door opener" which emerged with the Southern enlargement round (1981-1986). Just before Portugal and Spain became members of the European Union, the Council agreed on the Integrated Mediterranean Programmes (IMPs) which were set up in order to compensate the regions in the new member states for the increasing competition in the common market (Manzella/Mendez 2009: 12). The President of the European Commission, Jacques Delors, seized the opportunity and made use of a "policy window" that had opened-up with the accession of Portugal and Spain. In presenting the Commission's work programme for 1985, Delors outlined the rationale and the approach of an independent EU regional policy:

> "Over the last 15 years, regional disparities within the Community have widened. The underdeveloped regions on the periphery of the industrial heart of Europe have been joined by a number of old industrial regions whose traditional economic base is in structural decline. But the two are fundamentally different. The Community's structural Funds should – provided, of course, that they have sufficient resources – make it possible for the Community to support structural conversion and adjustment projects in regions in difficulty. […] The socio-economic disparities between North and South in Europe were heightened with the accession of Greece and will be accentuated further with the accession of Spain and Portugal. There is a danger that these disparities could become a permanent source of political confrontation if the South is not given a fairer share of the benefits of economic development. Indeed, the South could become Europe's 'new frontier', generating a dynamism which would benefit the old industrial regions of the North. This is the thinking behind the integrated approach advocated in the Mediterranean programmes (IMPs). These set three targets: to develop local potential, to adapt southern regions to the new conditions created by their incorporation in a large continental-scale market, and to maintain employment an incomes" (European Communities 1985: 15).

The institutionalization of the EU's regional policy took place between 1986 and 1988. With the Single European Act (1986), the first major revision of the Rome Treaties, the regional policy became "constitutionalized" through the insertion of a new chapter on "economic and social cohesion" (Art. 130 EC Treaty, now: Art. 174-178 TFEU). The Delors-I package of February 1988 provided the financial means for the regional policy by doubling the resources for the period 1988-1992. Its share to the overall budget increased from 17.2% to 27% (or 7.790 million ECU in 1988 to 13.450 million ECU in 1992).

A major invention made in the EU's regional policy was the so-called partnership principle introduced with the 1988 reform. The principle required the formal involvement of regional and local actors into the formulation and implementation of the support programmes. Although not foreseen in the treaty, the partnership principle changed the traditional "state-centric" perspective on European integration as a process determined by interactions between EU institutions and member states. A new understanding of the integration process subsequently emerged also in scientific research considering the EU as a system of multi-level governance (see Chapter 2) in which actors and arenas – from the European to the regional/local levels – are increasingly interlinked in joint policy coordination. (Marks 1992; Marks et al. 1996).

Since that time, the cohesion policy is characterized by three main aspects.

Firstly, it has a significant, albeit highly different, impact on public investments in the member states of the European Union. As table 7.1 shows, the share of EU funds to the overall public investments at the national level is highest in Portugal (84.2%) and lowest in Luxembourg (0.3%). Basically, the European Union falls apart into two clusters of member states in which the share of EU regional funding is above or below 5%. The latter group consists of 10 member states that are, unsurprisingly, mostly the net-payer countries.

*Table 7.1: Share of EU cohesion policy per member state to public investment 2015-2017 in percent*[103]

| *Member State* | *Share of Cohesion Policy on total public investments 2015-2017 in %* | *Member State* | *Share of Cohesion Policy on total public investments 2015-2017 in %* |
|---|---|---|---|
| | | | |
| *Portugal* | 84.2 | *Cyprus* | 26.9 |
| *Croatia* | 79.6 | *Spain* | 16.6 |
| *Lithuania* | 74.4 | *Italy* | 12.7 |
| *Poland* | 61.2 | *Germany* | 3.8 |
| *Latvia* | 59.9 | *Ireland* | 3.0 |
| *Hungary* | 55.5 | *Belgium* | 2.9 |
| *Slovakia* | 54.6 | *France* | 2.7 |
| *Bulgaria* | 48.6 | *United Kingdom* | 2.4 |
| *Romania* | 44.9 | *Finland* | 2.2 |
| *Estonia* | 44.8 | *Austria* | 1.3 |
| *Czech Republic* | 42.5 | *Sweden* | 1.2 |
| *Greece* | 35.1 | *Netherlands* | 0.6 |
| *Malta* | 32.1 | *Denmark* | 0.5 |
| *Slovenia* | 29.4 | *Luxembourg* | 0.3 |

Secondly, Europe's investments in the cohesion policy, and thus the share of the respective expenditures to the overall budget, has been steadily increasing until 2014. Even the MFF 2014-2020, which reduced the expenditures for the regional policy by 8.5%, privileged cohesion over agriculture since the CAP spending was reduced by more than 11%. Based on the Eu-

103 Data obtained from the European Union's website information on the EU cohesion policy see: https://cohesiondata.ec.europa.eu/Other/Share-of-Cohesion-Policy-per-Member-State-to-publi/drqq-sbh7/data (accessed 31 March 2019).

ropean Commission's proposal for the MFF 2021-2027, cohesion policy would now even replace for the first time the agricultural policy as the main spending area.

And thirdly, contrary to constantly recurring calls for a concentration of the regional and cohesion funds on the less and least developed regions, the policy has always been designed in a way that allowed for supporting all regions across the European Union regardless of their economic and social performance. Funding criteria were targeted (with some changes of the description of the targets) at less-developed and more-developed regions as well as regions in transition. It would be a surprise if this would change for the post-2020 period. It is at least not foreseen in the Commission's proposal.

### *7.2 Territorial cohesion under the MFF 2014-2020*

After 1992, reforms of the regional policy have led to incremental institutional adjustments at the instrumental level. With regard to the accession of Austria, Finland and Sweden in 1995, new objectives were added aimed at supporting regions with sparse population and regions confronted with the restructuring of the fishing industry. The 2004 enlargement round that involved 10 new member states with significant lower levels of income and economic performance demanded a major shift of resources to a newly designed funding line for regions with a GPD per capita of less than 75% of the EU average. Moreover, regional and cohesion policy became linked to the EU's cross-policy agenda for competitiveness, the Lisbon Agenda (and later on the Agenda Europe 2020).

In the period 2014-2020, the European Union invests €351.8 billion in programmes directly related to the EU's regional and cohesion policy.[104] This amount is divided into €182.2 billion for the less developed regions which have a GDP of less than 75% of the EU27 GDP. The respective funding line has a share of 50.5% to the overall budget. €35.4 billion are available for regions in transition which have a GDP of 75-90% of the EU27 average. This compares to 9.9% of the total budget. More developed regions (GDP higher than 90% of EU27 average) receive €54.3 billion, which is a share of 15.1%. The remaining resources are divided into

---

104 Some publications mention the amount of 450 billion Euro. This includes €99.6 billion for rural development that comes from the agricultural budget and €.7 billion provided by the Common Fisheries Policy.

programmes for European territorial cooperation (€10.2 billion), for Urban innovation actions (€0.4 billion), the youth employment initiative (€3.2 billion), allocations for outermost and sparsely populated regions (€1.6 billion), a technical assistance programme (€1.2 billion) and the Cohesion Fund (€63.3 billion).

The Cohesion Fund is, in contrast to the resources available for less developed regions, targeted at member states' level. However, it can be stated that in the end about 70% of the total investments are delegated to less developed regions and/or member states. Those less developed regions are largely situated in net-recipient member states. The only exemptions are the French overseas territories (Guadeloupe, Martinique, Guyane, Réunion, and Mayotte), the Southern Italian regions of Campania, Puglia, Basilicata, Calabria, and Sicilia, as well as Cornwall and Isles of Scilly, West Wales and The Valleys in the UK (European Commission 2015e).

The MFF 2014-2020 left the EU's regional and cohesion policy structure largely unchanged. It is still based on financial support provided by three funds: the European Regional Development Fund (ERDF) which is targeted at strengthening regional economic growth and social cohesion (also for trans-border projects), the European Social Fund (ESF) which focusses on the improvement of employment and education, and the Cohesion Fund which provides investments for member states with a GDP below 90% of EU27 average. These three funds address different policy priorities that were defined for the 2014-2020 programme phase:

- The ERDF is mainly targeted at the priorities of strengthening research, technological development and innovation, the enhancing of access to information and communication technologies, the enhancing of competitiveness of small and medium-sized enterprises (SMEs), and the supporting of the shift towards a low-carbon economy.
- Funds available under the ESF are targeted at promoting employment and supporting labour mobility, at promoting social inclusion, at investing in education, training and lifelong learning, and at improving the efficiency of public administrations.
- The Cohesion Fund provides resources (for the countries that are eligible) for the shift towards a low-carbon economy, for promoting climate change adaption, for protecting the environment, for promoting sustainable infrastructures, and for the improvement of the efficiency of public administrations.

In contrast to the agricultural funding under pillar I, financial resources provided by the funds for regional development require co-financing from the regions or member states. In the 2014-2020 period, the co-financing rates were largely stable: 50-85% under the ERDF and the ESF (depending on the category of the region) and 85% under the European territorial cooperation and in respect to the Cohesion Fund (European Commission 2015e).

The 2014-2020 funding period also saw an "expansion" of conditionality, meaning the requirement for member states not only to address their programmes to the policy-specific objectives of the regional and cohesion policy, but also to recommendations developed at the European level in the context of the European semester (see Chapter 3). Member states were asked to "take into account" already in the programme development phase the National Reform Programmes (where appropriate), the country-specific recommendations and any relevant Council recommendation (ibid.: 22). Moreover, the partnership principle became legally binding in the sense that actors involved in planning and implementing regional programmes (such as public authorities, trade unions, employer organisations, NGOs, etc.) were obliged to subscribe to a new "European Code of Conduct on Partnership".

All in all, under the MFF 2014-2020, the regional and cohesion policy experienced only very limited changes at the instrumental level. There was apparently hardly any need for reform. The integration of the East European countries was sufficiently managed already under the two preceding financial frameworks. In terms of the overall budget, the cuts were – compared to agricultural funding – less severe.

This may not hide the fact that the impediments to reform are quite similar both in the agricultural as well as in the regional and cohesion policy. One could even argue that the cleavage between net-payers and net-recipients is more distinct in the field of regional policy. As table 7.2 shows, the net-payers' balance is generally more negative in this area compared to agricultural funding. This holds especially for France (to a lesser extent also for Germany and Italy) that has a much higher rate of revenues from the CAP. Moreover, 12 member states (all net-recipients) manage to get higher revenues from the regional funds compared to their total expenditures for the overall EU budget. Among the net-recipients, Poland is in a very favourable position as the country has a significant surplus both in agricultural and regional funding. Assuming the traditional "juste retour" logic of the member states' governments, one could argue that there is an increasing need for a larger number of member states to calculate their burden and benefits in a cross-sectoral perspective as net-recipients of the total MFF could soon become net-payers to the budget for regional and cohesion policy. This holds already for countries like Cyprus, Hungary or Slovenia which are – in contrast to the classical net-payers – also less compensated by funds from research and innovation policies.

*Table 7.2: Financing the regional policy – contributions and receipts by member states, fiscal year 2017 in EUR million*[105]

| *Member State* | *Total national contribution to EU budget* | *Total receipts from sub-heading 1.2: Economic, social and territorial cohesion* |
|---|---|---|
| | | |
| *Belgium* | 2 978 | 307 |
| *Bulgaria* | 379 | 627 |
| *Czech Republic* | 1 282 | 2 583 |
| *Denmark* | 1 927 | 78 |
| *Germany* | 19 587 | 2 061 |
| *Estonia* | 154 | 282 |
| *Ireland* | 1 777 | 51 |
| *Greece* | 1 248 | 1 550 |
| *Spain* | 8 080 | 2 194 |
| *France* | 16 234 | 1 227 |
| *Hungary* | 359 | 272 |
| *Italy* | 12 000 | 1 632 |
| *Cyprus* | 137 | 64 |
| *Latvia* | 184 | 292 |
| *Lithuania* | 274 | 685 |
| *Luxembourg* | 307 | 48 |
| *Hungary* | 821 | 2 141 |
| *Malta* | 82 | 103 |
| *Netherlands* | 3 384 | 192 |
| *Austria* | 2 429 | 85 |
| *Poland* | 3 048 | 7 514 |
| *Portugal* | 1 375 | 2 347 |
| *Romania* | 1 229 | 1 256 |
| *Slovenia* | 293 | 128 |
| *Slovakia* | 600 | 815 |
| *Finland* | 1 595 | 258 |
| *Sweden* | 2 629 | 215 |
| *United Kingdom* | 10 575 | 649 |

105 Data obtained from the European Union's website information on the 2014-2020 budget, see: http://ec.europa.eu/budget/graphs/revenue_expediture.html (accessed 31 March 2019).

## 7.3 Perspectives on the EU's regional and cohesion policy post-2020

Under the Commission's proposal for the MFF 2021-2027, the EU's regional policy would be organized under budget heading 2 ("cohesion and values") with a total amount of expenditures of €391.974 million or 34.5% of the total budget. The composition of this new heading has changed in so far as it now includes the Erasmus+ and other smaller support measures. Anyway, if we just consider the three funds of the traditional regional and cohesion policy, the total expenditures amount to €331.684 million. This makes regional and cohesion policy the largest EU expenditure area surpassing the agricultural policy by €7 billion (the two pillars of the CAP would amount to €324.284 million with €254.274 million for the EAGF and €70.037 million for the EAFRD). The proposal also includes significant shifts between the different regional funds, because the regional development fund would increase by 2% while the cohesion fund faces a loss of 45% and the European Social Fund would decrease by 7% (European Parliamentary Research Service 2018).

On the Commission's side, the preparation for the new regional and cohesion policy proposal was mainly based on the ex-post evaluation of the 2007-2013 funding period (European Commission 2016i) and an impact assessment for the new funding period (European Commission 2018y). In terms of the impact assessment, the main result lies in the reduction of economic disparities between the EU member states and regions. Albeit they are still large and had even increased temporarily due to the financial crisis, they have narrowed again (even if marginally) since the 2014. This is mainly because net-recipient countries had significantly higher GDP growth than the net-payer countries (European Commission 2016i: 19). The assessment indicated, however, that there is room for improvement. Overall, 90% of the financial means provided by the ERDF were used to directly support enterprises. As the report states, an even better result could have been achieved if a larger part of the expenditures was delegated to financial investments in energy efficiency, renewable energy or transport infrastructure (ibid.: 44). The impact assessment for the regional and cohesion policies 2021-2027 was made particularly on the basis of consultations of stakeholders and the public. It appeared that the reduction of regional disparities is still the prime goal of the policy. Apart from that, stakeholders (including the member states) argued that the policy should develop into a more forward-looking and pro-active intervention offering sufficient flexibility to address new challenges. It was also stressed that the financial means should be used in a way that promotes the objectives of the broader EU policy framework (European Commission 2018y: 14).

The Commission's proposal (European Commission 2018z) responses to these findings. Compared to the 2014-2020 funding period, the programmes' targets have been streamlined (meaning they were reduced from 11 to 5) and better linked with the overall EU policy objectives. The regional and cohesion policy would, therefore, focus on:

1. "A smarter Europe", in terms of an "innovative and smart economic transformation",
2. "A greener, low-carbon Europe",
3. "A more connected Europe" in terms of mobility and regional ICT connectivity,
4. "A more social Europe" through implementing the European Pillar of Social Rights, and
5. "A Europe closer to citizens" through the promotion of a sustainable and integrated development of urban, rural, and coastal areas.

Compared to the prior programme objectives, it is not yet fully clear whether the new policy objectives will induce significant qualitative change. It still appears to be a "catch-all"-strategy that leaves enough room (or flexibility) for regions of all level of economic development to conceptualize regional strategies that fit with the European objectives. There are, however, some aspects in the regulation of the regional and cohesion funds that could have an impact on how regions will have to design their programmes.

The Commission has, for example, regulated that 30% of the resources provided by the ERDF have to be linked with the climate change targets of the European Union. The thematic re-reorientation will most likely lead to a reduction of funds available for infrastructural investments. The new programme objectives indicate a preference for innovation, modern communication and support for SMEs. This clearly constitutes an advantage of the better developed regions. Member states with more less developed regions will have to shift away from classical infrastructure investments. This mainly holds for Romania, Malta, the Czech Republic, Lithuania and Slovakia where those kinds of investments played a major role in earlier funding periods.

The Commission also proposes changes of the EU's co-funding shares. For less developed regions, the EU's share would be reduced significantly (in the case of less developed regions from 80-85% to 70%). More developed regions would suffer a decrease of 10% (from 50% to 40%). Only for the regions in transition, the EU's co-funding share would stay relative stable with a loss of only 5% (from 60% to 55%).

Furthermore, there is a qualitative change in terms of the programming procedures. The Commission's proposed regulation states that programming will take place only for the first five years of the MFF in order to allow for adjustments in case that they have been found necessary after the mid-term evaluation (European Commission 2018z: 7). Apart from that, there are hardly any changes compared to the 2014-2020 programme structure. In terms of resources, financial means for urban development have been increased. They now amount to 6% of the ERDF budget.

Given that, the debates around the future regional and cohesion policy will most probably revolve around two specific topics.

The first concerns the method that will be applied to define the amount of resources (the "envelopes") each country can expect from the regional funds. Traditionally, the measurement is done on the basis of the gross national income per capita of population ("The Berlin Method"[106]). This could, however, lead to changes (compared to the 2014-2020 period) individual member states will find difficult to accept. Hungary, for example, has already brought up the issue in the Council arguing that the method used for determining the allocations along with the cuts of the budget for cohesion would cost the country 24% percent of its envelope.[107] The German government expects a reduction of financial means of about €20 billion.[108] The European Court of Auditors (2019) prepared an assessment of how the revenues from the regional and cohesion policy would change in terms of the recategorization of regions and the overall member states' envelopes. A re-categorization of regions would concern:

- Estonia and Lithuania as well as some regions in the Czech Republic, Poland and Bulgaria which would change from less developed regions to regions in transition,

---

106 The Berlin method takes data of economic development for the last three years collected at the NUTS II level in order to classify regions as less developed, more developed regions or regions in transition. Other criteria (such as size of the population may also being taken into account.

107 See "Uncertainty over timetable for Council's adoption of 2021-2027 multiannual financial framework", Agence Europe, 19 September 2018.

108 Deutscher Bundestag: Die Kohäsionspolitik der EU im Mehrjährigen Finanzrahmen 2021-2027 und deren Bedeutung für Deutschland, Antwort der Bundesregierung auf die Kleine Anfrage der Abgeordneten Markus Tressel, Britta Haßelmann, Stefan Schmidt, Dr. Franziska Brandtner und der Fraktion Bündnis90/Die Grünen, Drucksache 19/3337, Berlin, 6 July 2018.

- The number of regions with less developed status would increase in Greece, Italy, Portugal and Spain,
- Several countries have regions that will be re-classified from more developed regions to regions in transition. This holds for Finland, France, Germany, the Netherlands, Slovenia, Austria, Belgium, Italy, Spain, Greece, Cyprus and Ireland.

Overall, under the allocation mechanism proposed by the Commission, the 2021-2027 regional and cohesion policy would produce seven member states that can expect higher revenues (Bulgaria, Romania, Greece, Italy, Spain, Finland and Cyprus). 14 member states would face a decrease that is especially significant for Malta, Estonia, Hungary, the Czech Republic and Lithuania, because their losses are limited by a -24% safety net. No impact would exist only for Sweden, Austria, the Netherlands, Luxembourg, Belgium and Denmark. It is also remarkable that among the remaining net-payer countries the decrease of revenues is much higher in Germany (about -20%) compared to "only" about -5% in France (European Court of Auditors 2019).

In times of overall budget cuts, we can thus expect not only a discussion about the vertical distribution of funds across budget headings, but also about the horizontal distribution between member states within budget headings. In this respect, it is yet unclear what effects the proposed changes to the "Berlin Method" could have. The Commission has suggested to apply not only the GDP indicator, but also the criteria of regional performance in terms of the level of youth unemployment, the educational level, contributions to the prevention of climate change as well as the number and the measures to support migrants.

In sum, the Commission's proposal keeps the principle of supporting all regions across Europe independent of their economic performance. There is, however, as table 7.3 shows, also a clear message especially to member states with less developed regions. The level of funding will, on average, stay stable but change is needed in terms of the measures and programmes which will receive funding. Member states with more developed regions will have to face significant cuts. Regions in transition will benefit most. Although they have the smallest budget, the increase of expenditures for them is considerable, thus, indicating the Commission's intention to support regions that adapt to the overall EU's political objectives.

*Table 7.3: Commitment appropriations in regional and cohesion policy 2021-2027, compared to 2014-2020 (Bachtler et al. 2019: 53)*

| | *EU28, 2014-2020 in EUR million (2018 prices)* | *EU27, 2021-2027 in EUR million (2018 prices)* | *Change in %* |
|---|---|---|---|
| *Less developed regions* | 188 757 | 198 622 | 5.2 |
| *Transition regions* | 36 397 | 45 935 | 26.2 |
| *More developed regions* | 56 867 | 34 843 | -38.7 |
| *Territorial Cooperation* | 10 282 | 8 430 | -18.0 |
| *Cohesion Fund* | 76 250 | 41,349 | -45.8 |
| *Outermost regions and low population density* | 1 593 | 1 447 | -9.2 |
| *Youth Employment Initiative* | 3 447 | - | -100 |
| *Total* | 373 596 | 330 624 | -11.5 |

The second issue is conditionality. Conditionality is not a new phenomenon in the EU's regional policy. It exists since 2004 in form of a macroeconomic conditionality and an infringement conditionality. Macroeconomic conditionality has a conceptual problem insofar as the regions that receive EU funding are usually not responsible for macroeconomic policies. It is, therefore, not surprising that this form of conditionality has not been applied in a coherent way. Until 2013, there was only one case in which macroeconomic conditionality was applied when Hungary was suspended from cohesion funds because of an excessive deficit in 2012. Similarly, also the instrument of infringement conditionality was successfully used only once (Italy 2008), but it did not lead to better compliance of the country with the EU Waste Directive. In the period 2014-2020 more conditionality cases appeared, but they also showed that the respective rules are still not working properly, partly because of the difficult economic situation in the countries concerned (Spain and Portugal in 2016).

As for the 2021-2027 budget negotiations, the debate about conditionality will intensify. This is because the Commission intends to establish a third form of conditionality that would refer to compliance with the rule-of-law and it would concern all funding areas of the EU, not only the regional and cohesion policy. The discussions will most likely revolve around a number of issues that are not yet specified, such as the components of the principle of the rule-of-law that would be relevant, the appropriate financial sanctions, the EU institution that would enforce it (the Commission or the Council), and the role the European Parliament would have in respective procedures (European Parliament 2018e).

Initial reactions from the member states indicate that an application of a rule-of-law conditionality is not necessarily supported by a majority of countries. In the General Affairs Council meeting of 9 April 2019, only Finland, France, Germany and the Netherlands explicitly supported the Commission's approach.[109] On the cohesion and regional policy in general, member states' view are currently in line with expectations. Apart from Sweden which calls for a significant reduction of expenditures of the structural funds, most member states that have already formulated a position either criticizing the overall budget cuts or changes in the distribution of resources across cohesion budget lines.

The European Parliament, unsurprisingly, took the same position on regional and cohesion policy as on agriculture and demanded that the level of funding should at least be equal to the 2014-2020 budget. Even more, it called for a doubling of resources available for SMEs and the youth unemployment initiative. All in all, compared to the 2021-2027 budget proposal the European Parliament calls for expenditures under the "cohesion and values" heading of 456.077 million Euro, almost 12% more than the Commission's proposal (European Parliament 2018b).

The Committee of the Regions shared the criticism of the Parliament in terms of the budget cuts and called it "unacceptable" to fund new priorities at the expense of existing policies (Committee of the Regions 2018). Both the Parliament as well as the Committee of the Regions support the Commission's plan to establish a rule-of law conditionality.

Regional interest associations are more supportive to the Commission's proposal. Cohesion Alliance, a network of European regional interest associations, welcomed the sustained promotion of all European regions and the strengthening of the partnership principle. It also indicated that thanks to their involvement even more drastic cuts of the budget could have been prevented.[110]

109 "Member states reiterate their differences on CAP and cohesion after 2020", Agence Europe, 10 April 2019.

110 "EU-wide coalition welcomes proposals to cover all regions with a strong role for cities and regions, but warns against cuts impact", Cohesion Alliance Press Release, 31 May 2018, https://cor.europa.eu/en/news/Pages/Cohesion-Policy-2021-2027-EU-wide-coalition-.aspx (accessed 12 April 2019).

## *7.4 Conclusions*

Three decades after its constitutionalization, the European regional and cohesion policy will further on develop in the 2021-2027 period along an established institutional path. It is still based on three main principles:

1. The promotion of all regions across Europe,
2. A focus, but not an exclusive perspective on the less developed regions,
3. A strategy aimed at reducing regional disparities and supporting the Union's overall policy objectives.

The Commission's proposal for the post-2020 regional and cohesion policy clearly sustains these principles while giving clear indications of the needed change. Since 1988, the European Union has proofed its capability to mobilize enormous financial resources to support new member states either because of their below-average economic performance (after 1986 and 2004) or because of their country-specific needs (as in 1995). Almost twenty years after the accession of the Central and Eastern European countries the European Union moves gradually away from infrastructure improvement, thus forcing even less developed regions to adapt to the needs of a digitalized and low-carbon economy. Compared to the agricultural policy, the regional and cohesion policy seems to align easier to the Union's goals. This comes not as a surprise. Even though most of the regional funds finally support mainly companies, the support measures are still provided in the framework of more comprehensive regional development plans. This contrasts to income subsidies to farmers which are still the dominant distributional logic in the CAP.

At the end of the EP's legislative term 2014-2019 it is, however, still not fully clear as to what extent the Commission's proposal will survive in the negotiations between the Parliament and the Council. There are a number of issues on which a compromise will be difficult to reach. Notably, the overall budget for regional and cohesion policies will very likely not be the most difficult part, because the Commission took the traditional cleavages and the "juste retour" logic well into account. Net-recipient countries will find it difficult to veto the budget as funds for less developed regions are still stable. Net-payer countries will get over the decrease of resources for more developed regions as long as each region across Europe maintains the right to apply for EU funding. The new conditionality rules could, however, become the biggest obstacles to an agreement. This holds for macroeconomic conditionality, but especially for the newly proposed rule-of-law conditionality. Some net-recipient country could instrumentalize this aspect for a veto even if they are more interested in their individual envelopes. Net-payer countries could do the same by insisting on stronger conditionality even if their focus is on a further reduction of the overall and the sectoral budgets.

# 8. The growth promise: perspectives on the EU's research and innovation policies

## *8.1 Research and innovation: the "darling" of EU expenditure*

In 1981 research policy in Europe enjoyed a strategic turn when the European Commission proposed for the first time to set up a "framework programme" (FP) aiming at "reaping the social and economic benefits of scientific discoveries" (Commission of the European Communities 1981: 20). The Commission developed its rationale for making progress in research and development (R&D) on mainly two arguments: the economic and growth effects of a Community-wide approach and the already proven added-value of Community projects in terms of scientific output. Consequently, the Commission requested a doubling of the Community budget for R&D, which amounted to 1.8% (or €300 million in total[111]) of the overall Community budget in 1980 (ibid.: 3).

The economic literature considers research and innovation, but also education and infrastructure policies, as being core to sustainable economic growth, international competitiveness, and job creation (Cantwell 1999; Freeman/Soete 1997; Tobin 1964;). They are growth-oriented policies that are generally to be supported, also and in particular in times of crisis.

The European Commission has therefore kept its original lines of arguing for continuously expanding EU research and innovation funding and policies.[112] In 2014 the Commission declared that:

> "New growth opportunities come from providing new products and services derived from technological breakthroughs, new processes and business models, non-technological innovation and innovation in the services sector, combined with and driven by creativity, flair and talent, or, in other words, from innovation in its broadest sense." (European Commission 2014d: 2)

The so-called Barcelona-target of 2002 was a major signpost of this policy. The EU has set a target of 3% of GDP to be invested in research and development across the Union by 2010. This target was confirmed in the context of the Europe 2020 strategy, which defined strengthening

---

111 Actually, until the introduction of the Euro in 1999, the European currency was the ECU.

112 See also section 8.2.

knowledge and innovation as drivers for future growth as one of its priorities (European Commission 2010c). Additionally, in 2004, the Kok-Report requested governments to give research and innovation policies a core role in reforming their economies, thereby provided a major impetus for European growth policies (Kok Report 2004).

As part of the EU's response to the economic and financial crisis of 2008 the EU has set up a European Economic Recovery Plan equivalent to about 1.5% of the EU GDP (i.e. around €200 billion) with a strong focus on research and innovation investment in the areas of energy efficiency and clean technologies (see European Commission 2008). Under the European Semester, each year the Commission's Annual Growth Surveys emphasise the need to promote growth enhancing expenditures which "can increase both productivity and employment" (European Commission 2017u: 3)

Tracing back the development of research and innovation funding and policies in the EU it is fair to claim that this area is the "darling" of the EU's expenditure side. There has never been a single doubt that R&I investments, both in general and at EU level, are needed to "deliver jobs, prosperity and quality of life" (European Commission 2011e: 10). On the contrary, with each new long-term EU budget R&I saw an increase in funding.

Unsurprisingly, EU Budget Commissioner, Günther Oettinger, named research and innovation a "clear case of European added value"[113], therefore aiming at a substantial increase of the budget for the post-2020 R&I programme.[114]

## *8.2 The EU as an actor in research and innovation policies and funding*

The EU is an established actor in science and research policy and funding. Early attempts by European states to cooperate in research policies started with the Treaty constituting the European Coal and Steel Community

113 See, for example, Oettinger (2018).

114 Oettinger expressed this intention early on in the debate on the post-2020 MFF, for example in a discussion at the Bruegel think tank on 7 March 2018, in which he spoke of a doubling of R&I spending (available at http://bruegel.org/events/the-future-of-the-eu-budget-mff-post-2020; accessed 25 April 2018).

(ECSC) in 1951. In the following years, the 1957 European Economic Community Treaty linked research to improving agricultural productivity. However, science and research cooperation was implemented under the general purpose Article 235 (Stein 2002: 476, endnote 3). A significant Europeanization of research policy was realized with the Single European Act (SEA) of 1986, when competences for a common research policy were partly transferred to the European Community (for example, Elera 2006; Peterson/Sharp 1998). According to Jasper (1998), the strengthening of the European level mirrored the conviction that the European industry was not capable of developing scientific and technological inventions on its own at that time.

The Lisbon Treaty of 2009 finally defined research policy as a shared "parallel" competence (Article 4(3) TFEU), meaning that EU member states can carry out science and research policies in parallel to the EU. Member states do not have to stop their national activities when there is a Union policy, which is the case for policies of shared competence. The Treaty provides ample competences to the EU to pursue a European level research policy, ranging from the need to coordinate national and Union research activities (Article 181 TFEU), to the possibilities to participate in "research and development programmes undertaken by several member states" (Article 185 TFEU), to set up joint undertakings or any other structure necessary for the efficient execution of Union research, technological development and demonstration programmes (Article 187 TFEU), and to conclude international science and technology (S&T) agreements (Article 186 TFEU).

The most important competence of the EU in science and research is to set-up multi-annual Framework Programmes for research, technological development and innovation (Article 182 TFEU). The EU implements multi-annual Framework Programmes since 1983. This new policy abolished the old approach used since 1974 which sought to coordinate national research policies (Grande/Häusler 1994: 208).

The first Framework Programme (1984-1987) had a budget of €3.75 billion and focused on a few strategic technology fields such as information and communication technologies, materials, energy and environmental technologies. The SEA gave the Community a mechanism to become a more active player in science, research and technology policy by providing a decision-making procedure for implementing multi-annual FPs (former Chapter XV, Articles 130f-g; today Title XIX of the TFEU).

While the second FP (1987-1991; €5.4 billion[115]) and third FP (1990-1994; €6.6 billion) remained modest in terms of budget, research expenditures at the European level were doubled to €12.3 billion with FP4 (1994-1998). The main driver for this development was the 1993 Maastricht Treaty, which further "communitarized" research policy. The Treaty allowed pursuing research activities at the EU level that were necessary to achieve non-research-related goals of the Treaty. The following two FPs saw only moderate increases in budgets, with the fifth FP (1998-2002) providing an amount of €13.8 billion and the sixth FP (2002-2006) of €16.2 billion (both without EURATOM). The seventh FP featured a significant budget increase, providing an amount of €50 billion for a seven-year period (2007-2013), and new instruments with the aim to better coordinate research policies and programmes in Europe (for example European Research Area-Nets, Joint Technology Initiatives, Joint Programming Initiatives).

In particular, the sixth and seventh FPs had the political objective to underpin the establishment of a European Research Area (ERA). The ERA concept was launched in 2000 (Elera 2006; European Commission 2000) getting back to the idea of better coordinating national research policies. The 2000 Lisbon European Council made ERA a key component of the Lisbon Strategy (European Council 2000). The ultimate aim of the ERA is the creation of an "internal market for research" (Article 179 TFEU) with the free circulation of researchers, knowledge and technologies. While former Research Commissioner Janez Potočnik pushed ERA, for example, by accelerating the creation of joint research infrastructures, building a European partnership for researchers, and enhanced use of joint programming of research, the enthusiasm for a common research space quickly faded with his successor, Máire Geoghegan-Quinn – who with the Innovation Union (European Commission 2010d) introduced a new policy –, and finally virtually disappeared with the following Commissioner for Science, Research and Innovation, Carlos Moedas. Moedas again introduced new concepts, which he called the "3 O's", i.e. open innovation, open science, and open to the world.

---

115 It should be noted that Commissioner Narjes proposed an ambitious second Framework Programme with an envisaged budget of €10 billion (Commission of the European Communities 1986: 17). However, this proposal faced fierce opposition of reluctant member states, such as France, Germany and the UK, in the Council (Lawton 1999).

After all, policy coordination to "ensure that national policies and Union policy are mutually consistent" (Article 181(1) TFEU) has remained limited (Kaiser/Prange 2004). Neither the Commission's endeavour to use an innovative governance instrument for policy coordination, i.e. the Open Method of Coordination, nor the initiatives for enhanced joint programming between member states and the Union were strong enough to overcome the Treaty-based impediments for creating an ERA, namely the split and parallel competences between the EU and national (or even regional) levels. However, the continuous broadening of the Framework Programmes' objectives and endeavours to develop a genuine European research policy has over the decades led to a reduction of the share of FP funding for thematic research areas from 90% under FP1 to about 60% under Horizon 2020 (European Parliamentary Research Service 2017: 26). Other instruments (so-called "horizontal activities"), such as the European Research Council (ERC), the mobility programmes, research infrastructures, and support for SMEs, have been strengthened instead.

In sum, one can claim that the Framework Programme after 35 years still remains the core EU research policy instrument. It reflects the EU's mid-term priorities and objectives in science, research and innovation – and most importantly – funds its activities with an ever-growing budget. Unsurprisingly, negotiations – between the member states and between the EU-institutions – on the content and budget of new programmes regularly turn out to be complex, tedious and long, while there is nevertheless a basic consensus that a common research and innovation programme is for the benefit of Europe.

## *8.3 Research and innovation under the multiannual financial framework 2014-2020*

Horizon 2020 – the largest common research and innovation (R&I) programme worldwide – was adopted on 20 December 2013 with an initial budget of about €77 billion (in current prices), which made 8.5% of the total MFF (Council of the European Union 2013a; European Parliament & Council of the European Union 2013b, 2013c). The programme "focuses on three priorities, namely generating excellent science in order to strengthen the Union's world-class excellence in science, fostering industrial leadership to support business, including micro, small and medium-sized enterprises (SMEs) and innovation, and tackling societal challenges, in order to respond directly to the challenges identified in the Europe 2020 strategy by supporting activities covering the entire spectrum from research to market" (European Parliament & Council of the European Union 2013b: 105).

*Table 8.1: Horizon 2020 budget by priority (total funding for 2014-2020)*[116]

| *Priority "Excellent Science* | *€ million* |
|---|---|
| European Research Council | 13 095 |
| Future & emerging technologies | 2 696 |
| Marie Skłodowska-Curie actions (MSCA) | 6 162 |
| Research infrastructures (including e-infrastructure) | 2 488 |
| | |
| *Priority "Societal Challenges"* | |
| Health, demographic change & wellbeing | 7 472 |
| Food security, sustainable agriculture and forestry, marine/maritime/inland water research and the bio-economy | 3 851 |
| Secure, clean & efficient energy | 5 931 |
| Smart, green & integrated transport | 6 339 |
| Climate action, environment, resource efficiency & raw materials | 3 081 |
| Inclusive, innovative & reflective societies | 1 310 |
| Secure societies | 1 695 |
| | |
| *Specific objective "Spreading excellence & widening participation"* | *816* |
| *Specific objective "Science with and for society"* | *462* |
| *Non-nuclear direct actions of the JRC* | *1 903* |
| *The European Institute of Innovation and Technology (EIT)* | *2 711* |
| | |
| *TOTAL* | *77 028* |

Compared to the previous programme FP7, Horizon 2020 has a stronger focus on innovation and close-to-market activities. Moreover, the budget for the ERC has been doubled, and there are new instruments devoted to regions with less-developed science infrastructures (under the synonym "spreading excellence") and to small- und medium-sized enterprises (the special instrument under the "Industrial Leadership"-Priority plus the so-called "SME-Instrument" that will receive 7% of the combined budget of

116 Source: European Parliament & Council of the European Union (2013b: 173).

LEITs and the "Social Challenges", i.e. a total of approximately €2.7 billion). Activities such as "international cooperation" or "social sciences and humanities" have been "mainstreamed" across the programme, i.e. there are no specific sub-programmes anymore in these areas.

Preparations for Horizon 2020 formally started when the Commission finally published its "Budget Review" in October 2010 (European Commission 2010a) in which the institution proposed to bring the full range of Union instruments for research and innovation together in a so-called "common strategic framework". In a first reaction, the Council in November 2010 called for future Union funding programmes to focus more on Europe 2020 priorities, address societal challenges and key technologies, facilitate collaborative and industry-driven research, streamline the instruments, radically simplify access, reduce time to market and further strengthen excellence (Council of the European Union 2010a).

Based on a Green Paper, published in February 2011, the Commission launched the compulsory three-month-long public consultation for the future Framework Programme (European Commission 2011f). The results fed into the overall MFF 2014-2020 proposal of the Commission that followed in June 2011 (European Commission 2011e). The main component in terms of the future R&I programme was to merge the areas covered by the seventh Research Framework Programme, the innovation part of the Competitiveness and Innovation Framework Programme, and the EIT into one single framework. On 30 November 2011, the Commission finally adopted its proposals[117] for Horizon 2020 (European Commission 2011g), kicking-off an almost two-year-long negotiation phase. The proposal foresaw a budget for research and innovation of €87.7 billion.

During the first phase in 2012, both legislators, the European Parliament and the Council, had to fix their negotiation positions. The European Parliament started the First Reading immediately in December 2011 with no less than 11 Parliamentary Committees[118] submitting their opinions to

117 The Commission adopted set of legal texts consisting of the proposals for: (1) a Framework Programme for Horizon 2020 (TFEU), (2) a single set of Rules for Participation and Dissemination (TFEU), (3) a single specific programme to implement Horizon 2020 (TFEU), as well as (4) a single proposal for the parts of Horizon 2020 corresponding to the Euratom Treaty.

118 The Industry, Research and Energy (ITRE) Committee was the lead Committee. Opinions were received from the following Committees: Foreign Affairs; Development; Budgets; Environment, Public Health and Food Safety; Transport and Tourism; Regional Development; Agriculture and Rural Devel-

the Rapporteur, Teresa Riera Madurell, until January 2013. In total, almost 2.000 requests for amendments were tabled by Parliamentarians until July 2012. The leading ITRE Committee tabled its report (Draft European Parliament Legislative Resolution) to the EP Plenary about a year after the Commission's proposals on 20 December 2012 (European Parliament 2012). The EP requested finally 151 amendments to the Commission's proposal, most notably the EP did not bring forward a concrete budget suggestion but assigned percentage shares to each Horizon 2020 priority.

The Council had already defined its positions on the Commission's proposals between May (for the Horizon 2020 Regulation) and early December 2012[119] (for the Decision on the Specific Programme) enabling the conduct of formal and informal ("Trilogue") negotiations during 2013. In May 2012 the Council proposed a maximum Horizon 2020 budget of €80 billion. The Council had two more debates about the compromise texts in February and May 2013, while the EP held its final debate on 20 November 2013. Adoption in the EP took place on 21 November 2013 (European Parliament 2013) and in the Council on 3 December 2013 (Council of the European Union 2013b).

Horizon 2020 saw a major backslide when the EU created a European Fund for Strategic Investment (EFSI) in 2015 as part of the so-called Juncker-Plan. The Commission argued that the investment plan was needed to counter the negative effects of the economic and financial crisis (European Commission 2014c: 4). Guarantees provided through the EU budget of maximum €16 billion and by the European Investment Bank (EIB) of €5 billion are the backbone of the Fund. However, the Commission had to set up this new instrument without any fresh money. The way out was to redeploy funds from Horizon 2020 and the Connecting Europe Facility to EFSI, i.e. a reshuffling within heading 1A of the MFF. Horizon 2020 was cut by €2.2 billion (down to a total of €74.8 billion) and the Connecting Europe Facility by €2.8 billion. The European Research Council and the Marie Skłodowska-Curie actions were excluded from contributing to EFSI. In the context of the revision of the MFF 2014-2020, an amount of €200 million was finally reallocated to Horizon 2020 (Council of the European Union 2017i), while the Commission proposed a reallocation of €400 million (European Commission 2016b: 16). The follow-

---

opment; Fisheries; Culture and Education; Legal Affairs; Women's Rights and Gender Equality.

119 See http://www.europarl.europa.eu/oeil/popups/summary.do?id=1239039&t=e&l=en (accessed 3 April 2018).

ing table shows the EU research contribution (cut-off date 1 September 2017) distributed by EU member state.

*Table 8.2: EU contribution by member state (signed grants cut-off date by 1 September 2017) – in million Euro*[120]

| *Member state* | *2014* | *2015* | *2016* | *Share* |
|---|---|---|---|---|
| *Germany* | 1643,5 | 1265,7 | 1240,6 | 16.7% |
| *UK* | 1306,4 | 1302,9 | 1159,2 | 15.2% |
| *France* | 931,2 | 782,7 | 851,1 | 10.3% |
| *Spain* | 690,2 | 704,6 | 784,2 | 8.8% |
| *Italy* | 668,6 | 626,2 | 701,4 | 8.0% |
| *Netherlands* | 670,8 | 666,9 | 589,6 | 7.8% |
| *Belgium* | 337,8 | 337,4 | 517,0 | 4.8% |
| *Sweden* | 285,1 | 249,5 | 318,3 | 3.4% |
| *Austria* | 224,1 | 243,7 | 214,1 | 2.7% |
| *Denmark* | 190,8 | 198,3 | 192,8 | 2.3% |
| *Finland* | 178,7 | 152,0 | 202,4 | 2.1% |
| *Greece* | 181,3 | 143,7 | 203,1 | 2.1% |
| *Ireland* | 161,0 | 140,6 | 130,6 | 1.7% |
| *Portugal* | 144,4 | 130,6 | 122,7 | 1.6% |
| *Poland* | 72,2 | 69,7 | 78,8 | 0.9% |
| *Czech Rep.* | 51,0 | 54,1 | 60,5 | 0.7% |
| *Hungary* | 47,6 | 44,7 | 64,2 | 0.6% |
| *Slovenia* | 41,0 | 41,5 | 61,9 | 0.6% |
| *Romania* | 31,7 | 29,3 | 27,1 | 0.4% |
| *Cyprus* | 27,3 | 22,3 | 32,6 | 0.3% |
| *Estonia* | 31,3 | 26,7 | 13,0 | 0.3% |
| *Slovakia* | 10,4 | 29,9 | 30,3 | 0.3% |
| *Luxembourg* | 22,6 | 18,4 | 22,5 | 0.3% |
| *Bulgaria* | 12,2 | 10,3 | 22,3 | 0.2% |
| *Latvia* | 10,9 | 7,5 | 20,5 | 0.2% |
| *Croatia* | 14,2 | 13,2 | 10,6 | 0.2% |
| *Lithuania* | 7,4 | 10,0 | 9,6 | 0.1% |
| *Malta* | 3,4 | 6,5 | 6,4 | 0.1% |

In absolute terms Germany received most of the funds (€4.149,8 million; 16.7% of the total Horizon 2020 EU contribution), followed by the United Kingdom (€3.768,5 million; 15.2%), France (€2.565 million; 10.3%), Spain (€2.179 million; 8.8%), Italy (€1.996,2 million; 8.0%), and the

120 Source: Based on European Commission (2017v: 28).

Netherlands (€1.927,3 million; 7.8%). These six EU member states account for two-thirds of all Horizon 2020 funding. In total, the EU member states received 92.9% of the funding, while associated countries accounted for 6.5%, with Israel and Norway being the most active, and third countries received 0.6% of the funding, with USA and South Africa in the lead (European Commission 2017w: 64).

The obligatory interim evaluation of Horizon 2020 carried out by the European Commission in 2017 has unsurprisingly revealed that the EU R&I programme brings "clear EU added value", delivers value for money, and contributes significantly to the creation of jobs and growth (European Commission 2018k: 2f). Consequently, the Commission supported the European Parliament's request to endow the post-2020 programme with at least €120 billion (European Parliament 2017b: point 40). The EP reminded the Commission that "the cuts inflicted by the European Fund for Strategic Investments" have deepened the problem of oversubscription, which makes it impossible to fund a large number of high-quality projects (ibid.: point 10). Overall the Commission remained conservative in its suggestions for potential future programme changes. Proposals for further simplification, supporting breakthrough innovation, increasing synergies with other EU funding programmes and EU policies, or strengthening international cooperation (European Commission 2018k: 4-10) have been uttered before.[121]

The next section will analyse the proposal for the EU's post-2020 R&I programme and the process of its development in more detail.

## *8.4 Perspectives for research and innovation post-2020*

On 7 June 2018 the European Commission has tabled its proposal for the ninth EU Framework Programme for Research and Innovation, now called "Horizon Europe" (European Commission 2018l, 2018m). The proposal reflects what Jean-Eric Paquet, Director-General for Research and Innova-

121 See, for example, the 5-year-assesemnt of the so-called Davignon-Commission in 1997 (European Commission 1997), and the interim and ex-post evaluations of the seventh FP (European Commission 2010e; High Level Expert Group 2014). All FP evaluations are accessible on http://ec.europa.eu/research/evaluations/index.cfm?pg=home (accessed 29 March 2018)

tion, has labelled "evolution, not revolution".[122] As with Horizon 2020, there is a science "pillar" (called "Open Science") comprised of the European Research Council, the Marie Sklowdowska-Curie researcher grants and research infrastructures, a "Global Challenges and Industrial Competitiveness" part, under which so-called "missions" should be established aiming to achieve a pre-formulated objective, and, finally, an "Open Innovation" section, which includes the European Innovation Council (EIC) to promote breakthrough innovation at the EU level as well as the European Institute of Innovation and Technology (EIT). A fourth part called "Strengthening the European Research Area" combines mainly actions that have so far been featured under the headings "Spreading excellence & widening participation" and "Science with and for society", plus activities that were scattered across the Framework Programme, such as support to national research and innovation policy reform, researchers' careers, supporting gender equality and support to international cooperation.[123]

The Commission proposed a budget of €86.6 billion (in constant 2018 prices, which is €97.6 billion in current prices) for the period 2021-2027. Compared to the Commission proposal of 2011 for Horizon 2020 (which was at €80 billion in 2011 prices and €87.7 billion in current prices; European Commission 2011e: 25) this makes a moderate increase of 8% (for the overall MFF 2021-2027 the Commission proposed an increase of 13.6% in payments – in 2011, respectively 2018 prices). The programme's MFF share is 7.6%, going down from 8.5% under the MFF 2014-2020.

Moreover, the envelop includes €3.5 billion allocated to the InvestEU Fund (former EFSI and other financial instruments), which has been placed under the same MFF heading as the Framework Programme making it easy in the future to shift funds between the programmes, if deemed necessary. If one deducts the InvestEU price-tag, the new Framework Programme for research and innovation comes out at €83.5 billion (in 2018 prices; respectively €94.1 billion in current prices) or 7.4% of the overall post-2020 MFF, which is an increase of 4.4% compared to the Commission's Horizon 2020 proposal.

Additionally, the Commission proposed that up to 15% of a programme's budget can be transferred to another programme under the same

---

122 See https://sciencebusiness.net/framework-programmes/news/tear-down-silos-vows-new-commission-research-chief (accessed 3 April 2018).

123 Under FP6 these activities were clustered in the Specific Programme "Structuring the ERA" and the action "Strengthening the foundations of the ERA" (European Commission 2002).

heading as well as the possibility to blend different forms of funding, "moving between different modes of management" (European Commission 2018c: 26). This, on the one hand, opens the door for shifting more resources (i.e. up to €15 billion) in the future from Horizon Europe to the InvestEU Fund, on the other hand, it provides the Commission with the opportunity to swap more easily from grants to financial instruments under the Framework Programme.

As early as in the beginning of 2016 the European Commission started its preparations for the post-2020 programme. For the first time ever, the Commission triggered the deliberations on a new programme by conducting a foresight study, which involved the development of future scenarios "to sketch possible future settings and boundary conditions for the development of future R&I policy and funding", the execution of a Delphi survey "to gain new insights into future technologies, societal issues, and R&I practices"[124], and finally the presentation of policy recommendations on the future programme (European Commission 2018n). More or less in parallel, but formally in the context of the Horizon 2020 Interim Evaluation, the Commission had set up an independent expert group under the Chairmanship of former EU Trade Commissioner and WTO-Director General, Pascal Lamy, to "formulate a vision for future EU research and innovation and draw up strategic recommendations on maximising the impact of EU's future investment in this area".[125] The so-called Lamy-group, which was active between December 2016 and July 2017, brought forward eleven recommendations for future EU research and innovation programmes, one of which was to double its budget, but "at a minimum, the budget should maintain the average annual growth rate of Horizon 2020, taking the budget foreseen for the programme's final year as a starting point. This would lead to a seven-year budget of at least €120 billion in current prices" (European Commission 2017x: 9). The Commission used the report to legitimise some of its already existing plans, particularly on the European Innovation Council and the mission-oriented approach to address societal challenges, which both were strongly supported by the Lamy-group. Consequently, these ideas are again taken up in the Commission's political paper on the Horizon 2020 Interim Evaluation published in January 2018 (European Commission 2018k).

124 See https://ec.europa.eu/research/foresight/index.cfm?pg=strategic (accessed 5 April 2018).

125 See http://ec.europa.eu/research/index.cfm?pg=newsalert&year=2016&na=na-220916 (accessed 5 April 2018). See also European Commission (2016h).

Between January and March 2018, the Commission pursued a public consultation to seek the views of stakeholders and citizens in general on the future programme. The results revealed that a large majority of stakeholders and individuals have a positive attitude towards EU research and innovation programmes. EU-wide collaboration in research and innovation is mentioned most as an example of EU added value (European Commission 2018o: 3).

Already since the beginning of 2017, stakeholder organizations (including, for example, the European University Association, the European Association of Research and Technology Organizations, Science Europe, the European Consortium of Innovative Universities, the Universities of Applied Sciences for Europe, and a group or ten European Associations[126]), individual institutions (for example, the Helmholtz Association, the Fraunhofer Association, the National Research Council of Italy), and EU member states have published their position papers, respectively preliminary views, on the post-2020 Framework Programme. Particular east European interests have been articulated by the Academies of Sciences of the Visegrad Group and the Polish Science Contact Agency, who wish to see the introduction of a geographical selection criterion for cooperative research projects (i.e. having an EU-13 partner in the consortium would be an add-on) and the guarantee of a minimum salary for researchers participating in EU projects.[127] Concerning the possible budget of the post-2020 programme some member states remained vague by, for example, pointing simply to the need that funding must reflect a "European added value" or stayed completely silent. However, a number of EU member states, such as Belgium (Government of Belgium 2017), Cyprus (Republic of Cyprus 2018), Hungary (National Research, Development and Innovation Office Hungary 2017), Poland (Government of Poland 2017), Portugal (Government of Portugal 2017) and Sweden, proposed a general increase of R&I funding: "Proportionally, the FP9 budget's share of the total EU budget

126 The Coimbra Group, the European Alliance for Social Sciences and Humanities (EASSH), the European Association of Research Managers and Administrators (EARMA), the European University Association (EUA), the League of European Research Universities (LERU), The Guild of European Research-Intensive Universities and The Leiden Group.

127 Both position papers are available at: https://informacje.pan.pl /images /media/materialy/2018/03/V4_Position_statement.pdf and https:// sciencebusiness.net/sites/default/files/inline-files/Position%20paper_FP9_PolSCA.pdf (accessed 5 April 2018).

should increase, even in a scenario whereby the next multiannual financial framework decreases" (Government Offices of Sweden 2017).

Heads of States and Governments addressed the post-2020 EU budget for the first time at an informal meeting in Brussels on 23 February 2018. The Commission used that opportunity to present its vision for a future MFF (European Commission 2018p). As regards research and innovation the Commission was rather clear on defence research but remained at the level of "options" as concerns the overall Framework Programme. The Commission also saw priorities in the areas of the digital transformation and fulfilling the goals of the Paris Agreement. On defence research the Commission claimed a budget "of at least €3.5 billion" (ibid.: 7) for the period 2021-2027, while on the post-2020 Framework Programme it had put forward three options: i) "maintaining or even lowering current investment levels"; ii) "an increase in the Framework Programme by 50% to €120 billion"; iii) "doubling the Framework Programme to €160 billion" (ibid.: 9). While options ii) and iii) would come with huge job gains and growth effects, option i) would leave the "Union [...] fall further behind compared to the world leaders" (ibid.).

In the end, the European Commission has chosen none of its own options one-to-one, while the final proposal came in fact nearest to the "status-quo" option. In terms of content, structure, and instruments Horizon Europe resembles a mixture of its predecessors. The first pillar "Open Science"[128] remains more or less untouched form the Horizon 2020 priority "Excellent Science". Only the technology-related part on future and emerging technologies has been removed as innovation issues will be dealt with by the EIC. The tentative budget for pillar one is set at €25.8 billion (i.e. plus 18.6% compared to Horizon 2020).

Pillar two "Global Challenges and Industrial Competitiveness"[129] will be the biggest part of Horizon Europe with a tentative budget of €52.7 billion. It is comprised of five clusters (i.e. health; inclusive and secure society; digital and industry; climate, energy and mobility; food and natural resources), which mirror the "Societal Challenges" priority and the "Leadership in Enabling and Industrial Technologies"-sub-priority of Horizon 2020 (considering this, the proposed budget is 21.7% higher than under Horizon 2020). It will additionally include the non-nuclear direct actions

128 Member states suggested to call this pillar of Horizon Europe "Excellence Science".

129 Member states suggested to call this pillar of Horizon Europe "Global Challenges and European Industrial Competitiveness".

of the Joint Research Centre (JRC). This part of Horizon Europe shall be implemented by a number of "intervention areas" (called "thematic areas" under FP6, "activities" under FP7, and "specific activities" under Horizon 2020).[130] Moreover, within this pillar so-called missions will be launched. These missions "shall

(a) have a clear EU-added value and contribute to reaching Union priorities;

(b) be bold and inspirational, and hence have wide societal or economic relevance;

(c) indicate a clear direction and be targeted, measurable and time-bound;

(d) be centred on ambitious but realistic research and innovation activities;

(e) spark activity across disciplines, sectors and actors;

(f) be open to multiple, bottom-up solutions." (European Commission 2018l: 30)

The Commission does not give any indication about potential subjects for or number of missions. Instead, missions are supposed to be co-designed between the Commission, member states, the EP, stakeholders, and the public at large. The first missions shall be ready by the time the new Framework Programme is adopted. There will also be no dedicated budget ring-fenced for missions, which means that budgets will have to be identified through the work programmes implementing Pillar two. The Commission anticipates that "missions are normally [...] cross-cutting in nature and so receive their budget from more than one cluster" (European Commission 2018m: 3). This approach – at least in terms of funding – reminds of the so-called "Focus Areas" under Horizon 2020. "Focus Areas" linked several topics under a broader objective ("big ticket" challenges) and were endowed with significantly more money than usual calls for proposals.[131] Moreover, the Commission acknowledges that missions present

130 By way of example, in the cluster "Inclusive and Secure Society" the intervention areas are: Democracy; Cultural heritage; Social and economic transformations; Disaster-resilient societies; Protection and security; Cybersecurity – combining a rather heterogeneous mix of areas. By comparison, in the cluster "Digital and Industry" the areas are: Manufacturing technologies; Digital technologies; Advanced materials; Artificial intelligence and robotics; Next generation internet; High performance computing and Big Data; Circular industries; Low carbon and clean industry; Space – continuing Horizon 2020 priorities and showing a still rather closed (or silo) approach.

131 See "Horizon 2020 work programme 2018-2020 - Strategic Programme Overarching Document", available at http://ec.europa.eu/programmes/ horizon2020/sites/horizon2020/files/stratprog_overarching_version_for_publicatio n.pdf (accessed 7 June 2018).

substantial analogies with "FET flagships"[132]. Therefore, such flagships "will be supported [...] as missions geared towards future and emerging technologies" (European Commission 2018q: 2). In terms of governance the Commission proposes that for each mission, a mission board "of around 15 high level individuals" may be established. These boards will advise on the work programme content, potential evaluators, framework conditions to achieve the objectives of the mission, and communication issues (European Commission 2018m: 10).

The Commission's approach to missions, i.e. no indication of potential topics nor any pre-defined budget, is at best cloudy and has created serious distractions. First, while the participatory approach to define missions has been welcomed by several stakeholders and member states as a chance to place their "hobby horses" as missions, reaching an agreement on a limited number of missions failed during the negotiations in the Council and the EP. Instead, the institutions only agreed on broad 'areas for missions', such as 'adaption to climate change' or 'healthy oceans and natural waters'. The final missions will have to be identified during the so-called Strategic Programming process, in which the Commission presents its mid-term planning for Horizon Europe. Secondly, it can be assumed that missions – when having been identified – will exhaust huge shares of the cluster budgets sacrificing the other "intervention areas". The EP has, therefore, proposed to cap the mission budgets at 10% of the annual expenditures for Pillar two during the first three years of Horizon Europe. Both developments discussed bear a huge frustration potential either for those who "lost" in the missions' selection battle, or for those who see budgets vanishing away for "their" research areas.

Pillar three "Open Innovation"[133] with a tentative budget of €13.5 billion subsumes the EIC and the EIT. The EIC swallows all former activities in relation to future and emerging technologies and small- and medium-sized enterprises. It will mainly focus on breakthrough and disruptive innovations that have market-creating potential. Besides financial support, the EIC will also provide business advisory services, such as coaching,

---

132 "Flagships are visionary, science-driven, large-scale research initiatives addressing grand Scientific and Technological (S&T) challenges. They are long-term initiatives bringing together excellent research teams across various disciplines, sharing a unifying goal and an ambitious research roadmap on how to achieve it" (http://ec.europa.eu/programmes/horizon2020/en/h2020-section/fet-flagships; accessed 13 June 2018).

133 Member states suggested to call this pillar of Horizon Europe "Innovative Europe".

mentoring and technical assistance, and pairing innovators with peers, industrial partners and investors (European Commission 2018q: 61). A High-Level Advisory Board of 15 to 20 individuals will assist the Commission in implementing the EIC. Moreover, the Commission plans to engage EIC programme managers, which practically implement the EIC activities by serving as a kind of companion to the projects. Finally, the EIC will contribute to a "European innovation ecosystem". The core aim is to closer coordinate national and EU level innovation policy activities, including "co-fund[ing] joint innovation programmes managed by authorities in charge of public national, regional or local innovation policies and programmes" (ibid.: 69). The following table provides an overview of the Horizon Europe proposal.

*Table 8.3: Horizon Europe by priority (Commission proposal for 2021-2027)*[134]

| *Priorities* | *€ million* |
|---|---|
| *Pillar I "Open Science"* | |
| European Research Council | 16 600 |
| Marie Skłodowska-Curie actions | 6 800 |
| Research infrastructures | 2 400 |
| *TOTAL Pillar I* | *25 800* |
| *Pillar II "Global Challenges and Industrial Competitiveness"* | |
| Cluster "Health" | 7 700 |
| Cluster "Inclusive and Secure Society" | 2 800 |
| Cluster "Digital and Industry" | 15 000 |
| Cluster "Climate, Energy and Mobility" | 15 000 |
| Cluster "Food and Natural Resources" | 10 000 |
| Non-nuclear direct actions of the JRC | 2 200 |
| *TOTAL Pillar II* | *52 700* |
| *Priority "Open Innovation"* | |
| European Innovation Council | 10 500 |
| The European Institute of Innovation and Technology | 3 000 |
| *TOTAL Pillar III* | *13 500* |
| *Part "Strengthening the European Research Area"* | |
| Sharing excellence | 1 700 |
| Reforming and enhancing the European R&I System | 400 |
| *TOTAL "Strengthening the European Research Area"* | *2 100* |
| *TOTAL* | *94 100* |

134 Source: European Commission (2018l: 32).

In addition, to the Framework Programme research and innovation activities are scattered throughout the EU's new budget. The proposal for Horizon Europe, therefore, devotes some attention on synergies with other programmes. The draft regulation names 16 of those programmes with which Horizon Europe should work closely together (however, it does not say, how). Amongst those are the European Structural and Investment Funds, the Digital Europe Programme, the InvestEU Fund, the Space Programme, the Programme for the Environment and Climate Action (LIFE), and the European Defence Fund.

In conclusion, it has to be pointed out that the Commission's proposal for the Horizon Europe programme signals neither a changing direction in terms of content nor in terms of budget. Compared to the Commission's proposal for Horizon 2020 the nominal increase is marginal. In relation to the overall MFF the share for the programme is even decreasing. Taking into account previous negotiations on the EU's long-term budget one can expect that the proposed Horizon Europe budget might even be less at the end of the negotiations due to member states' path-dependent preferences for other policy areas. Usually, the European Parliament is not able to counter-weight the Council's position as its role is ambiguous.

This is not different this time. On the post-2020 MFF proposal the EP, on the one hand, advocates a budget for research and innovation of at least €120 billion, on the other hand, it wants to freeze the status of cohesion and agricultural policies. The EP's solution is "to set the 2021-2027 MFF at the level of 1.3% of the EU-27 GNI" (European Parliament 2018b: point 6), which brings it in sharp opposition to the member states.

Content-wise the Horizon Europe proposal has a high potential for conflicts in relation to its mission-approach. The selection process and the identification of related budgets could create disaccord amongst member states or other actors about which mission to choose. Moreover, there exists inevitably a trade-off between missions and other objectives of the programme. The identification of "negative priorities" is usually heavily conflict-laden. Very early in the negotiation process member states made clear that they will not accept the undefined treatment of missions in the Commission proposal but will request a list of missions defined in the legal text as well as a strong say in the implementation of the missions.[135]

135 See https://sciencebusiness.net/framework-programmes/news/eu-science-ministers-weigh-five-research-missions-ten-industry (accessed 2 December 2018).

Last but not least, the exit of an important voice for defending the excellence criterion, i.e. the UK, is likely to trigger demands for further softening that criterion in favour of additional geographical measures supporting member states that joint the EU after 2004 (see Council of the European Union 2018b: 5).[136]

136 See also Chapter 9.

# 9. Between stability and change: scenarios for the post-2020 EU budget

## 9.1 *Stability and change: two sides of the same coin*

As with all previous EU long-term budgets, the debate on the post-2020 MFF goes along with suggestions – both from the political and the academic angle – for its "modernization" or "reform". At the same time expectations are low that substantial change will really happen, i.e. the future MFF is supposed to reflect the status quo (for example, Begg 2018; in the context of the 2014-2020 MFF, see, for example, Becker 2014; Mijs/Schout 2012). Throughout this book we have contested this simplistic either-or dichotomy and argued that institutionalizing the EU budget in form of a MFF allows for stability and change at the same time. On the one hand, the MFF represents a stable, path-dependent structure guaranteeing security for the actors in terms of costs and benefits. On the other hand, it is a flexible instrument as change within the overall framework is a recurring feature in various MFFs.

Based on this argument, we can explore stability and change scenarios in two dimensions: first, in relation to the overall MFF structure (macro-level), and second, in relation to instruments and priorities of the MFF (micro-level). We argue that the emergence of either stability or change depends on a number of conditions, such as the order of events, the use of windows of opportunities, external shocks (for example, Brexit), leadership capabilities (for example, expressed through German-French compromises and their ability to build coalitions of member states), cleavage structures, as well as national and European politics. This chapter presents a reasoned forward-looking view on where and why to expect either stability or change in the post-2020 MFF.

Between March and June 2017, the European Commission attempted to break the path-dependent straitjacket of the MFF by tableing a set of non-exhaustive options – or scenarios as the Commission called them – on the future of Europe and their potential implications for the EU budget (European Commission 2017a 2017b). While scenarios are not intended to describe a certain future – and therefore no-one expects that a scenario really occurs – the Commission's reflection papers even failed to launch a substantial debate in the member states on the future of the EU in general, and on its finance in particular. This might be grounded in the quality of the scenarios, which were only vaguely developed or reasoned, with some judged as unrealistic from the beginning (see Begg 2017). However, what might at least equally be important in this case, was the timing of the Commission's initiative. With elections in bigger EU members, such as France (Presidential elections in April/May 2017), Germany (federal elections in September 2017; regional elections in several Länder) and the UK (June 2017) as well as in some smaller member states (such as Austria and the Czech Republic in October 2017) ahead, and the decision of the UK to leave the EU taken on 30 March 2017, national politics (and more precisely quite often right-wing, anti-EU populist pressure) dominated the attention of several member states' governments.

Moreover, reform debates at the European and the national level were not synchronized in the sense that proposals issued by French President Emmanuel Macron were not only criticised by some net-payer governments (see Chapter 10), they were also immediately dismissed by the European Commission. This holds especially for the proposal of a dedicated budget for the Eurozone which, from the perspective of the Commission, called into question the MFF as the single integrated European budget instrument. Unsurprisingly, the European Commission reacted to the idea with restraint. In its "Reflection Paper on the Deepening of the Economic and Monetary Union" (European Commission 2017y), the French proposal is only casually mentioned. The Commission points out that such a budget "may rather be a long-term goal, taking into account the relationship with the general EU budget over time with an increasing number of euro area countries" (European Commission 2017y: 26). A coordinated Franco-German initiative for a Eurozone budget could have generated more support for the plan, but despite the fact that there were also some concerns in Germany the country was simply not ready for it due to the long-lasting negotiations for a new coalition government.

### *9.2 Stability and change in the overall MFF structure*

Stability and change in the overall MFF structure represent the macro-level of our analysis. Generally, the macro-level appears rather change-resistant (or path-dependent) over the last decades, in particular in relation to the MFF ceiling, its duration, the budget lines, and the structure of revenues.

The overall MFF ceiling is the most obvious orientation point for member states during the negotiations and a core selling feature at home for their national electorates. The Commission proposal for the post-2020 MFF foresees a limit of 1.11% of the EU-27 GNI, under the 2014-2020 MFF the limit was 1.03% (commitments, 2018 prices, including the EDF). For net-payers to keep the 1%-paradigm has become a matter of principle. Except Germany, net-payers made already clear that it will hold also for the post-2020 MFF. Germany has considered to pay more into the next EU budget, but this does not automatically mean Germany would accept an increase of the MFF ceiling, as Germany might need to fill part of the Brexit gap. The willingness of some net-beneficiaries to increase the ceiling can be neglected as a decisive factor for change as long as they will stay net-beneficiaries. The request of the European Parliament for 1.3% of the EU-27 GNI is unlikely to materialize. Such as sharp increase, which would mean an MFF of €1.341 billion, would not only put considerable burden on many net-contributors, it would also mean that net-beneficiaries would have to agree to much higher national contributions. In a situation of anti-EU sentiment or economic difficulties in many of the net-beneficiary countries such an agreement looks out of reach. National elections in Sweden in September 2018, in Slovakia in March 2019, in Finland in May 2019, and in Poland in Winter 2019 (parliament) respectively April 2020 (President), i.e. in member states that are either net-payers defending the 1%-ceiling or show eurosceptical tendencies, make a stability scenario more likely. Additionally, a potentially more eurosceptical EP after the elections in May 2019 could be tempted to abandon the demand of its predecessor for raising the MFF significantly.

However, it is also not very likely that the post-2020 MFF will be cut exactly at the level of the British contribution. To keep the MFF ceiling at 1.03% after Brexit would mean a decrease of more than €80 billion over the whole MFF period compared to the previous MFF 2014-2020.[137] There is obviously enormous pressure to provide sufficient financial means for the new challenges. To a certain extent, funds could be taken from the agricultural budget, which will most likely further decrease (alternatively or additionally agricultural policy could be attributed a greater research and innovation component). But there is very little redistribution mass in the two other areas of cohesion and research and innovation.

137 Calculated based on figures in European Parliamentary Research Service (2018: 3).

An important aspect regarding the structure of the forthcoming MFF concerns its duration. Especially the EP had advocated in favour of a five years or even a five plus five years period. At first sight, the justification for a deviation from the current seven-year period seems reasonable. Without the change, the next two elected European Parliaments would have no chance to decide on a budget which they would also control afterwards. Nevertheless, we argued elsewhere (Kaiser/Prange-Gstöhl 2017) that we consider a change unlikely. First, it would provoke considerable technical adjustments to the most important EU funding programmes without providing a substantial functional advantage. Second, and probably more important, the change would intervene in the institutional equilibrium between the EP and the Council. It would provide the EP with the opportunity to politicize budget negotiations even more than it has already done in 2014 with regard to the selection of the European Commission's President. There is hardly any chance that EU member states would support such a proposal except it will be legally fixed that a five-year period for the upcoming MFF would be an extraordinary exception. Therefore, it is not surprising that the Commission's MFF proposal again foresees a seven-year period.

The budget lines will generally remain an element of stability. The Commission's proposal incorporates marginal changes in terms of renaming of some headings and creating new headings ("Migration and Border Management" and "Security and Defence"). Additionally, some programmes are proposed to be shifted between headings (see European Court of Auditors 2018: 7). As tables 9.1 shows, changes in terms of funding of new headings appear, at first sight, quite fundamental.

*Table 9.1: Changes in MFF headings 2014-2020 to 2021-2027 (European Court of Auditors 2018: 10)*

| *MFF headings* | *Changes in billion EUR* | *Changes in percent* | *Percent of the overall MFF 2021-2027* |
|---|---|---|---|
| *Natural Resources and Environment* | - 63 | - 16 | 29.7 |
| *Cohesion and Values* | + 4.7 | + 1 | 34.5 |
| *European Public Administration* | + 4.8 | +7 | 6.7 |
| *Neighbourhood and the World* | + 12.6 | + 13 | 9.6 |
| *Single Market, Innovation and Digital* | + 49.9 | + 43 | 14.6 |
| *Migration, Security and Defence* | +43.1 | + 359 | 4.9 |

Closer inspection, however, reveals that the increase of investments in areas of new priorities are largely realized by proposing fresh money. As table 9.2 indicates, the European Commission was much less motivated for reform in terms of a shifting of funds across budget lines. The respective changes are limited, and sometimes only of symbolic nature. They are significant, however, in terms of one specific pattern.

The EU Commission used substantial funds that were now delegated to the new heading of "cohesion and values" in order to prevent a substantial decrease of investments in regional policy. Apart from that, all other cases of redistribution of resources give proof to a very limited ambition to reorient the budget towards new challenges. This shows, on the one hand, that the path-dependent structure of the MFF is quite stable even at the level of established budget headings. On the other hand, it becomes obvious that the post-2020 MFF will mainly loose its innovative approach if member states should reject to fully compensate for the British budget contribution.

*Table 9.2: Proposed changes of MFF structure 2014-2020 to 2021-2027 (European Court of Auditors 2018: 7)*

| *Programme* | *Amount of investment in billion EUR* | *Moves from heading of MFF 2014-2020 ...* | *... to heading of MFF 2021-2027* |
|---|---|---|---|
| *Erasmus and others* | 16.6 | 1a: Competitiveness for Growth and Jobs | 2: Cohesion and Values |
| *Nuclear Safety* | 1.9 | 1a: Competitiveness for Growth and Jobs | 4/5: Migration, Security and Defence |
| *Food and Consumer* | 2.1 | 3: Security and Citizenship | 1: Single Market, Innovation and Digital |
| *Creative Europe* | 5.2 | 3: Security and Citizenship | 2: Cohesion and Values |
| *EU Aid initiative* | 0.3 | 4: Global Europe | 2: Cohesion and Values |
| *Union Civil Protection* | 0.1 | 4: Global Europe | 4/5: Migration, Security and Defence |

The direct linkage between the main expenditure lines and the three most important Union programmes (i.e. for agricultural policies, for structural and cohesion policies, and for research and innovation policies), generates significant reliability of expectations for the member states, but also for the European Commission as the administrator of the programmes. Therefore, the relative size of the different budget lines will still show the biggest portion for agriculture and cohesion policies (while certainly further decreasing in relative terms for the benefit of migration and security policies, which however come from a very low share).

The structure of the revenue side should remain stable. We do not consider increasing revenues from new own resources as a plausible outcome of the MFF negotiations. The simple reason is that all measures proposed by the Monti Group score lower than current own resources on the indicator of "limiting political transaction costs" (HLGOR 2016: 89). Apart from that, up to now there has not been a substantial discussion about the question of the need for new correction mechanisms if tax-based own resources for the European Union would be established. We therefore conclude that a change of the own resources system needs to be framed with a much broader reform that would render political transaction costs more acceptable. Such a broader EU reform, which might require substantial Treaty change, is an illusion in a situation of growing confrontation amongst member states and between member states and EU institutions.

Change in the overall MFF structure might stem from a potential Eurozone budget, respectively a financial stabilization mechanism, the budgetization of the European Development Fund (EDF), and the elimination of all correction mechanisms (i.e. the rebates).

However, the immediate establishment of a fully-fledged Eurozone budget is unlikely for the post-2020 MFF. First, because of the obvious distrust the European Commission has vis-à-vis the Eurozone budget. The European Parliament might consider it more open-minded, but only as an add-on to the MFF, and certainly not at the expense of funds foreseen for the MFF. However, a separate Eurozone budget outside the MFF endangers the principle of unity of the EU budget and leaves the role of the EU institutions unclear. Questions for the system of revenue, expenditure and governance have to be solved. The potential need for creating new, parallel institutions is not in the interest of the European Parliament and the Commission and raises legal concerns (European Parliament 2017c). Second, a short window of opportunity for such a major reform has existed after the German federal elections and the Sorbonne-Speech of French President Macron in September 2017. This window closed meanwhile due to the unusually long coalition talks in Germany which made it impossible to reach a French-German compromise on time, i.e. before the Commission was tableing its proposals on the reform of the Economic and Monetary Union in December 2017 and on the post-2020 MFF in May 2018. Only in June 2018, Germany and France agreed to present more concrete suggestion on a Eurozone budget to the European Council in December 2018. The Meseburg Declaration[138] contains, however, rather conflictual issues for funding the new budget, such as raising resources from tax revenues and relying on European resources, i.e. the MFF. Moreover, the funding of the Eurozone budget also through additional national contributions – as the third source – will likely be contested by Euro members in difficult socio-economic conditions, but possibly also by net-payers if the Greek financial crisis starts to glow again after it has been declared finished by the European Commission and the Greek government at the end of August 2018. There is no guarantee that Greece will not need another bail-out programme in case the people, companies and investors will not regain trust in the Greek economy and the Greek political system.[139] As all EU member states might want to avoid complicated and conflictual parallel negotiations (on the MFF and a separate Eurozone budget), it is more likely that a so-called Eurozone budget could be established stepwise over a longer period starting with the stabilization mechanism already proposed by the Commission for the post-2020 MFF.

The introduction of a European Investment Stabilization Function (EISF) would mark another step towards an EU budget more focused on macroeconomic stability.[140] The EU budget will guarantee loans of up to €30 billion for Eurozone members suffering from "large asymmetric macroeconomic shocks". Costs for member states will be generated through the accompanying interest rate subsidy. The Commission wants these €600 million to "be financed from contributions from euro area member states equivalent to a share of monetary income (seigniorage)" (European Commission 2018c: 11). It can be argued that compared to the ESM this is

138 Available at: https://www.bundesregierung.de/Content/EN/Pressemitteilungen/BPA/2018/2018-06-19-meseberg-declaration.html (accessed 13 August 2018).

139 The bail-out programme for Greece ended on 20 August 2018. The European Commission and Eurozone creditors have lent Athens about €240 billion (European Commission 2018r: 2). The recovery of Greece and its debt sustainability will depend on a rigorous growth strategy and prudent fiscal policies. However, the calculations by the Commission are based on the assumption that Greece maintains a primary surplus of 3.5% of GDP until 2022 and of 2.2% of GDP on average in the period from 2023 to 2060 (ibid). The IMF questioned these figures and called for more "realistic assumptions for primary balance targets and growth projections" (IMF 2018: 10).

140 According to the European Commission the Structural and Investment Funds, the Reform Support Programme, the InvestEU Programme, the EIB and the ESM are already part of a budgetary system for a stable Euro area (European Commission 2018c: 11).

a small instrument. However, as an instrument within the MFF, implemented and controlled by the Commission, the institution would receive more influence during crisis situations (the mechanism would be triggered automatically based on pre-defined parameters without the need to involve parliaments). As European integration history has shown in relation to other programmes and instruments, initially small initiatives might serve as a potential entrance to further developments with major effects in the future.

The so-called budgetization of the EDF – i.e. its inclusion into the MFF – would signal major change in the MFF structure. The Commission has proposed to integrate the €30 billion EDF into the new Neighbourhood, Development and International Cooperation Instrument. This is a long-standing idea (since the 1970s) mainly supported by the Commission and the EP, which argue that the budgetization would increase democratic control, legitimacy and transparency (European Parliament 2014b). Those member states that are traditionally against a budgetization, such as Italy and Spain, want to retain control over EDF decisions (ibid.). Budgetizing the EDF would give the Council and the EP co-legislative powers, thus "moving the EDF from member state competence to EU competence" (Døhlie Saltnes 2018). Moreover, budgetization would mean a change in the contribution key, leading to higher payments for member states that have higher shares in funding the EU budget.[141] Last but not least, the ACP group is an opponent of budgetizing the EDF. In sum, while shifting the EDF into the post-2020 MFF would be a major structural change, several components reduce its likelihood. The upcoming negotiations on a post-Cotounou Agreement, however, open a window of opportunity for structural changes in EU-ACP relations.

The UK's exit from the Union would be a political opportunity to eliminate all so-called rebates or correction mechanisms granted to the UK, Germany, Netherlands, Denmark, Austria and Sweden.[142] The removal of the rebates would lead to a sudden increase of these five countries' budget contributions. Therefore, the Commission intends to phase these rebates out over a period of five years. Nevertheless, immediate rejections of this plan by Austria, Denmark, and the Netherlands show that there is no automatism that Brexit results in the complete abolishment of rebates, espe-

141 Currently, the contribution key reflects the different historical ties of EU member states with ACP countries.

142 See Chapter 3 for details.

cially not if net-payers will have the impression that they have to step-in for both the Brexit gap and an increased MFF.[143]

In sum, we expect much stability in the post-2020 MFF at the structural level. Though there has been a small window of opportunity for more substantial changes, this window has closed due to national politics. In addition, the Commission's attempt to trigger a more fundamental discussion on the future of Europe, including its finance, has been badly timed. Brexit is unlikely to impact on the next MFF at this level, particularly if the EU reaches an agreement with the UK and the UK will be enabled to take part in some Union policies and programmes for which they would have to contribute into the EU budget. A "no-deal-scenario" would create a bigger impact on the 2014-2020 MFF as the UK could step back from paying its "divorce bill"[144] since it is part of the Withdrawal Agreement. In May 2019, such a no-deal scenario became again more likely with the announced resignation of Theresa May as Prime Minister and leader of the Conservative Party as well as the British results of the elections to the European Parliament. The latter brought forth those parties that are explicitly positioned either in favour of even a no-deal Brexit (as the newly-founded Brexit Party of Nigel Farage) or against a Brexit at all (especially the Liberal Democrats). More recent polls even assume that the Brexit Party could come close to an absolute majority if May's successor would call a general election.[145] Against this background, the ratification of the Brexit agreement is not a very plausible option anymore. It seems even more likely that the UK could stay in the EU if the House of Commons rejects to leave the European Union without a second referendum. Either way, the current situation produces a significant amount of uncertainty for the budget negotiations. If the UK should leave without an agreement, those

143 See Financial Times, "Wealthier EU states attack Brussels plan to end rebates", 2 May 2018, available at: https://www.ft.com/content/5ce33318-4e1e-11e8-a7a9-37318e776bab (accessed 13 August 2018).

144 The whole financial settlement is estimated by the British government at around €41 billion until 2064. For the 2014-2020 MFF the amount is estimated at around €18.5 billion (UK House of Commons 2018).

145 It has been estimated that, by winning 26% of the votes, the Brexit Party could obtain 306 seats in the House of Commons. This would leave the party only 20 seats short of an absolute majority. See The Guardian, "Brexit party tops Westminster election poll for the first time", 1 June 2019, available at: https://www. theguardian.com/politics/2019/jun/01/brexit-party-nigel-farage-lead-opinion-poll-conservatives-opinium (accessed 1 June 2019).

net-payers claiming that a smaller EU needs a smaller budget (mainly Austria, the Netherlands, Sweden) could again win the support of bigger net-payers such as Germany and France. If the UK stays, the established net-payer/net-recipient logic would be clearly reinforced and consequently also the existing rules for revenues and rebates.

### *9.3 Stability and change in instruments and priorities*

Instruments and priorities are usually linked to the sectoral programmes that underpin the overall MFF. As we have argued before, on this micro-level the MFF has shown more flexibility over the last decades and will continue to do so.

While with every new MFF a few new instruments might be introduced, some policy and programme objectives change, and programmes are re-named, merged, or moved between budget lines, the major expenditure programmes – such as agriculture, regional development and cohesion, as well as research and innovation – continue to exist (independent of whether the respective policy undergoes a reform or not). This will not change with the post-2020 MFF. Both the Structural Funds (i.e. the European Agricultural Guidance and Guarantee Fund, Guidance Section; the European Social Fund; the European Regional Development Fund) and the research and innovation programme have a Treaty base, meaning there is a legal obligation for the EU to realize policy objectives through these funding programmes.[146] For the post-2020 MFF the Commission mainly suggests a synchronization of programmes with budget lines by reorganizing some of the programmes under new headings within 17 "policy clusters". According to the Commission "this will provide greater clarity on how they will contribute to policy goals" (European Commission 2018c: 5).

Albeit stable as a financial framework, the MFF never prevented the EU from incremental reforms within the main expenditure programmes. The establishment of the European Research Council for the funding of basic research in 2007, the proposal for a European Innovation Council to support innovative start-ups under the post-2020 research and innovation programme, changes in terms of the priorities in regional and cohesion policy (especially in terms of including more science- and innovation re-

146 Together with the space and the development programmes, these are the only funding programmes explicitly mentioned in the TFEU.

lated targets[147]) and the "greening" of agricultural policy[148] were all possible without significantly changing the respective budget shares of these programmes.

Programme reforms usually go hand in hand with additional flexibility within and between budget lines. In general, the flexibility is greater within headings than between headings. Transfers between headings that exceed the margins, or the scope of special instruments would require revision of the MFF regulation, whereas transfers within headings can take place through the budgetary procedure, with the approval of the two arms of the budgetary authority. Nevertheless, there are several examples which show that even new activities can be financed either within the MFF structure or by individual member states' contributions outside the MFF. Examples for financing new activities within the MFF structure are the creation of the EFSI and the use of the flexibility instruments. Examples for new funding outside the MFF are the European Development Fund (EDF), the European Security and Defence Policy (Athena-Mechanism), and the European Union Regional Trust Fund in response to the Syrian crisis (the so-called Madad Fund). However, Mijs and Schout (2015) have shown that the flexibility of the MFF 2014-2020 has quickly reached its limits during the migration crisis.

For the post-2020 MFF the Commission proposed that "the EU budget must be flexible enough to allow the Union to respond quickly and effectively to unforeseen needs" (European Commission 2018c: 25). To create greater flexibility within and between programmes the Commission aims at increasing the amount that can be transferred from one programme to another within the same heading from 10% to 15%[149]. At the same time the Commission proposal foresees new "built-in reserves", "the possibility of 'blending' different forms of financial support, moving between different modes of management, 'reprogramming' funding at mid-term as well as specific revisions of national allocations to adjust to developments over

---

147 The proposal for the post-2020 Cohesion Policy includes the possibility for pan-European innovation clusters. "The aim is to scale up 'bankable' interregional projects that can create European value chains in priority sectors such as big data, bioeconomy, resource efficiency, connected mobility or advanced manufacturing" (European Commission 2018s).

148 "Greening" the CAP means that 30% of member states' budgets for direct payments and rural development may be spent only if mandatory greening measures are carried out.

149 For the 2014-2020 MFF this share had already been increased from 5% to 10%.

the period" (ibid.: 25f.). Further on, to enhance the flexibility between headings and years, the Commission suggests to increase the budget for the "flexibility instrument"[150] to €1 billion per year (from €600 million under the MFF 2014-2020), to continue and extend the possibility of transferring margins between headings and years – a novelty that had been introduced with the MFF 2014-2020 (European Parliament 2017d: 11) – as well as to establish a "Union Reserve" to tackle unforeseen events and to respond to emergencies. This reserve would consist of unspent funds, which so far flow back into member states' budgets (European Commission 2018c: 26).

While the need for more flexibility in and of the MFF is generally accepted amongst the actors, the Commission proposals contain two potentially controversial elements: the possibility for specific revisions of national allocations and the "Union Reserve". These proposals link directly to national budgets. While the first issue could meet resistance of both net-payers and net-beneficiaries as it would lead to an unsecure situation in terms of previously secure budget allocations, the second proposal might particularly be unpopular in net-payer countries who already have to cope with a possible financial Brexit gap, new challenges to be funded, and – if they are Eurozone members – additional instruments to stabilize their currency. The "Union Reserve" would be filled by unspent funds that are normally re-distributed back into national budgets. In 2016, member states had already rejected a similar proposal by the Commission – the so-called "Crisis Reserve" – in the context of the MFF mid-term review (European Parliament 2017d: 16). We, therefore, predict that another proposal to increase flexibility, i.e. the intensified use of financial instruments, will be less controversial.

Financial instruments, i.e. the backing of investments based on a guarantee from the EU budget, have become a stable feature of the MFF since 2007. Introduced, first, only to trigger investments in research and innovation under the 7th Framework Programme through the Risk-Sharing Finance Facility (RSFF; under Horizon 2020 renamed into InnoFin), the instrument was boosted in form of the EFSI since 2015.[151] Originally intro-

---

150 In case of clearly identified needs requiring expenditure above the maximum allocations of resources ("ceilings") set in the MFF, the European Commission can propose to use the Flexibility Instrument, after verifying that no reallocation of funds is possible under the relevant heading. The decision to mobilise the instrument is made jointly by the European Parliament and the Council.

151 See Chapter 3 for details on EFSI.

duced as an initiative in response to the economic crisis, it became soon popular both amongst the European Commission and the EU member states as a tool pretending higher investments with limited public funding. EFSI was extended in late 2017 aiming at mobilizing €500 billion by 2020 (EFSI 2.0). For the post-2020 MFF the Commission proposed a contribution from the EU budget of €15.2 billion for EFSI's successor, the InvestEU programme, hoping to mobilize more than €650 billions of additional investment across Europe by 2027 (European Commission 2018c: 7).

Meanwhile, similar financial instruments are applied in the EU's external actions. The first External Investment Plan had been adopted by the EU in September 2017. This model is supposed to be continued and expanded in the post-2020 MFF. The future Neighbourhood, Development and International Cooperation Programme should include an investment framework combining a European Fund for Sustainable Investment (EFSD+) and the External Action Guarantee to "allow for the 'crowding-in' of additional resources from other donors and from the private sector" (European Commission 2018c: 18).[152] Moreover, the Commission also wants the objectives of the European Defence Fund to be "addressed through financial instruments and budgetary guarantees under the policy window(s) [...] of the InvestEU Fund" (European Commission 2018i: 17).

There is no doubt that financial instruments will remain a stable element in the post-2020 budget as they easily allow actors to proliferate the narrative of efficient and effective spending of public money at EU level.

Macroeconomic conditionality had become a new mechanism under the MFF 2014-2020.[153] It aims to link the allocation of European structural and investment funds to good economic governance. The Commission is empowered to "request a member state to re-programme part of its funding when this is deemed necessary to maximise the 'growth and competitiveness impact' of the Funds. It also gives the possibility to the Commission to consider a suspension of payments when member states fail to address its reprogramming request" (Huguenot-Noël/Hunter 2017: 12). Therefore, macroeconomic conditionality is aiming at both, "providing incentives for member states to reduce fiscal and macroeconomic imbalances" (ibid.: 16), on the one hand, and serving as a "sanction mechanism

---

152 According to the European Commission "together with the private sector and thanks to the leverage effect, this may mobilise up to half a trillion euro in investments for the 2021-2027" (European Commission 2018t).

153 However, economic conditionality was already applied to Cohesion Policy during the financial period 2007-2013 (Huguenot-Noël/Hunter 2017).

to prevent the emergence of imbalances that could affect the resilience of the euro area" (ibid.), on the other hand. In the absence of a genuine budget capacity for the Eurozone of a similar volume – which we see unlikely to emerge under the post-2020 MFF (see above) – macroeconomic conditionality for the structural and investment funds will continue as an instrument for the EU's fiscal and macroeconomic surveillance framework.

However, to be conceived as a credible mechanism either the incentives to follow good fiscal and economic governance or the sanctions mechanisms or both have to be strengthened. Since member states will seek to keep the sanctions procedure in their own hands (i.e. Council decisions are needed to suspend funds, which has never been realized so far) it is likely that the Commission will aim at strengthening the part on which it has most influence, i.e. the programming part, which is usually characterized by negotiations of roadmaps and policy implementation strategies (so-called Partnership Agreement) between the Commission and each member state based on a number of conditions member states need to comply with to receive funding ("preventive arm").[154]

A more fundamental change for the next financial period would be the introduction of some kind of policy conditionality in the context of EU cohesion policy reform. This debate was mainly triggered during the 2015-2016 refugee crisis when some member states were accused of lacking solidarity with southern EU member states that were hit most by the inflow of migrants. At the same time concerns regarding the rule of law in some eastern EU member states further heated the discussions.

The proposed new "rule of law"-conditionality[155] looks, therefore, attractive at first sight to pressure those member states in which the rule of law is supposedly under attack by governments. Besides legal concerns[156] there are political impediments, which are likely to raise resistance amongst a number of member states – even in those for which rule of law concerns are currently not relevant, as there is always the possibility that in the future the new mechanism could be applied to any member state. First, the criteria for identifying a generalized deficiency have not been

154 In this context the Commission has proposed to consider the European Semester's Country-Specific Recommendations for the design and programming of the funds (European Commission 2018s).

155 See also Chapter 1 for more details on this proposal.

156 Kölling (2017: 4) notes the missing legal basis between specific conditionalities and financial support and that "there is no explicit treaty mandate for conditionality spending".

defined, yet. As Kölling (2017: 5) points out, "conditionality must rest on objective factors which are amenable to judicial review including, in particular, the aim and the content of the measure". This is certainly not the case in the proposed mechanism, which, thus, contains a high risk for member states if they would agree. The Commission's proposal simply acknowledges that the "assessment could be based on the information from all available sources and recognised institutions, including judgments of the Court of Justice of the European Union, reports of the Court of Auditors, and conclusions and recommendations of relevant international organisations and networks, such as the bodies of the Council of Europe and the European networks of supreme courts and councils for the judiciary" (European Commission 2018g: indent 12).

Secondly, the use of "reverse qualified majority" – which is not foreseen in the Treaty and is only used under the Excessive Deficit Procedure of the Stability and Growth Pact – as the decision-making procedure could be interpreted as a "power grab" by the Commission undermining the legislative prerogative of the Council.[157] It is certainly not in interest of member states that the Commission decides in a rather independent manner when and on which member states to launch this new instrument based on yet still unknown criteria. Agreement of member states on such an instrument is likely to be conditional upon a change of the decision-making rules and the provision of a set of clearly defined criteria when to trigger the mechanism.

Revised co-financing rules are another potential source of change in the post-2020 MFF. In normative terms, "larger national contributions might improve project selection, ownership and the management of these funds" (Claeys/Darvas 2018). However, the proposed change of co-financing rules is likely to meet resistance as a change would significantly affect the net position of individual member states, in particular in those where regions are at the brink of moving from a less developed status to a transition status (for example, the Baltic countries). In these countries the national financial contribution for projects under the European Regional Development Fund and the European Social Fund would rise from 15% to

157 In general, the Commission seems to seek greater control over EU spending, "reflected in the proposed shift from shared management to central management of funding, and greater influence for the Commission services in areas such as the European Semester, application of the proposed conditionality on the rule of law, and the introduction of structural reform programmes" (Bachtler et al. 2018: 5).

45%. At the same time member states would fall under new, stricter conditionality rules (see above).

Due to higher co-financing rates in combination with funding cuts in cohesion policy for a number of EU-13 countries (including the Baltic countries), compensation might be sought through a territorialisation of programmes that so far did not – or just to a very limited extent – apply such a criteria, such as the EU's research and innovation funding programme. A further softening of the principle that research and innovation funding must be based on excellence in favour of geographical criteria is likely to meet strong resistance of economically and scientifically stronger member states (usually net-payers) in the North.

However, the cleavage line is fuzzy and does not clearly run between net-payers and net-receivers in this case. As some net-payers (i.e. Austria, Belgium, Finland, the Netherlands, Sweden) will gain from the envisaged reform of cohesion policy (Bachtler et al. 2018), the traditional front of scientifically strong member states against softening the excellence principle in research and innovation policy might not be closed. France and Germany might find themselves separated from the other net-payers, being those countries losing from the cohesion policy reform, on the one hand, and, being confronted with a group of former allies that could be willing to trade their guaranteed advantages in cohesion policy for a softened excellence principle, on the other hand.

In sum, the likelihood for change of instruments and priorities is much higher than at the structural level. Member states have to use the micro-level to calibrate their future policies as they prefer to keep the overall framework (i.e. the macro-level) stable. Negotiations on programmes or instruments are more technical and specialized and less politicized, thus leaving more leeway for potential change and adaptation to new priorities (usually called "policy reforms") for actors. Issues of timing and constraints of European or national politics, therefore, play a much lesser role that at the structural level.

# 10. Conclusions: three worlds of European disintegration and the role of the long-term budget

## *10.1 Disintegration as an empirical phenomenon*

Given the political context in which the new MFF is negotiated as well as the changes and dynamics of the cleavage structure that impact on the negotiation process, we consider a comprehensive reform of the post-2020 budget not very likely. Claims for significant changes are inadequately justified as they often lack recognition of the stabilizing function of the framework's complex institutional structure, especially in times of uncertainty. We argue that potential outcomes of the MFF negotiations have to be evaluated primarily against two key requirements.

First, the multiannual financial framework has to reinforce the EU's problem-solving capacity in areas of integration that are largely undisputed. This holds especially for the functioning and integrity of the single market and its supporting policies (such as environmental policy, trade and competition policy, as well as infrastructural policies like energy and transport, etc.), but also for the main expenditure programmes, because they do not only support common measures in the fields of agriculture, regional development or research and innovation. Rather, these are the EU policies that organize financial compensations across member states and thus are an expression of solidarity among them. This first requirement concerns the structural level of the MFF, the financing and the revenue side as well as expenditures, either investment-related or (re-)distributive. Therefore, we find already sufficient reasons to assume that any reform of the budget will be – at best – of incremental instead of radical nature.

As we have seen, the Commission's proposal for the post-2020 budget made a clear choice in favour of stabilizing the existing large expenditure programmes. They have to face significant cuts as they assume a stronger financial involvement of the member states, both for net-payers and net-recipients. The "new European challenges", however, would be from the beginning clearly under-funded especially if the member states would refuse to increase the overall MFF budget ceiling. One could criticise the Commission (as many will certainly do) for a lack of ambition. The question is, however, what political room for manoeuvre the Commission actually had. As always, the European Parliament, a number of member states as well as NGOs and civil society groups came forward with the expected reactions, arguing that the next budget has to provide funding for this and that at least at the level of the current MFF. Hardly any of the statements presented show any willingness to support a re-orientation of the EU's policies towards the new challenges. The responsibility for a less ambitious post-2020 budget is spread again on many shoulders. While the MFF 2021-2027 is therefore a reasonable answer to the first requirement it remains to be seen as to what extent it offers solution for the second one.

Secondly, the post-2020 MFF needs to be an efficient instrument targeting the various dimensions of European disintegration. We have already referred to the multi-dimensional crisis phenomena with which the European Union is currently confronted. We have also argued that crises are certainly not a new aspect in the process of European integration. In recent years, however, these crises phenomena have assumed a new quality as they put into question earlier achievements of the integration process. This second requirement may indeed evoke dynamics for more substantial change, because political actors may become aware of certain strategies or policies that do not work anymore. For that reason, it is important to understand the nature of disintegration and to clearly distinguish between its causes and its effects.

There is, firstly, a process of socio-economic disintegration as member states (and regions within member states), despite the billions of European public investments that have been made over the last decades, are further drifting apart in terms of their economic capacity and their level of social welfare. Economic disintegration is also mirrored by the fact that intra-European trade (meaning the importance of the single market) is decreasing for many member states with above-average economic performance while it is the main market especially for some of the member state with a less developed economy.[158] Even much deeper economic integration through a common currency does not automatically provide for a stronger linking-up of European economies. As O'Neill and Terzi (2014: 26) have shown in their analysis of trade patterns of Euro member states, Germany and Italy will export more goods and services to emerging and developing countries in 2020 than to other Euro countries while the opposite trend can be assumed for Belgium, France, Spain, and the Netherlands. Socio-economic disintegration has political consequences which became appar-

158 Eurostat (2018): EU-intra trade in goods – recent trends, see: https://ec.europa.eu/eurostat/statistics-explained/index.php/Intra-EU_trade_in_goods_-_recent_trends (accessed 5 February 2019).

ent when the Heads of States and Governments of 17 member states signed a letter for the 2019 Spring European Council in which they formulated priorities for the strengthening of the European Single Market. It is remarkable that France, Germany and Italy (which have the three largest economies in the EU-27) did not sign this initiative.[159] There is also growing tension among EU institutions and member states on a relaunch of negotiations for an EU-U.S. trade agreement. Attempts to conclude a negotiation mandate for the European Commission have been contested by the French government and the European Parliament while the German government, having in mind the interests of its main export industries, strongly supports a new agreement.[160]

In terms of socioeconomic disintegration, the Commission's proposal has indeed something to offer. The definition of new, and limited, objectives for the regional and cohesion policy may support a more coherent development of regions across Europe in the direction of a "greener, innovative and carbon-free" economy. This approach seems to be more promising than infrastructure investments and company subsidies that mainly characterized the regional policy in the past. And it did not perform overwhelmingly good in terms of its contribution to economic and social cohesion. In this respect, the beginning of a "phasing-out" of the cohesion fund is a step in the right direction. The opposite holds for the future Union's research and innovation policy. The proposal for Horizon Europe offers hardly anything new as there is again the danger that it – in the end – becomes a victim of the budget fight. The uncertainty about the future relations between the EU and the United Kingdom is another problem. Being a strong supporter and profiteer of the research and innovation policies in the past, an ongoing UK's participation (in a certain form of association to Horizon Europe) would apparently stabilize the programme. Without the

159 "Preparing the March European Council. The future development of the Single Market and European digital policy in view of preparation for the next Strategic Agenda", Letter signed by the Heads of State and Governments of Belgium, Croatia, the Czech Republic, Denmark, Estonia, Finland, Ireland, Latvia, Lithuania, Luxembourg, Malta, the Netherlands, Poland, Portugal, Slovakia, Slovenia, and Sweden to the President of the European Council, 26 February 2019.

160 See "Parliament rejects opening trade talks with Trump", Euractiv, 14 March 2019, https://www.euractiv.com/section/economy-jobs/news/parliament-rejects-opening-trade-talks-with-trump/ and "France maintains blockade to opening EU-US trade negotiations", Euractiv, 3 April 2019, https://www.euractiv.com/section/economy-jobs/news/france-maintains-blockade-to-opening-eu-us-trade-negotiations/ (both accessed 4 April 2019).

UK, there is an eminent danger that the research and innovation policies could come under increasing pressure to support cohesion instead of excellence.

Secondly, the European Union faces territorial disintegration. This is apparently most visible in the Brexit case, in which – for the first time in integration history – a member state applied for termination of EU membership (see Chapter 4). Territorial disintegration has, however, assumed another characteristic in form of renewed dynamics of subnational mobilization, especially visible in initiatives for greater autonomy or even independence in Scotland, Catalonia, Flanders, South Tyrol, Lombardy and Veneto. As European integration progresses, the subnational level of member states has become more and more an addressee of European legislation but also an actor in policy formulation and decision-making. While European legislation cannot give much consideration to which state level is responsible for the relevant regulatory aspect, regional actors in specific policy areas (in particular in regional and environmental policy) are actively involved in policy-making at European level, although the EU Treaty makes no provision for that.

The fundamental problem of subnational mobilization in the European multi-level system is the heterogeneity of the regional structure. Basically, regional actors exist within federal member states (Austria, Belgium, Germany), within regionalized member states (Great Britain, Italy, Spain) and within decentralized states (Denmark, France, Finland, the Netherlands, and Sweden). It is noticeable that conflicts over autonomy and independence predominantly occur in the group of regionalized member states. There are reasons for this. In the federal systems, political conflicts over the involvement of the regional level in European politics were largely solved in the first half of the 1990s with constitutional reforms providing for comprehensive participation rights within the national and the European context. In decentralized member states, there is a lack of institutional preconditions at the regional level, but in most cases also a lack of political motivation of regional actors. That is why initiatives at the local level are more common in these cases.

Regionalized member states have the specific problem that they are generally denied full participation rights, but they are affected by European rulemaking in areas of their autonomy. In times of increasing economic competition, this is also problematic in a transnational perspective, because regions have much less to say in European politics than member states with a comparable size of population and economic power. Therefore, it is hardly surprising that autonomy and independence initiatives have gained momentum especially after the financial crisis of 2008 and primarily in regions with an above-average economic performance.

The European level generally assigns the responsibility for solving conflicts over regional autonomy or independence to the member states concerned. This is understandable, because the European Union has a constitutional obligation to respect the national identity of its member states, which is "reflected in their fundamental political and constitutional structures, including regional and local self-government" (Art. 4(2) TEU). Nevertheless, this "restraint" poses considerable problems for the integration process. Wherever regions already have substantial participation rights in European policy-making, they can, on the one hand, easily assume veto positions against strategic European projects (as the example of the attempt of the Parliament of Wallonia to prevent Belgium's approval of the EU-Canada Free Trade Agreement in 2016 impressively showed). On the other hand, where such opportunities for participation do not exist (currently in Catalonia and Scotland, in particular), there is an imminent risk that the economic and social costs of lengthy autonomy conflicts will ultimately have to be borne by all member states, especially if the respective country is a member of the European Monetary Union.

The European Union has yet not found a convincing institutional solution for the involvement of the subnational level into the integration process. Their participation in the formulation and implementation of EU funding programs can hardly compensate for the loss of legislative autonomy. The Committee of the Regions, established in 1994, is clearly underdeveloped, at least from the perspective of regions with legislative powers. Due to its heterogeneous structure, representing both regional and local interests, and its merely advisory role it is an ineffective instrument for the representation of interests.

Territorial disintegration mainly refers to constitutional problems that can be solved to a very limited extent by budgetary means. Nevertheless, the post-2020 MFF proposal provides for some measures which could have a calming effect on territorial disintegration. Both the agricultural policy as well as the regional and cohesion policy will put more responsibility to member states and regions in implementing the respective programmes. That allows, in principle, for strategies that are more linked with the specific needs at the domestic level. This would require, however, that member states invest in these policies by compensating reduced EU-cofinancing shares and/or by making use of the flexibility options that exist for shifting funds to programme pillars that promote regional development.

Thirdly, there is political disintegration that has emerged in two variants: as increasing divergence of interests about internal EU policies but also in view of the strategic positioning of the European Union in global affairs. Undoubtedly, there is a growing number of cases in which EU member states' governments disagree on (and pursue "national interest-based agendas" in) key policy issues that are of strategic importance for the future of the European Union.

In energy policy, for example, Germany is currently the only member state that has implemented a comprehensive strategy to abolish in the foreseeable future both nuclear and coal-based power generation. Given that the share of renewable energy will not exceed 40% of the overall energy production, natural gas is likely to be the country's most important energy source by 2040. Germany has, however, only very limited natural gas resources and therefore has to import roughly 90% of its total consumption. In order to guarantee sufficient supply from Russia, which is by far the most important import country, the German government supports an infrastructure project ("North Stream 2") through which natural gas is delivered directly to Germany via a pipeline in the Baltic Sea. The project has met considerable resistance from Baltic countries, Poland and Denmark, the European Commission and France, even though a French company has a significant share in the North Stream consortium. Strategically, the project is hardly compatible with the establishment of a single European energy market. On the contrary, the German government exerted enormous political pressure on the European Commission, but also on other member states, in order to make sure that European energy market regulations apply to the North Stream project only under very specific circumstances.

In trade and economic policy, the European Union is currently reviewing basic principles for its bilateral relations with China. There is a growing concern that a "more balanced and reciprocal conditions governing the economic relationship" is needed (European Commission & High Representative of the Union for Foreign Affairs and Security Policy 2019: 1). Given China's increasing power and economic role, the European Union has acknowledged that "neither the EU nor any of its member states can effectively achieve their aims with China without full unity. In cooperation with China, all member states [...] have a responsibility to ensure consistency with EU law, rules and policies" (ibid.: 2). The claim for unity and consistency is, however, not necessarily shared by all member states. With its "New Silk Road Initiative" (also called the "Belt and Road Initiative", BRI), China has quite successfully driven a wedge between EU member states. Already in 2012, China invited 11 EU member states and five candidate countries from South and Central Europe to establish the "16+1 platform" aimed at joint planning of transcontinental infrastructure projects. Since then, three more EU member states aligned with the BRI initiative: Greece in August 2018, Portugal in January 2019 and Italy in March 2019. Especially the Italian engagement into a comprehensive memorandum of understanding with China provoked some outrage among EU partners. German foreign minister Heiko Maas, for example, warned Italy that countries that believe "they do clever business with the Chinese will wonder when they suddenly weak up in dependency".[161] The German EU budget commissioner Günther Oettinger even called for an EU veto on the Italy-China deal, in order to prevent, "that infrastructure of strategic importance like power networks, rapid rail lines or harbours are no longer in European but in Chinese hands".[162]

Political disintegration also has occurred in more general terms in view of the need to reform the European Union. At first sight, different positions on constitutional reforms seem to indicate a considerable weakening of the Franco-German axis which always played a significant role in pushing European integration forward. Since 2017, French President Emmanuel Macron has repeatedly called for comprehensive steps to further develop the Eurozone, a "Social Europe" and the EU's foreign and security policy. The German reaction has always been at best lukewarm. Closer inspection, however, reveals that there is not much support for Macron's agenda even outside Germany. In March 2018, the finance ministers of Denmark, Estonia, Finland, Ireland, Latvia, Lithuania, the Netherlands and Sweden wrote a joint letter in which they clearly dismissed Macron's plans for a deepening of the currency union. Austrian chancellor Sebastian Kurz along with the party leader of the German Christian Democratic Party, Annegret Kramp-Karrenbauer (a likely candidate for the succession of Chancellor Angela Merkel), issued strong criticism on plans to intensify integration in the field of social policy (without explicit reference to Macron's ideas for a common European social security framework or a European minimum wage regulation).[163]

161 See "Einige lachen über uns", Welt am Sonntag, 24 March 2019.

162 See "Oettinger calls for EU veto on Italy-China deal", Euractiv, 25 March 2019, https://www.euractiv.com/section/eu-china/news/oettinger-calls-for-eu-veto-on-italy-china-deal/ (accessed 25 March 2019).

163 See Sebastian Kurz: "Europa wirkt satt, selbstzufrieden und träge", Die Welt, 14 March 2019; Annegret Kramp-Karrenbauer: „Europa jetzt richtig machen", Die Welt, 10 March 2019.

Last but not least, the severe conflict over a coordinated European migration policy (see Chapter 4) constitutes a unique and unprecedented example of divergent interests and actions of member states that goes far beyond "normal" disputes over EU policies. In the past, the problem of unwillingness of a limited number of member states to participate in a common European policy was solved by offering an opting-out that allowed a majority to go on while few countries abstained. Opting-out solutions were used, inter alia, for the Schengen Agreement (in terms of Denmark, Ireland and the UK), for membership in the Eurozone (in terms of Denmark and the UK) or for the application of the EU's Charter of Fundamental Rights (in terms of Poland and the UK). In the case of migration policy, however, member states did not back off from a denial of implementation of a distribution mechanism for asylum seekers, a unilateral suspension of the Dublin regulation, the prolongation of border controls and from putting common measures on the shelf, such as the expansion of the Frontex operational staff until 2027. This case, therefore, illustrates both the limits of integration as well as the risk of disintegration. Limits of integration increasingly exist when measures taken at the European level impact heavily on political competition and conflicts within the national political systems of EU member states. A risk of disintegration emerges if such a measure would be needed to stabilize elements of integration that have already been achieved. In this respect, the failure to agree on a common European migration policy certainly poses a danger for the functioning of the European Area of Freedom, Security and Justice, and – in the end – even for free movement of people within the single market.

The post-2020 MFF will most probably fail to contain the problem of political disintegration. While the future challenges receive limited budgetary support, new instruments, such as the rule-of-law conditionality could even amplify the discord among member states. This could become evident after the May 2019 elections to the European Parliament. Up to now, the Parliament did not contribute much in favour of far-reaching reforms of the EU's budget, but it has always been a strong voice in terms of providing the EU with the needed financial resources for policies the Parliament considered to have a clear European added value. Depending on the result of the election, this voice could fade thus making it easier for member states (especially the net-payers) to refuse the EU the fresh money which is required to finance the new challenges.

## *10.2 The potential of the post-2020 MFF to counter disintegration*

As said before, we are well aware that a prevention of disintegration will not be possible by utilizing budgetary means only. However, given that the post-2020 MFF will define the EU's policy and spending priorities for a considerable number of years and taking also into account that mid-term revisions of a multiannual financial framework never have produced significant changes to the original structure, we can still argue that the next financial perspective will have an enormous impact on how Europe will face the current crises.

In this respect, the delay of the Brexit until 31 October 2019 has to be taken into account as an event that could impact on the budget negotiations in an unforeseeable way. On 10 December 2018, the European Court of Justice had already ruled that the UK is free to revoke unilaterally its withdrawal from the European Union (Court of Justice of the European Union 2019). Due to a lack of a majority for the ratification of the Withdrawal Agreement in the House of Commons, the British government had to ask the European Council twice for a prolongation of the exit date. On 11 April 2019 a Special European Council decided to provide another extension (European Council 2019). The UK may leave the EU at any time after successful ratification, but the extension will be no longer than end of October. Without doubt, this relatively long time-span could support new dynamics in the British domestic Brexit discussion, especially since the country is obliged to hold elections to the European Parliament in May 2019 if the UK is still a member state. Even a revocation of the Brexit has to be taken into consideration which could be the result of national elections or a second referendum. In this case, the consequences for the post-2020 MFF would be significant. There would be no need any more for net-payers to compensate for the missing British contribution. The dualism between net-payers and net-recipients could be reinforced. And any discussion about a phasing-out of rebates and correction mechanisms would be choked before they had even started.

Against this background, we find that the overall MFF structure will largely stay confirming its change-resistant and path-dependent nature especially in terms of the budget ceiling, its operational duration, the budget lines, and the structure of the revenues.

At the instrumental level, the MFF has always shown more flexibility over the last decades and it will continue to do so. With every new MFF a few new instruments have been introduced, some policy and programme objectives have changed, and programmes were re-named, merged, or moved between budget lines. The major expenditure programmes – such as agriculture, regional development and cohesion, as well as research and innovation – continued to exist (independent of whether the respective policy undergoes a reform or not). This will not change with the post-2020 MFF.

Given that, incremental adjustment and adaption to new challenges describes best the potential changes for the future budget. Far-reaching innovations, such as a provision of significant resources for totally new policy priorities would require either a significant increase of national contributions and/or a re-definition of established financing instruments in form of more public-public a or public-private co-financing arrangements. We do not see this happen to a substantial degree nor do we consider significant changes of the EU's own resource system very likely.

This does not mean that incremental reform is not a sufficient way to address the problem of disintegration. With its change-resistant nature, the post-2020 MFF meets our first requirement as it helps to stabilize the undisputed achievements of European integration. In terms of the various forms of disintegration, the European Union certainly has to proof the added-value of common and coordinated action. Sufficient financial resources are important for that, but it is often at least equally important how the money is spent. That is why there are always two well-known performances during the "theatre-season". The first one, mainly performed by the European Parliament and the Commission, claims that the EU's problem-solving capacity mostly depends on the amount of money that is available for European policies. The second play is given by (net-payer-) member states arguing that there is more than enough money on the table which could, however, be used in a much smarter way. It would come as a surprise if we would have to miss them during the post-2020 budget negotiation period.

# References


Aksoy, Deniz (2010), Who gets what, when, and how revisited: Voting and proposal powers in the allocation of the EU budget, in: European Union Politics, 11(2), pp. 171-194.

Anderson, Charles (1978), The Logic of Public Problems. Evaluation in Comparative Policy Research, in: Ashford, Douglas E. (ed.): Comparing Public Policies. New Concepts and Methods, Beverly Hills: Sage, pp. 19-43.

Angeloni, Chiara/Merler, Silvia/Wolff, Guntram B. (2012), Policy Lessons from the Eurozone Crisis, in: The International Spectator, 47(4), pp. 17-34.

Arnull, Anthony (2007), Me and My Shadow: The European Court of Justice and the Disintegration of European Union Law, in: Fordham International Law Journal 31(5), pp. 1173-1210.

Arthur, Brian W. (1994), Increasing Returns and Path Dependence in the Economy, Ann Arbor: University of Michigan Press.

Auer, Stefan (2014), The Limits of Transnational Solidarity and the Eurozone Crisis in Germany, Ireland and Slovakia, in: Perspectives on European Politics and Society, 15(3), pp. 322-334.

Bachtler, John/Mendez, Carlos/Wishlade, Fiona (2018), Ambitious and pragmatic? First reflctions on the reform of cohesion policy, European Policies Research Centre, Delft/Strathclyde.

Bachtler, John/Mendez, Carlo/Wishlade, Fiona (2019), Reforming the MFF and Cohesion Policy 2021-27: pragmatic drift or paradigmatic shift?, European Policy Research Paper No. 107, University of Strathclyde Publishing, January 2019.

Baldwin, Richard/Giavazzi, Francesco (2017), The Eurozone crisis: A consensus view of the causes and a few possible solutions, available at: http://voxeu.org/article/eurozone-crisis-consensus-view-causes-and-few-possible-solutions (accessed 8 November 2017).

Barker, Alex (2017), The €60 billion Brexit bill: How to disentangle Britain from the EU budget, Center for European Reform, London.

Barnier, Michel (2017), Press statement by Michel Barnier following the fifth round of Article 50 negotiations with the United Kingdom, 12 October 2017, Brussels.

Beauregard, Robert A./Pierre, Jon (2000), Disputing the Global: A Sceptical View of Locality-based International Initiatives, in: Policy and Politics 28(4), pp. 465-78.

Becker, Peter (2014), Lost in Stagnation: The EU's Next Multiannual Financial Framework (2014–2020) and the Power of the Status Quo, SWP Research Paper 14, Berlin: SWP.

Becker, Peter (2017), Der Brexit und die Folgen für den Europäischen Haushalt, Schriftliche Stellungnahme zur öffentlichen Anhörung des Ausschusses für die Angelegenheiten der Europäischen Union des Deutschen Bundestages, 24 April 2017, Berlin.

Begg, Iain (2007), The 2008/9 EU Budget Review, EU-Consent EU-Budget Working Paper No. 3.

Begg, Iain (2017), The EU budget after 2020, SIEPS European Policy Analysis, Issue 2017: 9, Stockholm.

Begg, Iain (2018), Plus ça change…the Commission's budget proposals for 2021-27, ETUI Policy Brief, N° 9/2018, Brussels.

Begg, Iain/Heinemann, Friedrich (2006), New Budget, Old Dilemmas, London: Centre for European Reform.

Bendel, Petra (2017), EU Refugee Policy in Crisis: Blockades, Decisions, Solutions, Politics for Europe Project, Bonn: Friedrich-Ebert-Stiftung.

Benedetto, Giacomo (2012), Budgetary Reform and the Lisbon Treaty, in: Benedetto, Giacomo/Milio, Simona (eds), European Union Budget Reform: Institutions, Policy and Economic Crisis, Basingstoke: Palgrave MacMillan, pp. 40-58.

Biscop, Sven (2016), The EU Global Strategy: Realpolitik with European Characteristics, Egmont Royal Institute for International Relations, Security Policy Brief No 75, June 2016, Brussels.

Blankart, Charles B./Köster, Gerrit B. (2009), Refocusing the EU Budget: An Institutional View, Working paper 2009:16, Basel: Crema.

Blavoukos, Spyros/Pagoulatos, George (2011), Accounting for coalition-building in the European Union: Budget negotiations and the south, in: European Journal of Political Research, 50(4), pp. 559–581.

Bosco, Anna/Verney, Susannah (2016), From Electoral Epidemic to Government Epidemic: The Next Level of the Crisis in Southern Europe, in: South European Society and Politics, 21(4), pp. 383-406.

Buananno, Laurie (2017), The European Migration Crisis, in: Dinan, Desmond/Nugent, Neil/Paterson, William E. (eds), The European Union in Crisis, London: Palgrave MacMillan, pp. 100-130.

Buti, Marco/Carnot, Nicholas (2012), The EMU Debt Crisis: Early Lessons and Reforms, in: Journal of Common Market Studies, 50(6), pp. 899–911.

Cantwell, John (1999), Innovation as the principal source of growth in the global economy, in: Archibugi, Daniele/Howells, Jeremy/Michie, Jonathan (eds), Innovation policy in a global economy, Cambridge: Cambridge University Press, pp. 225-241.

Cipriani, Gabriele (2007), Rethinking the EU Budget: Three Unavoidable Reforms, Brussels: CEPS.

Cipriani, Gabriele (2014), Financing the EU budget: moving forward or backwards?, London, Rowman & Littlfield.

Citi, Manuele (2013), EU budgetary dynamics: incremental or punctuated equilibrium?, in : Journal of European Public Policy, 20(8), pp. 1157-1173.

Citi, Manuele (2015), European Union budget politics: Explaining stability and change in spending allocations, in : European Union Politics, 16(2), pp. 262–280.

Claeys, Grégory/Darvas, Zsolt (2018), The Commission's proposal for the next MFF: A glass half-full, Bruegel Blog-Post, 25 May 2018, available at: http://bruegel.org/2018/05/the-commissions-proposal-for-the-next-mff-a-glass-half-full (accessed 22 August 2018).

Collignon, Stefan (2011), The Governance of European Public Goods, in: Tarschys, Daniel (ed), The EU Budget: What Should Go In? What Should Go Out?, Stockholm: Swedish Institute for European Policy Studies, pp. 42-57.

Commission of the European Communities (1981), Scientific and technical research in the European Community – Proposals for the 1980s, COM(81) 574 final, 12 October 1981, Brussels.

Commission of the European Communities (1985), European Regional Development Fund. Tenth Annual Report (1984), COM(85) 516 final, 04 October 1985, Brussels.

Commission of the European Communities (1986), The Science and Technology Community – Guidelines for a new Community Framework Programme of technological research and development 1987-1991, COM(86) 129 final, 17 March 1986, Brussels.

Committee of the Regions (2018), Opinion on the Multiannual Financial Framework package for the years 2021-2017, COTER-VI/042, 10 October 2018, Brussels.

Copsey, Nathaniel (2015), Rethinking the European Union, Basingstoke: MacMillan Palgrave.

Correa, Ricardo/Sapriza, Horacio (2014), Sovereign Debt Crises, International Finance Discussion Papers 1104, Board of Governors of the Federal Reserve System, Washington.

Council of the European Union (2002), Council Regulation (EC) No 332/2002 of 18 February 2002 establishing a facility providing medium-term financial assistance for Member States' balances of payments, Official Journal of the European Union, L 53, 23 February 2002.

Council of the European Union (2003), Council Regulation (EC) No 343/2003 of 18 February 2003 establishing the criteria and mechanisms for determining the Member State responsible for examining an asylum application lodged in one of the Member States by a third-country national, Official Journal of the European Union, L 50, 25 February 2003, pp. 1-10.

Council of the European Union (2005), Financial Perspective 2007-2013. Doc. 15915/05, 19 December 2005.

Council of the European Union (2010a), Conclusions on Innovation Union for Europe, 26 November 2010, Brussels.

Council of the European Union (2010b), Council Regulation (EU) No 407/2010 of 11 May 2010 establishing a European financial stabilisation mechanism, OJ L 118, 12 May 2010.

Council of the European Union (2011a), Council Implementing Decision of 7 December 2010 on granting Union financial assistance to Ireland, Official Journal of the European Union, L 30, 4 February 2011.

Council of the European Union (2011b), Council Implementing Decision of 30 May 2011 on granting Union financial assistance to Portugal, Official Journal of the European Union, L 159, 17 June 2011.

Council of the European Union (2013a), Council Decision establishing the specific programme implementing Horizon 2020 - the Framework Programme for Research and Innovation (2014-2020) and repealing Decisions 2006/971/EC, 2006/972/EC, 2006/973/EC, 2006/974/EC and 2006/975/EC, Official Journal of the European Union L 347, 20 December, pp. 965-1041.

Council of the European Union (2013b), 3276th Council meeting, Competitiveness (Internal Market, Industry, Research and Space), 17141/1/13 REV 1, Press Release, Brussels, 2/3 December 2013.

Council of the European Union (2014), Council Decision of 26 May 2014 on the system of own resources of the European Union, OJ L 168, 7 June 2014, pp. 105-111.

Council of the European Union (2015a), Statement on Banking Union and bridge financing arrangements for the Single Resolution Fund, Press Release, 884/15, 8 December 2015.

Council of the European Union (2015b), Council Decision (EU) 2015/1523 of 14 September 2015 establishing provisional measures in the area of international protection for the benefit of Italy and of Greece, Official Journal of the European Union, L 239, 15 September 2015, p. 146.

Council of the European Union (2015c), Council Decision (EU) 2015/1601 establishing provisional measures in the area of international protection for the benefit of Italy and Greece, Official Journal of the European Union, L 248, 24 September 2015, pp. 80-94.

Council of the European Union (2016), Conclusions on a Roadmap to complete the Banking Union, Press Release, 353/16, 17 June 2016.

Council of the European Union (2017a), Outcome of the Council Meeting, 3552nd Council meeting, General Affairs Council, 10502/17, Luxembourg, 20 June 2017.

Council of the European Union (2017b), The Rome Declaration, Declaration of the leaders of the 27 member states, the European Parliament and the European Commission, Presse Release, 149/17, Brussels, 25 March 2017.

Council of the European Union (2017c), The Rome Declaration, Presse Release, 149/17, 25 March 2017.

Council of the European Union (2017d), Good Friday Agreement and Peace Process, Information Note from Ireland to the Article 50 Working Party, XT 21055/17, Brussels, 7 September 2017.

Council of the European Union (2017e), Common Travel Area, Information Note from Ireland to the Article 50 Working Party, XT 21056/17, Brussels, 7 September 2017.

Council of the European Union (2017f), Directives for the negotiation of an agreement with the United Kingdom of Great Britain and Northern Ireland setting out the arrangements for its withdrawal from the European Union, 22 May 2017.

Council of the European Union (2017g), Council conclusions on the strategic approach to resilience in the EU's external action, 14191/17, 13 November 2017, Brussels.

Council of the European Union (2017h), Council Decision (CFSP) establishing Permanent Structured Cooperation (PESCO) and determining the list of Participating Member States, Official Journal of the European Union, L 331, 14.12.2017, pp. 57-77.

Council of the European Union (2017i), Outcome of the Council Meeting, 3552nd Council meeting, General Affairs Council, 10502/17, Luxembourg, 20 June 2017.

Council of the European Union (2018a), Political declaration setting out the framework for the future relationship between the European Union and the United Kingdom, doc. XT 21095/18, 22 November, Brussels.

Council of the European Union (2018b), Multiannual Financial Framework (2021-2027) : State of play, doc. 11871/18, 10 September, Brussels.

Court of Justice of the European Union (2019), The United Kingdom is free to revoke unilaterally the notification of its intention to withdraw from the EU, Press Release 191/18, 10 December 2018, Luxembourg.

Danell, Torbjörn/Östhol, Anders (2008), The EU Long-term Budget. Reform and New Priorities, Östersund: Swedish Institute for Growth Policy Studies.

David, Paul (1985), Clio and the Economics of QWERTY, in: American Economic Review 75, pp. 332-337.

De Feo, Alfredo (2017), The European Budget: Motor or Brake of European Integration? A Walk through 40 Years of Budgetary Decisions, in: Becker, Peter/Bauer, Michael W./De Feo, Alfredo (eds), The New Politics of the European Union Budget, Baden-Baden: Nomos, pp. 33-82.

den Hertog, Leonhard (2016), Money Talks: Mapping the funding for EU external migration policy, CEPS Papers in Liberty and Security in Europe, No. 95 / November 2016, Brussels.

Deutscher Bundestag (2010), Stenografischer Bericht, 42. Sitzung, Plenarprotokoll 17/42, 19. Mai 2010, Berlin.

Deutscher Bundestag (2017), Gesetz über die Feststellung des Bundeshaushaltsplans für das Haushaltsjahr 2017 (Haushaltsgesetz 2017), 20 December 2016, BGBl. 1.

De Wilde, Pieter/Zürn, Michael (2012), Can the Politicization of European Integration Be Reversed?, in: Journal of Common Market Studies, 50(1), pp. 137-153.

Diamond, Patrick/Liddle, Roger/Sage, Daniel (2015), The social reality of Europe after the crisis: trends, challenges and responses, London: Rowman & Littlefield.

Dinan, Desmond (2017), Crises in EU History, in: Dinan, Desmond/Nugent, Neill/Paterson, William E. (eds), The European Union in Crisis, London: Palgrave, pp. 16-32.

Døhlie Saltnes, Johanne (2018), Why the debate over the European Development Fund is a question of politics, available at: http://blogs.lse.ac.uk/europpblog/2018/06/29/why-the-debate-over-the-european-development-fund-is-a-question-of-politics (accessed 13 August 2018).

Draghi, Mario (2012), Speech at the Global Investment Conference in London, 26 July 2012, available at: http://www.ecb.int/press/key/date/2012/html/sp120726.en.html (accessed 16 November 2017).

Elera, Álvaro de (2006) The European Research Area: On the Way towards a European Scientific Community?, in: European Law Journal, 12(5), pp. 559-574.

Enderlein, Henrik/Letta, Enrico/Asmussen, Jörg/Boone, Laurence/De Geus, Aart/Lamy, Pascal/Maystadt, Philippe/Rodrigues, Maria João/Tumpel-Gugerell, Gertrude/Vitorino, António (2016), Repair and Prepare: Growth and the Euro after Brexit, Gütersloh/Berlin/Paris: Bertelsmann Stiftung/Jacques Delors Institut.

EPSC (2015), The Euro Plus Pact: How Integration into the EU Framework can Give New Momentum for Structural Reforms in the Euro Area, EPSC Strategic Notes, Issue 3 / 2015, Brussels.

Euro2030 (2014), Towards a true European Investment Fund, available at: http://fr.euro2030.eu/upload/euro2030-towards-true-european-investment-fund.pdf (accessed 13 June 2018).

European Central Bank (2012), Technical Features of Outright Monetary Transactions, 6 September 2012, available at: http://www.ecb.int/press/pr/date/2012/html/pr120906_1.en.html (accessed 16 November 2017).

European Central Bank (2014), Decision ECB/2014/34 of 29 July 2014 on measures relating to targeted longer-term refinancing operations, Frankfurt, ECB.

European Central Bank (2015), ECB announces expanded asset purchase programme, 22 January 2015, available at: https://www.ecb.europa.eu/press/pr/date/2015/html/pr150122_1.en.html (accessed 16 November 2017).

European Central Bank (2016), Decision ECB/2016/10 of 28 April 2016 on a second series of targeted longer-term refinancing operations, Frankurt, ECB.

European Central Bank (2017), Monetary Policy Decisions, Press Release, 26 October 2017, available at: https://www.ecb.europa.eu/press/pr/date/2017/html/ecb.mp171026.en.html (accessed 16 November 2017).

European Commission (1997), Five-year assessment of the European Community RTD framework programmes, Brussels: European Commission.

European Commission (2000) Towards a European Research Area, COM(2000) 6 final, Brussels, 18 January 2000.

European Commission (2002), The 6th Framework Programme in brief, Brussels: European Commission.

European Commission (2004), Building our common future. Policy challenges and Budgetary means of the Enlarged Union 2007-2013, COM(2004) 101 final, Brussels, 26 February 2004.

European Commission (2008), A European Economic Recovery Plan, COM(2008)800 final, 26 November 2008, Brussels.

European Commission (2010a) The EU Budget Review, COM(2010) 700 final, 19 October 2010, Brussels.

European Commission (2010b), Communication from the Commission to the Council and the Economic and Financial Committee on the European Financial Stabilisation Mechanism, COM(2010) 713, 30 November 2010, Brussels.

European Commission (2010c), Europe 2020 - A strategy for smart, sustainable and inclusive growth, COM(2010) 2020 final, 3 March 2010, Brussels.

European Commission (2010d), Europe 2020 Flagship Initiative Innovation Union, COM(2010) 546 final, 6 October 2010, Brussels.

European Commission (2010e), Interim Evaluation of the Seventh Framework Programme Report of the Expert Group, Brussels.

European Commission (2011a), Investing today for growth tomorrow, IP/11/799, 29 June 2011, Brussels.

European Commission (2011b), Proposal for a Council Decision on the system of own resources of the European Union, COM(2011) 510 final, 29 June 2011, Brussels.

European Commission (2011c), European Economic Forecast Autumn 2011, Brussels: European Commission.

European Commission (2011d), Innovation Union Competitiveness Report, 2011 edn, Brussels: European Commission.

European Commission (2011e), A Budget for Europe 2020, COM(2011) 500 final, 29 June 2011, Brussels.

European Commission (2011f), From Challenges to Opportunities: Towards a Common Strategic Framework for EU Research and Innovation funding, COM(2011) 48 final, 9 February 2011, Brussels.

European Commission (2011g), Proposal for a Regulation of the European Parliament and of the Council establishing Horizon 2020 – The Framework Programme for Research and Innovation (2014-2020), COM(2011) 809 final, 30 November 2011, Brussels.

European Commission (2012), Communication from the Commission to the European Parliament and the Council "Roadmap towards a Banking Union", COM (2012) 510 final, 12 September 2012, Brussels.

European Commission (2014a), Taking stock of the Europe 2020 strategy for smart, sustainable and inclusive growth, COM(2014)130 final, 5 March 2014, Brussels.

European Commission (2014b), European Economic Forecast Winter 2014, Brussels: European Commission.

European Commission (2014c), An Investment Plan for Europe, COM(2014) 903 final, 26 November 2014, Brussels.

European Commission (2014d), Research and innovation as sources of renewed growth, COM(2014) 339 final, 10 June 2014, Brussels.

European Commission (2015a), Proposal for a Regulation of the European Parliament and of the Council on the European Fund for Strategic Investments and amending Regulations (EU) No 1291/2013 and (EU) No 1316/2013, COM(2015)10 final, 27 January 2015, Brussels.

European Commission (2015b), Proposal for a Regulation of the European Parliament and of the Council amending Regulation (EU) 806/2014 in order to establish a European Deposit Insurance Scheme, COM(2015) 586 final, 24 November 2015, Brussels.

European Commission (2015c), Eighth biannual report on the functioning of the Schengen area, 1 May - 10 December 2015, COM (2015) 675 final, 15 December 2015, Brussels.

European Commission (2015d), A European Agenda on Security, COM (2015)185 final, 28 April 2015, Brussels.

European Commission (2015e), European Structural and Investment Funds 2014-2020: Official texts and commentaries, November 2015, Brussels.

European Commission (2016a), Adaptation of the ceiling of own resources and of the ceiling for appropriations for commitments following the entry into force the Council Decision 2014/335 on the system of own resources of the European Union, COM(2016) 829 final, 21 December 2016, Brussels.

European Commission (2016b), Mid-term review/revision of the multiannual financial framework 2014-2020: An EU budget focused on results, COM(2016)603 final, 14 September 2016, Brussels.

European Commission (2016c), Science, Research and Innovation performance of the EU, Brussels: European Commission.

European Commission (2016d), EU budget 2015 – Financial Report, Brussels: European Commission.

European Commission (2016e), Proposal for a Regulation of the European Parliament and of the Council establishing a Union Resettlement Framework and amending Regulation (EU) No 516/2014 of the European Parliament and the Council, COM (2016) 468 final, 13 July 2016, Brussels.

European Commission (2016f), Strengthening European investments for jobs and growth: Towards a second phase of the European Fund for Strategic Investments and a new European External Investment Plan, COM(2016) 581 final, 14 September 2016, Brussels.

European Commission (2016g), European Defence Action Plan, COM(2016) 950, 30 November 2016, Brussels.

European Commission (2016h), Commission Implementing Decision of 2.9.2016 on the approval of the Terms of Reference for the Interim Evaluation of Horizon 2020, C(2016) 5546 final, 2 September 2016.

European Commission (2016i), Ex post evaluation of the ERDF and the Cohesion Fund 2007-13. Commission Staff Working Paper, SWD(2016) 318 final, 19 September 2016, Brussels.

European Commission (2017a), White Paper on the Future of Europe. Reflections and scenarios for the EU27 by 2025, COM(2017) 2025 final, 1 March 2017, Brussels.

European Commission (2017b), Reflection Paper on the Future of EU Finances, COM (2017) 358 final, 28 June 2017, Brussels.

European Commission (2017c), Autumn Economic Forecast, Statistical Annex European Economic Forecast – Autumn 2017, Brussels: European Commission.

European Commission (2017d), Vade Mecum on the Stability and Growth Pact, 2017 Edition, Directorate-General for Economic and Financial Affairs, Brussels: European Commission.

European Commission (2017e), Communication from the Commission "The Fiscal Compact: Taking Stock", COM(2017) 1200 final, 22 February 2017, Brussels.

European Commission (2017f), Proposal for a Council Directive laying down provisions for strengthening fiscal responsibility and the medium-term budgetary orientation in the Member States, COM(2017) 824 final, 6 December 2017, Brussels.

European Commission (2017g), Communication to the European Parliament, the Council, the European Central Bank, the European Economic and Social Committee and the Commitee of the Regions on completing the Banking Union, COM(2017) 592 final, 11 October 2017, Brussels.

European Commission (2017h), New budgetary instruments for a stable euro area within the Union framework, COM(2017) 822 final, 6 December 2017, Brussels.

European Commission (2017i), Proposal for a Regulation of the European Parliament and of the Council amending Regulation (EU) No 1303/2013 of the European Parliament and of the Council of 17 December 2013 laying down common provisions on the European Regional Development Fund, the European Social Fund, the Cohesion Fund, the European Agricultural Fund for Rural Development and the European Maritime and Fisheries Fund and laying down general provisions on the European Regional Development Fund, the European Social Fund, the Cohesion Fund and the European Maritime and Fisheries Fund and repealing Council Regulation (EC) No 1083/2006 as regards support to structural reforms in Member States, COM (2017) 826 final, 6 December 2017, Brussels.

European Commission (2017j), Proposal for a Council Regulation on the establishment of the European Monetary Fund, COM(2017) 827 final, 6 December 2017, Brussels.

European Commission (2017k), Guiding principles for the Dialogue on Ireland/Northern Ireland, TF50 (2017) 15, 20 September 2017, Brussels.

European Commission (2017l), Joint report from the negotiators of the European Union and the United Kingdom Government on progress during phase 1 of negotiations under Article 50 TEU on the United Kingdom's orderly withdrawal from the European Union, TF50 (2017) 19 – Commission to EU 27, 8 December 2017, Brussels.

European Commission (2017m), EU budget 2016 – Financial Report, Brussels: European Commission.

European Commission (2017n), Proposal for a Regulation of the European Parliament and of the Council amending Regulation (EU) 2016/399 as regards the rules applicable to the temporary reintroduction of border control at internal borders, COM(2017) 571 final, 27 September 2017, Brussels.

European Commission (2017o), EU budget for the refugee crisis and improving migration management, Factsheet, Brussels: European Commission.

European Commission (2017p), Progress report on the European Agenda on Migration, Annex 6 Relocation, COM(2017) 669 final, 15 November 2017, Brussels.

European Commission (2017q), Fifteenth report on relocation and resettlement, COM(2017) 465 final, 6 September 2017, Brussels.

European Commission (2017r), Reflection Paper on the Future of European Defence, COM(2017) 315, 7 June 2017, Brussels.

European Commission (2017s), Launching the European Defence Fund, COM(2017) 295 final, 7 June 2017, Brussels.

European Commission (2017t), Proposal for a Regulation of the European Parliament and of the Council establishing the European Defence Industrial Development Programme aiming at supporting the comnpetitiveness and innovative capacity of the European defence industry, COM(2017) 294 final, 7 June 2017, Brussels.

European Commission (2017u), Annual Growth Survey 2018, COM(2017) 690 final, 22 November 2017, Brussels.

European Commission (2017v), Horizon 2020 in full swing - Three years on, Key Facts and Figures 2014-2016, Brussels: European Commission.

European Commission (2017w), In-depth Interim Evaluation of Horizon 2020, SWD(2017) 220 final, 29 May 2017, Brussels.

European Commission (2017x), LAB – FAB – APP: Investing in the European future we want, Report of the independent High-Level Group on maximising the impact of EU Research & Innovation Programmes, Brussels: European Commission.

European Commission (2017y): Reflection Paper on the Deepening of the Economic and Monetary Union, COM(2017)291, 31 May 2017, Brussels.

European Commission (2018a), EU budget: Commission proposes a modern budget for a Union that protects, empowers and defends, IP/18/3570, 2 May 2018, Brussels.

European Commission (2018b), Proposal for a Council Decision on the system of Own Resources of the European Union, COM(2018) 325 final, 2 May 2018, Brussels.

European Commission (2018c), A modern budget for a Union that protects, empowers and defends, The Multiannual Financial Framework for 2021-2027, COM(2018) 321 final, 2 May 2018, Brussels.

European Commission (2018d), Proposal for a Council Regulation laying down the multiannual financial framework for the years 2021 to 2027, COM(2018) 322 final, 2 May 2018, Brussels.

European Commission (2018e), Proposal for a Interinstitutional Agreement between the European Parliament, the Council and the Commission on budgetary discipline, on cooperation in budgetary matters and on sound financial management, COM(2018) 323 final, 2 May 2018, Brussels.

European Commission (2018f), Proposal for a Council Regulation on the methods and procedure for making available the Own Resources based on the Common Consolidated Corporate Tax Base, on the European Union Emissions Trading System and on Plastic packaging waste that is not recycled, and on the measures to meet cash requirements, COM(2018) 326 final, 2 May 2018, Brussels.

European Commission (2018g), Proposal for a Regulation of the European Parliament and of the Council on the protection of the Union's budget in case of generalised deficiencies as regards the rule of law in the Member States, COM(2018) 324 final, 2 May 2018, Brussels.

European Commission (2018h), Compliance Report - ESM Stability Support Programme for Greece, Fourth Review, June 2018, Brussels: European Commission.

European Commission (2018i), Proposal for a Regulation of the European Parliament and of the Council establishing the European Defence Fund, COM82018) 476 final, 13 June 2018, Brussels.

European Commission (2018j), A modern budget for a Union that protects, empowers and defends, The Multiannual Financial Framework for 2021-2027, COM(2018) 321 final, 2 May 2018, Brussels.

European Commission (2018k), Horizon 2020 interim evaluation: maximising the impact of EU research and innovation, COM(2018)2 final, 11 January, Brussels.

European Commission (2018l), Proposal for a Regulation of the European Parliament and of the Council establishing Horizon Europe – the Framework Programme for Research and Innovation, laying down its rules for participation and dissemination, COM(2018) 435 final, 7 June 2018, Brussels.

European Commission (2018m), Proposal for a Decision of the European Parliament and of the Council on establishing the specific programme implementing Horizon Europe – the Framework Programme for Research and Innovation, COM(2018) 436 final, 7 June 2018, Brussels.

European Commission (2018n), Transitions on the Horizon: Perspectives for the European Union's future research and innovation policies, Final report from project BOHEMIA, Brussels: European Commission.

European Commission (2018o), Horizon Europe Stakeholder Consultation - Synopsis Report, SWD(2018) 309 final, 7 June 2018, Brussels.

European Commission (2018p), A new, modern Multiannual Financial Framework for a European Union that delivers efficiently on its priorities post-2020, COM(2018) 98 final, 14 February 2018, Brussels.

European Commission (2018q), Annexes to the Proposal for a Decision of the European Parliament and of the Council on establishing the specific programme implementing Horizon Europe – the Framework Programme for Research and Innovation, COM(2018) 436 final, 7 June 2018, Brussels.

European Commission (2018r), Compliance Report ESM Stability Support Programme for Greece, Fourth Review, July 2018, Brussels: European Commission.

European Commission (2018s), Regional Development and Cohesion Policy beyond 2020: Questions and Answers, Fact Sheet, 29 May 2018, Strasbourg.

European Commission (2018t), Questions and answers: the EU budget for external action, Fact Sheet, 14 June 2018, Brussels.

European Commission (2018u), Facing the EU budget: report of the operation of the own resource system, SWD(2018) 172 final, 2 May 2018, Brussels.

European Commission (2018v), European Union. Statistical Factsheet, May 2018.

European Commission (2018w), Impact Assessment. Commission Staff Working Document, SWD(2018) 301 final, 01 June 2018, Brussels.

European Commission (2018x), Proposal for a Regulation of the European Parliament and the Council on the financing, management and monitoring of the common agricultural policy, COM(2018) 393 final, 01 June 2018, Brussels.

European Commission (2018y), Impact Assessment. Commission Staff Working Paper, SWD(2018) 282 final, 29 May 2018, Brussels.

European Commission (2018z), Proposal for a Regulation of the European Parliament and the Council laying down common provisions on the European Regional Development Fund, the European Social Fund Plus, the Cohesion Fund, and the Maritime and Fisheries Fund and financial rules for those and for the Asylum and Migration Fund, the Internal Security Fund, and the Border Management and Visa Instrument, COM(2018) 375 final, 29 May 2018, Brussels.

European Commission & High Representative of the Union for Foreign Affairs and Security Policy (2019), EU-China. A Strategic Outlook, Joint Communication to the European Parliament, the European Council and the Council, JOIN(2019) 5 final, 12 March 2019, Strasbourg.

European Communities (1985), Programme of the Commission for 1985. Statement by Jacques Delors, President of the Commission, to the European Parliament and his reply to the ensuing debate, Strasbourg, 12 March 1985, Bulletin of the European Communities, Supplement 4/85.

European Communities (2003), Farm Structure. 1999/2000 survey, Luxembourg.

European Community (1997), Convention determining the State responsible for examining applications for asylum lodged in one of the Member States of the European Communities - Dublin Convention, OJ C 254, 19 August 1997, pp.1-12.

European Council (1984), European Council Meeting at Fontainebleau, Conclusions of the Presidency, 25-26 June 1984.

European Council (2000), Presidency Conclusions, Lisbon European Council, 23 and 24 March 2000.

European Council (2011), Conclusions 24-25 March 2011, Brussels.

European Council (2013), Conclusions, EUCO 217/13, 20 December 2013, Brussels.

European Council (2016a), The Bratislava Declaration, Bratislava, 16 September 2016.

European Council (2016b), Decision of the Heads of State or Government, meeting within the European Council, concerning a new settlement for the United Kingdom within the European Union, OJ C 69, 23 February 2016, pp. 1-16.

European Council (2016c), EU-Turkey statement, 18 March 2016, 144/16, 18 March 2016, Brussels.

European Council (2016d), European Council meeting – Conclusions, EUCO 26/16, 28 June 2016, Brussels.

European Council (2017a), European Council (Art. 50) meeting, Guidelines, 15 December 2017.

European Council (2017b), Migration: way forward on the external and the internal dimension, Leaders' Agenda, December 2017, Brussels.

European Council (2019), European Council Decision taken in agreement with the United Kingdom extending the period under Article 50(3) TEU, EUCO XT 20013/19, 11 April 2019, Brussels.

European Court of Auditors (2017), Greening: a more complex income support scheme, not yet environmentally effective, Special Report 21, Luxembourg.

European Court of Auditors (2018), Opinion No. 7/2018 concerning Commission proposal for regulations relating to the common agricultural policy in the post-2020 period, ECA_OPI_2018_7, 25 October 2018.

European Court of Auditors (2019), Allocation of Cohesion Policy Funding to Member States 2021-2027, Rapid case view, March 2019, Luxembourg.

European Parliament (2012), Report on the proposal for a regulation of the European Parliament and of the Council establishing Horizon 2020 - The Framework Programme for Research and Innovation (2014-2020) COM(2011)0809 – C7-0466/2011 – 2011/0401(COD)), A7-0427/2012, 20 December 2012, Brussels.

European Parliament (2013), European Parliament legislative resolution of 21 November 2013 on the proposal for a regulation of the European Parliament and of the Council establishing Horizon 2020 - The Framework Programme for Research and Innovation (2014-2020) (COM(2011)0809 – C7-0466/2011 – 2011/0401(COD)), P7_TA(2013)0499, 21 November 2013, Brussels.

European Parliament (2014a), Report on negotiations on the MFF 2014-2020: lessons to be learned and the way forward (2014/2005(INI)), A7-0254/2014, 26 March 2014, Brussels.

European Parliament (2014b), European Development Fund. Joint development cooperation and the EU budget: out or in?, In-depth Analysis, PE 542.140 – November 2014, Brussels.

European Parliament (2016a), European Parliament resolution of 26 October 2016 on the mid-term revision of the MFF 2014-2020, (2016/2931(RSP)), Brussels.

European Parliament (2016b), European Parliament resolution of 6 July 2016 on the preparation of the post-electoral revision of the MFF 2014-2020: Parliament's input ahead of the Commission's proposal, (2015/2353(INI)), Brussels.

European Parliament (2016c), Overview on the Use of EU Funds for Migration Policies, In-Depth Analysis for the European Parliament's Committee on Budgets, PE 572.682, Brussels.

European Parliament (2017a), Report on budgetary capacity for the Eurozone, A8-0038/2017, 13 February 2017, Brussels.

European Parliament (2017b), European Parliament resolution of 13 June 2017 on the assessment of Horizon 2020 implementation in view of its interim evaluation and the Framework Programme 9 proposal (2016/2147(INI)), P8_TA(2017)0253, 13 June 2017, Brussels.

European Parliament (2017c), The next Multiannual Financial Framework (MFF) and the Unity of EU budget, In-depth Analysis requested by the BUDG Committee, PE 603.796 - November 2017, Brussels.

European Parliament (2017d), The next Multiannual Financial Framework (MFF) and its Flexibility, In-depth Analysis requested by the BUDG Committee, PE 603.799 - November 2017, Brussels.

European Parliament (2018a), European Parliament resolution of 14 March 2018 on the reform of the European Union's system of Own Resources P8_TA(2018)0076.

European Parliament (2018b), European Parliament resolution of 30 May 2018 on the 2021-2027 multiannual financial framework and own resources (2018/2714(RSP)), Brussels.

European Parliament (2018c), Opinion of the Committee on Agriculture and Rural Development for the Committee on Budgets, 2018/0166R(APP), 10 October 2018.

European Parliament (2018d), Towards the Common Agricultural Policy beyond 2020: comparing the reform package with the current regulation, Briefing for the AGRI committee, PE617.494, September 2018.

European Parliament (2018e), Conditionalities in Cohesion Policy, Policy Department for Structural and Cohesion Policies, PE617.498, September 2018.

European Parliament & Council of the European Union (2013a), Regulation (EU) No 604/2013 of the European Parliament and of the Council of 26 June 2013 establishing the criteria and mechanisms for determining the Member State responsible for examining an application for international protection lodged in one of the Member States by a third-country national or a stateless person (recast), Official Journal of the European Union, L 180, 29 June 2013, pp. 31-58.

European Parliament & Council of the European Union (2013b) Regulation (EU) No 1291/2013 of the European Parliament and of the Council of 11 December 2013 establishing Horizon 2020 - the Framework Programme for Research and Innovation (2014-2020) and repealing Decision No 1982/2006/EC, Official Journal of the European Union, L 347, 20 December, pp. 104-173.

European Parliament & Council of the European Union (2013c), Regulation (EU) No 1290/2013 of the European Parliament and of the Council of 11 December 2013 laying down the rules for participation and dissemination in 'Horizon 2020 - the Framework Programme for Research and Innovation (2014-2020)' and repealing Regulation (EC) No 1906/2006, Official Journal of the European Union, L 347, 20 December, pp. 81-103.

European Parliament & Council of the European Union (2016), Regulation (EU) 2016/399 of the European Parliament and of the Council of 9 March 2016 on a Union Code on the rules governing the movement of persons across borders (Schengen Borders Code), Official Journal of the European Union, L 77, 23 March 2016, pp. 1-51.

European Parliament & Council of the European Union (2017), Regulation (EU) 2017/1601 of the European Parliament and of the Council of 26 September 2017 establishing the European Fund for Sustainable Development (EFSD), the EFSD Guarantee and the EFSD Guarantee Fund, Official Journal of the European Union, L 249, 27 September 2017, pp. 1-16.

European Parliamentary Research Service (2016), The UK "rebate" on the EU budget: An explanation of the abatement and other correction mechanisms, Briefing, February 2016, Brussels.

European Parliamentary Research Service (2017), EU framework programmes for research and innovation - Evolution and key data from FP1 to Horizon 2020 in view of FP9, In-depth Analysis, Brussels.

European Parliamentary Research Service (2018), 2021-2027 multiannual financial framework and new own resources. In-depth analysis, July 2018, Brussels.

European Union (2015), Implementation of the First Pillar of the CAP 2014-2020 in the EU Member States, July 2015.

European Union (2016), Shared Vision, Common Action: A Stronger Europe. A Global Strategy for the European Union's Foreign And Security Policy, Brussels.

European Union (2017), From Shared Vision to Common Action: Implementing the EU Global Strategy - Year 1, Brussels.

Fabbrini, Federico (2016), How Brexit Opens a Window of Opportunity for Treaty Reform in the EU, spotlight europe #2016/01, Gütersloh/Berlin/Paris: Bertelsmann Stiftung/Jacques Delors Institut.

Faure, Raphaëlle/Gavas, Mikaela/Knoll, Anna (2015), Challenges to a comprehensive EU migration and asylum policy, Report, London/Maastricht/Brussels: Overseas Development Institute & European Centre for Development Policy Management.

Fernandes, Sofia/Rubio, Eulalia (2012), Solidarity within the Eurozone: how much, what for, for how long?, Notre Europe Policy Paper 51, Paris: Institut Jacques Delors.

Frankel, Jeffrey (2015), Causes of Eurozone crises, available at: http://voxeu.org /article/causes-eurozone-crises (accessed 8 November 2017).

Freeman, Chris/Soete, Luc (1997), The Economics of Industrial Innovation, Cambridge: MIT Press.

Gerodimos, Roman/Karyotis, Georgios (2015), Austerity Politics and Crisis Governance: Lessons from Greece, in: Georgios Karyotis and Roman Gerodimos (eds), The Politics of Extreme Austerity: Greece in the Eurozone Crisis, London: Palgrave MacMillan, pp. 259-271.

Gourevitch, Peter A. (1992), Politics in Hard Times: Comparative Responses to International Economic Crises, New York, NY: Cornell University Press.

Government of Belgium (2017), Position of Belgium (BE) on the next Framework Programme for Research and Innovation ("FP9"), Brussels.

Government of Poland (2017), Polish Position Paper on Future Framework Programme - EU support for scientific, technological and social development, Warsaw.

Government of Portugal (2017), On the evolving nature of EU research funding: H2020 interim evaluation and directions towards the next framework program (FP9) in an increasingly diverging Europe, Lisbon.

Government Offices of Sweden (2017), Opinions in view of the discussion of the next EU Framework Programme for Research and Innovation, Stockholm.

Grande, Edgar (2000), Multi-Level Governance: Institutionelle Besonderheiten und Funktionsbedingungen des europäischen Mehrebenensystems, in: Grande, Edgar and Markus Jachtenfuchs (eds.): Wie problemlösungsfähig ist die EU? Regieren im europäischen Mehrebenensystem, Baden-Baden: Nomos, pp. 11-30.

Grande, Edgar (2001), The erosion of state capacity and the European innovation policy dilemma: A comparison of German and EU information technology policies, in: Research Policy 30, pp. 905-921.

Grande, Edgar/Häusler, Jürgen (1994), Industrieforschung und Forschungspolitik: Staatliche Steuerungspotentiale in der Informationstechnik, Frankfurt/New York: Campus.

Grande, Edgar/Kriesi, Hanspeter (2015), The Restructuring of Political Conflict in Europe and the Politicization of European Integration, in: Risse, Thomas (ed), European Public Spheres: Politics is Back, Cambridge: Cambridge University Press, pp. 190-223.

Gstöhl, Sieglinde (2015), The European UInion's Approach tot he Neighbours of its Neighbours : From Fragmentation to Strategy?, in: Studia Diplomatica: The Brussels Journal of International Relations, LXVIII(1), pp. 35-48.

Gstöhl, Sieglinde (2017), Theoretical approaches to the European Neighbourhood Policy, in: Gstöhl, Sieglinde/Schunz, Simon (eds), Theorizing the European Neighbourhood Policy, Abingdon: Routledge, pp. 3-21.

Haas, Jörg/Gnath, Katharina (2016), The Euro Area Crisis: A Short History, Jacques Delors Institut, Policy Paper 172, Berlin.

Haas, Jörg/Rubio, Eulalia (2017), Brexit and the EU budget: Threat or Opportunity, Policy Paper, No. 183, Jacques Delors Institute, Berlin.

Haas, Jörg/Rubio, Eulalia/Schneemelcher, Pola (2018), The MFF Proposal: What's New, What's Old, What's Next ?, Policy Brief May 2018, Jaques Delors Institute, Berlin.

Habermas, Jürgen (1973), Legitimationsprobleme im Spätkapitalismus, Frankfurt am Main: Suhrkamp Verlag.

Hall, Peter A. (1993), Policy Paradigms, Social Learning, and the State: The Case of Economic Policymaking in Britain, Comparative Politics, 25(3), pp. 275-296.

Hall, Peter A. (2014) Varieties of capitalism and the Euro crisis, in: West European Politics, 37(6), pp. 1223-1243.

Hall, Peter A./Soskice, David (eds) (2001), Varieties of Capitalism: The Institutional Foundations of Comparative Advantage, Oxford: Oxford University Press.

Hancké, Bob (2013), Unions, Central Banks, and EMU: Labour Market Institutions and Monetary Integration in Europe, Oxford: Oxford University Press.

Heinemann, Friedrich/Mohl, Phillip/Osterloh, Steffen (2010), Reforming the EU Budget: Reconciling Needs with Policy-Economic Constraints, in: European Integration, 32 (1), pp. 59-76.

High Level Expert Group (2014), Committment and Coherence, Ex-Post-Evaluation of the 7th EU Framework Programme (2007-2013), Brussels.

High Level Group on Own Resources [HLGOR] (2016), Future Financing of the EU - Final report and recommendations of the High-Level Group on Own Resources, December 2016, Brussels.

Hix, Simon (2015), Democratizing the Macroeconomic Union in Europe, in: Cramme, Olaf/Hobolt, Sara B. (eds), Democratic Politics in a European Union under Stress, Oxford: Oxford University Press, pp. 180-198.

HM Government (2016), The best of both worlds: the United Kingdom's special status in a reformed European Union, London.

HM Government (2017), The United Kingdom's exit from and new partnership with the European Union, February 2017, London.

HM Government (2018), Explainer for the agreement on the withdrawal of the United Kingdom of Great Britain and Northern Ireland from the European Union, 14 November, London

Hodson, Dermot (2015), Policy-making under Economic and Monetary Union: Crisis, Change, and Continuity, in: Wallace, Helen/Pollack, Mark A./Young, Alasdair R. (eds), Policy-making in the European Union, 7th edition, Oxford: Oxford University Press, pp. 166-196.

Hooghe, Liesbet/Marks, Gary (2001), Multi-Level Governance and European Integration, Lanham: Rowman & Littlefield.

Hooghe, Liesbet/Marks, Gary (2009), A Postfunctionalist Theory of European Integration: From Permissive Consensus to Constraining Dissensus, in: British Journal of Political Science, 39(1), pp. 1-23.

Huguenot-Noël, Robin/Hunter, Alison (2017), Can the EU structural funds reconcile growth, solidarity and stability objectives? A study on the role of conditionalities in spurring structural reforms and reducing macroeconomic imbalances, European Policy Center, Issue Paper, No. 83, October 2017, Brussels.

IMF (2018), 2018 Article IV Consultation and Proposal for Post-Programme Monitoring – Presse Release; Staff Report; and Statement by the Executive Director for Greece, IMF Country Report No. 18/248, Washington.

Jasper, Jörg (1998), Technologische Innovationen in Europa: ordnungspolitische Implikationen der Forschungs- und Technologiepolitik der EU, Wiesbaden: Deutscher Universitätsverlag.

Juncker, Jean-Claude (2014), Political Guidelines for the European Commission, Brussels.

Juncker, Jean-Claude (2016), State of the Union Address 2016: Towards a better Europe - a Europe that protects, empowers and defends, Brussels.

Juncker, Jean-Claude (2017), State of the Union Address 2017, Brussels.

Kaiser, Robert/Prange, Heiko (2004), Managing Diversity in a System of Multi-Level Governance: The Open Method of Coordination in Innovation Policy, in: Journal of European Public Policy, 11(2), 249-266.

Kaiser, Robert/Prange-Gstöhl, Heiko (2010), A paradigm shift in European R&D policy? The EU budget review and the economic crisis, in: Science and Public Policy, 37(4), pp. 253-265.

Kaiser, Robert/Prange-Gstöhl, Heiko (2012), European growth policies in times of change: budget reform, economic crisis and policy entrepreneurship, in: Benedetto, Giacomo/Milio, Simona (eds), European Union Budget Reform: Institutions, Policy and Economic Crisis, Basingstoke: Palgrave/Macmillan, pp. 59-78.

Kaiser, Robert/Prange-Gstöhl, Heiko (2017), The Future of the EU Budget - Perspectives for the Funding of Growth-Oriented Policies post-2020, SIEPS 2017:6, Stockholm.

Kingdon, John W. (1984), Agendas, Alternatives, and Public Policies. Boston: Little, Brown &Co.

Kölling, Mario (2014), Reform options for the EU budget – First reflections on the new departure for a new EU budget, in : Perspectives on Federalism, 6(3), pp. 218-237.

Kölling, Mario (2017), Policy conditionality – a new instrument in the EU budget post-2020?, SIEPS European Policy Analysis, Issue 2017:10epa, Stockholm.

König, Nicole/Walter-Franke, Marie (2017), France and Germany: Spearheading a European Security and Defence Union?, Policy Paper 2020, Berlin: Jacques Delors Institute.

Kohler-Koch, Beate (1999), The Evolution and Transformation of European Governance, in: Kohler-Koch, Beate/Eising, Rainer (eds) The Transformation of Governance in the European Union, London/New York: Routledge, pp. 14-35.

Kok-Report (2004), Facing the Challenge – The Lisbon Strategy for Growth and Employment, Report from the High-Level Group, Brussels.

Laffan, Brigid (2000), The big budgetary bargains: from negotiation to authority, in: Journal of European Public Policies, 7(5), pp. 725-743.

Laffan, Brigid (2016), Europe's union in crisis: tested and contested, in: West European Politics, 39(5), pp. 915-932.

Laffan, Brigid/Lindner, Johannes (2014), The Budget: who gets what, when, and how?, in: Wallace, Helen/Pollack, Mark A./Young, Alasdair R. (eds), Policy-Making in the European Union, Oxford: Oxford University Press, pp. 220-242.

Lawton, Thomas C. (1999), Fostering Invention and Innovation: Europe's collaborative R&TD initiatives, in: Lawton, Thomas C. (ed), European Industrial Policy and Competetiveness: Concepts and Instruments. Basingstoke: MacMillan Press, pp. 23-48.

Liebowitz, Stan J./Margolis, Stephen E. (1995), Path dependence, lock-in, and history, in: Journal of Law, Economics and Organization 11(1), pp. 205.226.

Lindberg, Leon N./Scheingold, Stuart A. (eds.) (1971), Regional Integration. Theory and Research, Cambridge: Harvard University Press.

Lindner, Johannes (2006), Conflict and Change in EU Budgetary Politics, London: Routledge.

Longo, Michael/Murray, Philomena (2015), Europe's Legitimacy Crisis: From Causes to Solutions, New York: Palgrave MacMillan.

Macron, Emmanuel (2017), Initiative for Europe, Speech, Sorbonne, 26 September 2017.

Majone, Giandomenico (1996), Regulating Europe, London: Routledge.

Manzella, Gian Paolo/Mendez, Carlos (2009), The turning points of EU cohesion policies, Working Paper written in the context of the report "An Agenda for a Reformed Cohesion Policy", January 2009.

March, James G./Olsen, Johan P. (1995), Democratic Governance, New York: The Free Press.

Marks, Gary (1992), Structural Policy in the European Community, in: Sbragia, Alberta M. (ed.), Europolitics. Institutions and policymaking in the new European Community, Washington D.C.: Brookings, pp. 191-223.

Marks, Gary/Hooghe, Liesbet/Blank, Kermit (1996), European Integration from the 1980s. State-Centric v. Multi-level governance, in: Journal of Common Market Studies 34(3), pp. 341-378.

Matthews, Alan (2018a), The CAP in the 2021-2027 MFF Negotiations, in: Intereconomics 2018(6), pp. 306-311.

Matthews, Alan (2018b), The greening architecture in the new CAP, in: capreform.eu, http://capreform.eu/the-greening-architecture-in-the-new-cap/ (accessed: 05 April 2019).

Matthijs, Matthias (2014), Mediterranean Blues: The Crisis in Southern Europe, in: Journal of Democracy, 25(1), pp. 101-115.

May, Theresa (2017), Letter to the President of the European Council, Donald Tusk, 29 March 2017.

Mayntz, Renate (1999), Multi-level governance: German federalism and the European Union, in: Lankowski, Carl F. (ed) Governing Beyond the Nation State. Global Public Policy, Regionalism, or Going Local?, Washington D.C.: American Institute for Contemporary German Studies, pp. 101-14.

Mayntz, Renate/Scharpf, Fritz W. (1995), Der Ansatz des akteurzentrierten Institutionalismus, in: Mayntz, Renate/Scharpf, Fritz W. (eds), Gesellschaftliche Selbstregelung und Steuerung, Frankfurt a.M.: Campus, pp. 39-72.

McGowan, Lee/Phinnemore, David (2017), The UK: membership in crisis, in: Dinan, Desmond/Nugent, Neil/Paterson, William E. (eds), The European Union in Crisis, London, Palgrave MacMillan, pp. 77-99.

Mijs, Arnout/Schout, Adriaan (2012), Views on the Commission's Draft EU Budget: Excessively Ambitious or Overly Timid?, EPIN Working Paper No. 32, available at: http://dx.doi.org/10.2139/ssrn.2001362.

Mijs, Arnout/Schout, Adriaan (2015), Flexibility in the EU Budget: Are There Limits?, Clingendael Report, Netherlands Institute of International Relations Clingendael, The Hague.

Mogherini, Federica (2017), Building on vision, forward to action: delivering on EU security and defence, Speech, 13 December 2017, Brussels.

Molino, Elisa/Zuleeg, Fabian (2011), The EU budget in an era of austerity: setting the example or compensating for national spending cuts?, Paper presented at the workshop ´The post-2013 financial perspectives: re-thinking EU finances in times of crisis`, 7-8 July 2011, Torino.

Moravcsik, Andrew (2001), Federalism in the European Union: Rhetoric and Reality, in: In Nicolaidis, Kalypso/Howse, Robert (eds): The Federal Vision: Legitimacy and Levels of Governance in the United States and the European Union, Oxford: Oxford University Press, pp. 161-87.

Mourlon-Druol, Emmanuel (2014), Don't Blame the Euro: Historical Reflections on the Roots of the Eurozone Crisis, in: West European Politics, 37(6), pp. 1282-1296.

National Research, Development and Innovation Office Hungary (2017), Position paper of Hungary on the next EU Framework Programme for Research and Innovation, Budapest.

Newman, Abraham (2015), The Reluctant Leader: Germany's Euro Experience and the Long Shadow of Reunification, in: Matthijs, Matthias/Blyth, Mark (eds), The Future of the Euro, Oxford: Oxford University Press, pp. 117-135.

North, Douglass C. (1990), Institutions, Institutional Change and Economic Performance, Cambridge: Cambridge University Press.

Núñez Ferrer, Jorge/Le Cacheux, Jaques/Benedetto, Giacomo/Saunier, Mathieu (2016), Study on the potential and limitations of reforming the financing of the EU budget. Expertise commissioned by the European Commission on behalf of the High-Level Group on Own Resources, 3 June 2016.

OECD (2017), Evaluation of Agricultural Policy Reforms in the European Union. The Common Agricultural Policy 2014-2020, Paris: OECD.

Oettinger, Günther (2018), A Budget Matching our Ambitions, speech given at the conference "Shaping our Future" on 8 January 2018, available at: https://ec.europa.eu/commission/commissioners/2014-2019/oettinger/blog/budget-matching-our-am–bitions-speech-given-conference-shaping-our-future-812018_en (accessed 25 April 2018).

O'Neill, Jim/Terzi, Alessio (2014), Changing Trade Patterns, Unchanging European and Global Governance, Bruegel Working Paper 2014/02, February 2014.

Overbeek, Henk (2012), Sovereign Debt Crisis in Euroland: Root Causes and Implications for European Integration, in: The International Spectator, 47(1), pp. 30-48.

Pantazatou, Katerina (2015), Promoting solidarity in crisis times: building on the EU budget and the EU funds, in: Perspectives on Federalism, 7(3), pp. 49-76.

Peters, Guy B./Pierre, Jon (2002), Multi-Level Governance: A View from the Garbage Can. Manchester Papers in Politics: EPRU Series, 1/2002.

Peterson, John/Sharp, Margret (1998), Technology Policy in the European Union, Basingstoke: Macmillan.

Pierson, Paul (2000), Increasing Returns, Path Dependence, and the Study of Politics, in: American Political Science Review 94(2), pp. 251-267.

Pisani-Ferry, Jean (2011), The Euro crisis and its aftermath, Oxford: Oxford University Press.

Pisani-Ferry, Jean (2018), The EU's Seven-Year Budget Itch, available at: http://bruegel.org/2018/03/the-eus-seven-year-budget-itch (accessed 23 May 2018).

Preunkert, Jenny (2015), Double Trust: Creditor's and Peopples' Confidence in the Euro Crisis, in: Champeau, Serge/Closa, Carlos/Innerarity, Daniel/Poiares Maduro, Miguel (eds.), The Future of Europe: Democracy, Legitimacy and Justice after the Euro Crisis, London/New York: Rowman & Littlefield, pp. 157-170.

Republic of Cyprus (2018), Position Paper of Cyprus on the next EU Framework Programme for Research and Innovation (FP9), Nikosia.

Roeger, Werner/in 't Veld, Jan (2010), Fiscal stimulus and exit strategies in the EU: a model-based analysis, European Economy Economic Papers 426, September 2010. Brussels: European Commission.

Rosamond, Ben (2016), Brexit and the Problem of European Disintegration, in: Journal of Contemporary European Research 12(4), pp. 864-871.

Rubio, Eulalia (2008), EU Budget Review: Addressing the Thorny Issues, Policy Paper 32, Notre Europe.

Runciman, David (2016) What Time Frame Makes Sense for Thinking about Crises?, in Kjaer, Poul F./Olsen, Niklas (eds), Critical Therories of Crises in Europe, London/New York: Rowman & Littlefield, pp. 3-16.

Samuelson, Paul A. (1954), The Pure Theory of Public Expenditure, in: Review of Economics and Statistics, 36(4), pp. 387-389.

Sapir, André (2014), Still the Right Agenda for Europe? The Sapir Report Ten Years On, in: Journal of Common Market Studies, 52(Supplement S1), pp. 57-73.

Scharpf, Fritz W. (1988), The Joint Decision Trap: Lessons from German Federalism and European Integration, in: Public Administration 66(3), pp. 239-78.

Scharpf, Fritz W. (2003), Problem-solving effectiveness and democratic accountability in the EU, MPIfG working paper, No. 03/1, Cologne.

Scharpf, Fritz W. (2013), Monetary Union, Fiscal Crisis and the Disabling of Accountability, in: Schäfer, Armin/Streeck, Wolfgang (eds), Politics in the Age of Austerity, Cambridge: Polity Press, pp. 108-142.

Schild, Joachim (2008), How to shift the EU's spending priorities? The multiannual financial framework 2007-13 in perspective, in: Journal of European Public Policy, 15(4), pp. 531-549.

Schimmelfennig, Frank (2014), European Integration in the Euro Crisis: The Limits of Postfunctionalism, in: Journal of European Integration, 36(3), pp. 321-337.

Schmidt, Vivien A. (2013), Democracy and Legitimacy in the European Union Revisited: Input, Output and 'Throughput', in: Political Studies, 61(1), pp. 2-22.

Schmidt, Vivian A. (2015), The Forgotten Problem of Democratic Legitimacy: 'Governing by the Rules' and 'Ruling by the Numbers', in: Matthijs, Matthias/Blyth, Mark (eds), The Future of the Euro, Oxford: Oxford University Press, pp. 90-113.

Schmitter, Philippe C./Lefkofridi, Zoe (2016), Neo-Functionalism as a Theory of Disintegration, in: Chinese Political Science Review 1, pp. 1-29.

Schneider, Christina J. (2013), Globalizing electoral politics: Political competence and distributional bargaining in the European Union, in: World Politics, 65(3), pp. 452-490.

Schuknecht, Ludger/Moutot, Philippe/Rother, Philipp/Stark, Jürgen (2011), The Stability and Growth Pact - crisis and reform, ECB Occasional Paper No. 129, Frankfurt/Main.

Seng, Kilian/Biesenbender, Jan (2012), Reforming the Stability and Growth Pact in Times of Crisis, in: Journal of Contemporary European Research, 8(4), pp. 451-469.

Single Resolution Board (2017), Banking Union - Single Resolution Board collects €6.6 billion in annual contributions to the Single Resolution Fund, now reaching €17 billion in total, Press Release, 19 July 2017.

Stenbaeck, Jorgen/Jensen, Mads D. (2016), Evading the joint decision trap: the multiannual financial framework 2014-20, in: European Political Science Review, 8(4), pp. 615-635.

Tassinari, Fabrizio (2016), The Disintegration of European Security: Lessons from the Refugee Crisis, in: PRISM 6(2), pp. 70-83.

Tarschys, Daniel (2011a), European Public Goods: Which Selection Criteria for the Multiannual Financial Framework?, in: Tarschys, Daniel (ed), The EU Budget: What Should Go In? What Should Go Out?, Stockholm: Swedish Institute for European Policy Studies, pp. 12-41.

Tarschys, Daniel (2011b) (ed), The EU Budget: What Should Go In? What Should Go Out?, Stockholm: Swedish Institute for European Policy Studies.

TF50 (2017), Joint report from the negotiators of the European Union and the United Kingdom Government on progress during phase 1 of negotiations under Article 50 TEU on the United Kingdom's orderly withdrawal from the European Union, 8 December 2017, Brussels.

Thatcher, Mark/Stone Sweet, Alec (2002), Theory and Practice of Delegation to Non-Majoritarian Institutions, in: West European Politics 25(1), pp. 1-22.

Thillaye, Renaud (2016), Can the EU Spent Better? An EU Budget for Crisis and Sustainability, London/New York: Rowman & Littlefield.

Tobin, James (1964), Economic Growth as an Objective of Government Policy, in: The American Economic Review, 54(3), pp. 1-20.

Toje, Asle (2005), The 2003 European Union Security Strategy: A Critical Appraisal, European Foreign Affairs Review, 10(1), pp. 117-133.

Tsebelis, George (2002), Veto Players. How Political Institutions Work. Princeton: Princeton University Press.

UK House of Commons (2017), The UK's contribution to the EU budget, Briefing Paper, Number CBP 7886, 4 January 2018, London.

UK House of Commons (2018), Brexit: the exit bill, Briefing Paper, Number 8039, 30 July 2018, London.

UK Prime Minister's Office (2017), Confidence and Supply Agreement between the Conservative and Unionist Party and the Democratic Unionist Party, 26 June 2017, London.

Verdun, Amy (2015), A historical institutionalist explanation of the EU's responses to the euro area financial crisis, in: Journal of European Public Policy, 22(2), pp. 219-237.

Vollaard, Hans (2018), European Disintegration. A Search for Explanations, London: Palgrave Macmillan.

Webber, Douglas (2017), Can the EU Survive?, in: Dinan, Desmond/Nugent, Neill/Paterson, William E. (eds), The European Union in Crisis, London: Palgrave, pp. 336-359.

Wolff, Guntram B. (2018), What does Europe care about? Watch where it spends, available at: http://bruegel.org/2018/05/what-does-europe-care-about-watch-where-it-spends (accessed 23 May 2018).

Wolfstädter, Laura Maria/Kreilinger, Valentin (2017), European integration via flexibility tools: the cases of EPPO and PESCO, Jacques-Delors-Institute Berlin, Policy Paper 209, Berlin.

Woodruff, David M. (2014), Governing by Panic: The Politics of the Euro Crisis, LEQS Paper No. 81/2014, London School of Economics and Political Science.